MW00849216

Merry Christmas Tim
2013

Sitting Pretty

HOLLYWOOD LEGENDS SERIES

CARL ROLLYSON, GENERAL EDITOR

Sitting Pretty

THE LIFE AND TIMES OF

CLIFTON WEBB

Clifton Webb with David L. Smith

Foreword by Robert Wagner

UNIVERSITY PRESS OF MISSISSIPPI • JACKSON

www.upress.state.ms.us

The University Press of Mississippi is a member of the Association of
American University Presses.

Lyrics from "Picture You Without Me" by Cole Porter, p. 117, reprinted
by permission of the Cole Porter Estate.

Letter from Noel Coward to Clifton Webb, p. 177, © NC Aventales AG
1946; by permission of Alan Brodie Representation, Ltd,
www.alanbrodie.com www.noelcoward.com.

Copyright © 2011 by University Press of Mississippi
All rights reserved
Manufactured in the United States of America

First printing 2011
∞
Library of Congress Cataloging-in-Publication Data

Webb, Clifton, 1893–1966.
Sitting pretty : the life and times of Clifton Webb / Clifton Webb with
David L. Smith ; foreword by Robert Wagner.
p. cm. — (Hollywood legends series)
Includes bibliographical references and index.
ISBN 978-1-60473-996-1 (cloth : alk. paper)
— ISBN 978-1-60473-997-8 (ebook) 1. Webb, Clifton, 1893–1966.
2. Motion picture actors and actresses—United States—Biography.
I. Smith, David L. (David Lee), 1929– II. Title.
PN2287.W4549A3 2011
791.4302′8092—dc22
[B]   2010049423
British Library Cataloging-in-Publication Data available

To John and Betsy Neylon,
who came to know and love Clifton Webb through his estate collection,
and without whose kindness this book would not have been possible

Contents

Foreword

I made two pictures with Clifton Webb, *Titanic* and *Stars and Stripes Forever*, but I really got to know him when he invited me into the social circle that centered around the house that he shared with his mother, Mabelle.

Mabelle ruled the roost, and Clifton was happy that she did, but he had his own eccentricities. I remember an African gray parrot bundled carefully into a large brandy snifter at dinner parties.

Clifton actually had several quite different careers—as a gifted dancer on Broadway during the 1920s, as a theatre star in such plays as Noel Coward's *Blithe Spirit*, as a distinctively acerbic movie star—but to me he will always be remembered as a wonderful host and friend to my family and myself. It was a job he took seriously, because Clifton's friends were the elite of their time: Jeanne Eagels, Cole Porter, Harpo Marx. It was Clifton who introduced me to Noel Coward.

People who read this book will get to know Clifton as an adoring son, as a dancer, as an actor. And to be perfectly honest, they will also get to know him as an endearing snob, for the names drop fast and furiously.

After reading the book, I feel honored to have been included in Clifton's circle, for his chapters read as if they were written by Elliot Templeton, the character he played so beautifully in *The Razor's Edge*. Templeton was supposedly based by Somerset Maugham on an English social butterfly named "Chips" Channon, but to me Elliott Templeton *is* Clifton Webb.

It's a loss that Clifton abandoned the writing of his autobiography, but it's a blessing that David L. Smith has rescued it from the scrap heap and finished Clifton's story.

I'm grateful that Clifton was my friend, and I'm grateful that this book exists.

ROBERT WAGNER

Preface

When I started my research on Clifton Webb, I soon discovered that he had begun an autobiography. But where was it? It was mentioned in several sources, but no one quoted from it. Then one day I purchased a few Webb items from a collector. I asked him if he had more. He said he had Webb's entire estate collection. I asked if he happened to have Webb's autobiography. He did. I told him I was researching Webb for a biography and would love to be able to use material from his autobiography. He replied that I could use as much as I wanted. We agreed that I would come to his house and see the collection. Then nothing. I tried to get in touch, but there was no answer. I eventually found that he had died suddenly of a heart attack. Months passed before I was able to make contact with his widow. She was very kind and said she would honor her husband's promise to me. I drove to her home in Ohio and went through the collection.

I discovered six chapters of an autobiography Webb wrote over the years, plus many notes and photographs. Using the six chapters that Webb wrote, I have written seven additional chapters using his notes and my research. This book provides the first look at this multi-talented man's life and times. No biography has ever been written on Clifton Webb. That void is now filled.

Webb was an important participant in what has been called, "The Great Broadway Period." His stage career began as a seven-year-old in 1896. His last stage appearance was in 1946. He was a contemporary and friend of Jeanne Eagels, the Dolly Sisters, Marilyn Miller, Libby Holman, Rudolph Valentino, Noel Coward, Cole Porter, Bea Lillie, Moss Hart, Irving Berlin, Gertrude Lawrence, Grace Moore, Alfred Lunt, Lynn Fontanne, and many others. Clifton Webb, indeed, knew and mingled with "everybody who was anybody."

When he moved to Hollywood in 1944, Clifton and his mother, Mabelle, became an integral part of what has come to be known as the "glamorous" Hollywood era. Webb bought and remodeled his house on

Rexford Drive in Beverly Hills with the distinct purpose of making it ideal for parties. Everyone came to Clifton and Mabelle's.

Clifton Webb was part of the great age of theatre as well as the golden age of Hollywood. This is an eyewitness account of possibly the most and best that the legitimate stage and Hollywood has ever seen or ever will see again. The six autobiographical chapters he wrote plus his huge collection of meticulous notes relate stories of the great and near great that have never been told. This biography sheds new light on the entertainment world of yesteryear through Webb's insightful and delightful writing and recollections.

DAVID L. SMITH

Acknowledgments

This book is primarily a product of Clifton Webb's marvelous unfinished autobiography. Webb wrote just as he spoke. As you read his words you can almost hear him speaking. Therefore, putting my words next to his was a daunting task.

I am grateful to Helen Matthews, Webb's secretary, for saving the Webb manuscript from oblivion. I am equally grateful to John and Betsy Neylon, who rescued the manuscript and Webb's collection of personal memorabilia from ten years in a basement. I am deeply indebted to the Neylon's generosity in allowing me to use the manuscript, photos, and other memorabilia in that collection.

I owe Robert Wagner many thanks for his kindness, generosity, and availability. Photos and memorabilia from his personal collection of Webb memorabilia contributed greatly to this book. Richard Zanuck was also very generous with his time and a very valuable eyewitness source. Jill St. John provided additional insight into the character of this unique man.

I am grateful to Bob Newhart, who took the time to write and tell me about his unusual first and only encounter with Webb. Victoria Price provided insight into the friendship between her father and Webb.

David Stenn provided extremely valuable information from his own research of the life of Jeanne Eagels. His meticulous research included ship manifests and important dates, as well as providing guidance for locations of photos and newspaper articles.

Leonard Leff shared his research and his publications covering Webb's life. Dennis Hollenbeck provided information on the Hollenbeck family and his personal research on the life of Clifton Webb, beginning in childhood, when he once sat on the lap of his distant relative.

Charles Hooey kindly shared his research on the fascinating life and career of Orville Harrold. Scott Eyman, who was the literary collaborator for Robert Wagner's memoir "Pieces of My Heart," provided important information from that book and helped steer me to Wagner, resulting in several valuable interviews.

Charles F. Engel and Mark E. Engel were valuable resources in that their father, Samuel G. Engel, wrote and delivered the wonderful eulogy for Clifton Webb found at the end of this book. Webb was a close family friend of the Engels and as such they were able to provide me with valuable insight into the true nature of this man.

As always, much credit should go to my dear wife, Lucy Ann, who acted as proofreader, grammar coach, and critic for my first book as well as this one.

The task of encompassing and defining a man's life is awesome. However, much of this was done for me. Webb's own writing gives us a delightful and authentic firsthand account of his life and times that, in effect, is also a history of theatrical performance in twentieth-century America.

Despite the presence of Webb's six chapters, there were many holes to fill and much research to be done. Unfortunately, many important people who were close to Clifton Webb have passed on. Because of this, one feels extraordinary affection and gratitude for those who were interested enough to help the book eventually see print.

After spending so much time reading and researching the life of Clifton Webb, I began to feel I knew him personally. Although I am very happy to see this book finished, it sometimes feels as though I have lost a wonderful and most unique friend.

Introduction

In his eulogy for Clifton Webb, producer Samuel Engel said, "No responsible historian of the theatre and the motion picture dealing with the last three decades can do even a remotely creditable job without the name Clifton Webb appearing on many a page of his work."

When the name *Clifton Webb* surfaces, many think only of his film career. Even then, many will think of him as a character actor, relegated to supporting roles in low-budget films. The truth is he was a top box-office draw and one of the most consistent moneymakers in the history of Twentieth Century Fox. He received top billing in most of his films. For more than fifteen years he was an unlikely leading man who rivaled the more typical leading men of the postwar years. His good friend Robert Wagner said, "At Fox, the elite circle was presided over by Clifton Webb."

Long before his film career began, Webb was a child actor and later a suavely effete song-and-dance man who introduced such songs as *Easter Parade, How's Chances? I've Got a Crush on You, At Long Last Love, Alone Together*, and *Something to Remember You By*. None of these are identified with him today. He became so popular in Broadway musicals and revues that in 1933 critic Brooks Atkinson said, "It's almost impossible to produce a smart revue without putting Clifton Webb in it somewhere."

Webb was a stage star when revues dominated Broadway. These were a unique form of entertainment built around stars, current events, or just plain laughs. Shortly after Florenz Ziegfeld died in 1932, Clifton Webb helped cast off the Ziegfeld spell in a show that stood out as a milestone in the post-Ziegfeld era. *As Thousands Cheer* was a tour de force for Irving Berlin. It was also a spectacular life-changing event for Webb.

After Webb's multifaceted appearance in *As Thousands Cheer* in 1933, critic John Mason Brown said, "In addition to his dancing and his sure instinct for comedy, he has now become a master of make-up." Brown said that Webb had accomplished "astonishing achievements in grease paint and mimicry."

It was about this time that RKO had developed Fred Astaire into a big box-office draw. MGM thought it would be a good idea to provide some competition for Astaire. They looked at Webb and came to the conclusion that he was more handsome than Fred Astaire and just as good a dancer. Unfortunately, after calling him to Hollywood, they had second thoughts about how a somewhat prissy, rather effeminate star would play as a leading man. No picture was made.

Undeterred, Webb went back to his beloved stage. It would be ten years before the movie industry was ready to take a chance on Webb. The turning point in his career came in 1941 when his good friend Noel Coward cast him in *Blithe Spirit*. Reflecting on the casting Coward said, "He is a beautiful comedian and the slight hint of preciousness won't matter and I think he will give it distinction." It also didn't matter to Otto Preminger, who saw Webb in *Blithe Spirit* and cast him in *Laura*.

That "slight hint of preciousness" would be with Webb throughout his career. Most of his performances were brittle and bitchy. More than any other male movie star, the effete Clifton Webb caused the moviegoing public to change their image of a leading man by challenging and reconfiguring our concept of masculinity.

Leonard Leff in his article on Clifton Webb in the *Cinema Journal* (Spring 2008) states that director Jean Negulesco asked Webb in 1952, "Clifton, a personal question, are you a homosexual?" Negulesco said Webb drew himself to full height and replied, "Devout, my boy . . . Devout." However, this anecdote appears only in the manuscript of Negulesco's 1984 memoir but not in the memoir itself, perhaps because the story was fabricated or the author was unwilling to "out" a man who had never "outed" himself.

Webb's sexuality is still a matter of dispute. He talked rather frequently of getting married and said he almost married twice. Robert Wagner recalled, "I never saw Clifton with another man. He was not involved with anyone. . . . [H]e had no relationship . . . no live-in person. There was no one coming in the back door. His mother was an overpowering influence."

Wagner's wife, Jill St. John, appeared in two films with Webb (*The Remarkable Mr. Pennypacker* and *Holiday for Lovers*), both in 1959. She said she saw no signs of homosexuality in him. "He was wonderful to work with. He had a devilish, wicked sense of humor. But he had good rapport with children. I would describe him as an effete type of person." One definition of "effete" is over-refined, effeminate. Indeed, the word "effete" appears in many descriptions of Clifton Webb.

It was obvious Webb had no great love other than his mother, Mabelle. Whether in New York or Hollywood, Webb and Mabelle were very much a part of the social scene. Their parties were legendary. Mabelle is remembered for sitting on a bar stool, holding her hand on the bun atop her head, while downing straight whiskey. She was renowned for her own special version of the can-can, which she would perform, even into her nineties, at the slightest provocation.

Henry Willson was a leading Hollywood agent in the 1940s and 1950s. Willson was gay and had a stable of gay actors, including Rock Hudson. When one of his clients complained that he needed the love and companionship of another man, Willson shouted, "So get a dog! You can live with your mother but not with your lover!" This was a pointed reference to Clifton Webb.

Webb had no girlfriends, but he managed to retain his position in Hollywood by having no boyfriends. The general consensus in Hollywood at that time was that it simply was not possible to be openly gay, but a celebrity's friends would tolerate homosexuality if the star were discreet. Webb may have been more asexual than homosexual. He enjoyed the company of both men and women but never seemed to be sexually attracted to either.

Richard Zanuck said, "I would come down on the side of his being asexual. You never saw him with a pretty girl on his arm, but you never saw him with a man either. Mabelle was always there."

In 1944, Otto Preminger approached Webb about appearing in a movie he was about to produce. Preminger asked Webb what kind of character he would most like to play. Webb replied, "A charming son of a bitch." Webb got his wish. Preminger cast him as Waldo Lydecker in *Laura*. Seldom in the history of motion pictures has an actor been so perfectly matched to a part.

Lydecker was supposed to be obviously gay, but Webb's portrayal made it possible to read him as both a spurned heterosexual lover and a woman-hating queen. In his first major movie, and at the age of fifty-five, he was nominated for an Oscar for best supporting actor.

In a day when all leading men were supposed to be strong, virile, and brave, Clifton Webb projected an image of flip aseptic arrogance. Most male movie stars of his day were supposed to have women melting in their arms. Webb had a considerably different approach. He said proudly, "I have destroyed the formula completely. I'm not young. I don't get the girl in the end and I don't swallow her tonsils, but I have become a national figure."

Critics and moviegoers alike were fascinated with this new and unique star. Webb reported that while shooting *Laura*, he overheard one of the crew say, "Where has this guy been?" Author Richard Barrios said, "The voice alone would have carried the performance: the tone a courtly buzz saw, the razor diction dining on consonants as if they were truffled squab." Critic Bosley Crowther said, "Mr. Webb is an actor who fits like a fine suede glove. He plays a creature of silky elegance whose caustic wit and cold refinements display him as a super-selfish man."

Webb's on-screen persona was that of a "super-selfish man," but in reality he was no such thing. He was a man of great compassion who "hated to see people fighting with each other." He was a staunch defender of people he thought were unfairly treated or misunderstood, people like Greta Garbo, Tallulah Bankhead, Marilyn Monroe, James Dean. He even settled a feud between columnists Hedda Hopper and Louella Parsons. He provided a helping hand to those who needed it. Vincent Price, who benefited from Webb's largesse when he was trying to make his mark in show business, said, "Clifton was the kindest man I ever knew in my life."

Webb's off-screen personality was much the same as his on-screen performances. He played Clifton Webb very well. Although this seeming lack of range might have damaged other actors, audiences were enchanted by Webb's urbane, caustic, and arrogant personality. In reality, his acting range was more than it seemed.

He was able to play everything from an effete columnist (*Laura*) to a fertile father (*Cheaper by the Dozen* and *The Remarkable Mr. Pennypacker*). Columnist William E. Sarmento said, "To be sure no one could deliver a verbal thrust with more venom than Mr. Webb and he could handle comedy well. But Clifton Webb was more than a stereotype. He was a fine actor."

Webb had a way of delivering lines in a suavely clipped, acidly dry manner. His leisured timing was impeccable. His delivery was as funny and entertaining as the lines themselves. All these things are the mark of a professional master of dialogue borne from years of experience on the stage, starting as a juvenile actor.

When asked about an autobiography, Webb told Hedda Hopper, "So thoroughly (was Mabelle) the gay companion of my life and travels that any autobiography would have to be a story of two people and their adventure with life." When he finally undertook the writing of his memoirs, Mabelle was omnipresent. Webb told reporters many times he had begun writing his memoirs. The proposed title was *Mabelle and Me*, verification, if such a thing was ever needed, that Webb's life could never be separated from his mother's.

In 1950, he spoke of working on his autobiography. He said he compiled a collection of papers and clippings for his "collaborator" (unnamed) and "talked myself hoarse for a week." At the end of that time the collaborator had taken no notes and had, as Webb put it, "written a masterpiece which made me out to be an egomaniac." It was at this point that he decided to write his own autobiography. He even contacted his friend, Bennett Cerf, at Random House about publishing the autobiography. Cerf was delighted and wrote to Webb in 1962, "It has been some months since I have talked to you about the autobiography you were contemplating. I earnestly hope that you got started on this project or at least have given it some further serious consideration. I know this will be a fine book if you ever get it finished, and one that we will be very proud to publish under our Random House imprint."

Unfortunately, Webb said he eventually had gotten "bogged down" in the process. "Truth is a desirable quality in an autobiography," he said, "though obviously not indispensable, and candor, I have found, compels me to put certain persons and events in a revealing, rather than a flattering light." This seemed to indicate there would be no autobiography.

However, Webb did write six chapters and left a hefty collection of notes that he intended to use in the proposed book. His writing is as witty and urbane as his on-screen persona. Those six chapters as well as information from his voluminous notes and personal letters from such close friends as Noel Coward, Gloria Swanson, and Darryl Zanuck are included in this book. They provide an intimate view of an amazingly talented man's life and times.

Webb certainly acquired much of his theatrical air and talent from his mother, who was a stage-struck young woman who attended performances of every stock company that ever played in Indianapolis. She was a feisty, headstrong woman who longed to become an actress, even changing her name from the plain Mabel to the more dramatic Mabelle.

Webb describes his mother, "The theatrical world was her universe from the beginning. Her father, a solid Southern gentleman, used the classic phrase to her: 'I'll see you in your coffin before you go on the stage.' Mabelle swore then and there that if she ever had a child that showed the slightest inclination toward such a career, she would further it heart and soul. I promptly appeared, to become that child."

Mabelle's hopes for a career of her own in drama ended when, on January 18, 1889, she married Jacob G. Hollenbeck. Ten months later she gave birth to her one and only child at the couple's home at 305 Mississippi Street in Indianapolis. (Other sources list Webb's birth date as 1891; however, the birth records of Marion County, Indiana, show he was born November 19, 1889, in Indianapolis, Indiana.)

She named him Webb Parmelee Hollenbeck and called her son by his first name all of her life. He, in turn, called her Mabelle. It has been said they were Hollywood's happiest couple. This is their story, with six chapters in Webb's own words.

Sitting Pretty

May I jingle Merry Christmas
Clifton Webb!

1.1. Clifton Webb's Christmas card. The John
and Betsy Neylon Collection.

1.2. Clifton Webb at two years. Elite Studios, Indianapolis,
Indiana. The John and Betsy Neylon Collection.

CHAPTER 1

The Noses Have It

According to all accounts, which I have no reason to disbelieve, I was a disgustingly fat baby. I was an out-sized Hoosier with no perceptible neck and such thick rolls of fat dispersed about my person that I had to be probed clean. Other than that, I was blonde, curly haired, and hazel-eyed like my mother, and the nose budding between my fatuous cheeks began immediately to turn up towards my forehead.

Of the facts I have set down above, only the last is of great consequence. Although time has worked upon the others, the nose has remained. If I were even slightly whimsical, I would insist that the course of my life has been determined by Mabelle Parmelee's nose. I am Mabelle Parmelee's son, and within the normal limits of genes and chromosomes her nose is my nose. It is not something to be worn lightly.

Once upon a time, for example, I was smuggled into a wicked Parisian party. It was the annual Bal des Quat'z Arts, and I was smuggled because nobody but French artists and models was supposed to be there.

The Bal des Quat'z Arts, the art students' ball, took place in the spring. The theme was changed every year: Incas, Aztecs, Phoenicians, Egyptians, Gauls, and Babylonians. The costumes were almost always non-existent and there wasn't much historical authenticity. Everyone, male and female, was covered with vivid colored paint: red, bronze, gold, and silver. Even great painters like Henri Matisse attended this Roman Saturnalia, where every license was permitted.

Having been told that the evening's motif was Babylonian, I attired myself in a ratty toga and a great deal of brown makeup, which an old

dressing-room crone lathered on me with a sponge. At that, I turned out
to be overdressed. Some of the artists wore nothing but blue paint and
a small tin cup, while there was one model costumed exclusively in a
bunch of cherries hung at the most obvious spot. Along about midnight
she astonished everybody by launching into a routine of bumps and
grinds, extremely professionally executed, as a man in a long black beard
pranced about on all fours, snapping at her costume with his teeth.

Without warning, some hour and bottles of champagne later, she
climbed a ladder to the box where I was sitting. Before I could move
she was in my lap. "Tiens! Quell nez extraordinaire!" she exclaimed,
and, seizing my nose between her thumb and forefinger, she gave it a
dreadful wrench. The only point of the incident is that at the height of a
bacchanal, surrounded by a horde of pickled Babylonians, the first thing
that lady noticed was my nose.

As far as design goes, Mabelle's nose is not a headliner. Cyrano de
Bergerac would have ignored it completely. It is merely a nice, functional
feature, constructed for blowing, sniffing, and the occasional dramatic
snort. There is nothing flamboyant about our nose. The essential factor
is its tilt. Although I have never applied a protractor, I am certain that
the angle described by the tip of Mabelle's nose and her brief upper lip is
considerably greater than 135 degrees.

Since one's birth is a purely involuntary part of one's life, and since
the root of everything that happens in this world is imbedded in the past,
I must digress for a while to the period when I was merely a coming
event.

Mabelle was sixteen and thoroughly saturated with Southern charm
when her parents moved from Lexington, Kentucky, to Indianapolis in
1885. The indirect result was their daughter's romance and my advent.

The 1880 census shows Mabelle and her family living in Indianapolis. In 1870
they were living in Coles County, Illinois. Mabelle had two brothers; Marvin
was six years younger and Edwin was older. Webb never mentions them. The
family moved to Indianapolis when Mabelle was about eleven years old. The
Indianapolis Evening News noted Mabelle's early theatrical career with articles
on her performances (April 18, 1882, and May 30, 1882) at the St. Nichol's
Hotel in Indianapolis. She gave readings of "Painter of Seville," "Mrs. Candle's
Lecture," and "Order for a Picture." A reporter stated, "All the recitations were
well delivered but those of Miss Mabel Parmelee deserve special attention."
This means Mabelle was living in Indianapolis from age eleven to at least age

1.3. Mabelle Parmelee. The John and Betsy Neylon Collection.

thirteen. Apparently, there was a move to Lexington, Kentucky, and then back to Indianapolis when Mabelle was sixteen.

Mabelle's early romping in the blue grass had provided her with a tantalizing lisp, a habit of fluttering her eyelids, and various other accessories of blooming belledom, none of which sat well with Grandfather Parmelee. He was the son of a Presbyterian minister and the victim of chillingly Calvinistic convictions, and I am told that Mabelle's conduct made him spend many hours reflecting on the integrity of his wife's supposedly Quaker forebears.

In Indianapolis, where she was queen of a front-porch court, Mabelle exercised the lisp and flutter with devastating effect. She had the local swains delicately balanced between hope and despair when it began to be rumored behind fans at taffy-pulls that a tall, dark, and handsome stranger had hit town. To add to the intriguing possibilities of the situation, it was whispered that "he had something to do with railroads." Just why railroads had such a powerful grip on the girlish imagination is not clear to me, but the fact is indisputable. A little later, against the background of an eminently fashionable dance, one Mr. Jake Grant Hollenbeck was presented to Miss Mabelle Parmelee. He looked at her dance card, saw it was full, and frowned with disappointment. She tossed the card elegantly over her left shoulder and made a silent wish. Then Mr. Hollenbeck smiled and Miss Parmelee smiled. Such portents were of incalculable significance.

Nobody need be surprised that Mabelle's nose eventually carried the day. After a year of informing her parents in the delightful diction of the day, "I'll marry Jake Hollenbeck . . . or die!" Mabelle found it unnecessary to die.

The house in Indianapolis where I was born, and which I dimly remember as enormous, high-ceilinged, with dark closets to strike terror into a child, had a long, curved, black-walnut staircase and banister. The last was more than young Mrs. Hollenbeck, despite her interesting condition, could resist. She landed in a limp heap in the lower hall one afternoon, and the family doctor was hastily summoned. What weighed with Mabelle when he arrived was not his tart comment on the advisability of sliding down banisters while pregnant, but what the spiteful girl across the street might say. Mabelle envisioned her counting on her fingers and gloating cheerfully: "Of course, she says it's premature . . . but . . . I guess this will bring that damn nose down a peg!"

Mabelle accordingly allowed herself to be carried up the long staircase to bed, and there she obdurately remained—one eye on the calendar, determinedly holding up my entrance—until precisely ten months from her wedding day. On that day she produced Webb Parmelee Hollenbeck, an infant endowed with the revolting physical characteristics which I have already described.

––––––––––

Since Webb does not describe how he got to New York from Indianapolis, the following information is provided. After Webb's birth, Mabelle continued to see as many plays as possible in Indianapolis. Her husband never accompanied her. He cared nothing for the theatre and worried that his wife's love for the stage might be transferred to their son. Jacob had cause to worry. When Jacob was away at work, Mabelle impetuously boarded a train for New York with her child in tow. Upon their arrival, she immediately enrolled him in dancing, acting, and music schools. Eventually, Jacob found his wayward family. He did not, however, force their return to Indianapolis. Instead, he allowed Mabelle and Webb to stay in New York for what he thought would be a brief adventure for the pair.

1.4. George Bellows's portrait of Clifton Webb. Courtesy of Richard Zanuck.

Mabelle had other ideas; she wanted to remain in New York, where she could vicariously participate in the theatre through her son. It became apparent to Jacob Hollenbeck that his wife would never return to Indianapolis. He had no desire to move to New York. Mabelle and Jacob finally divorced sometime prior to 1897, when Mabelle remarried.

Webb talks of his public school education. However, most of his schooling was through private tutors. When he was accepted into the Children's Theatre, teachers were provided for the children.

My nose continued turning up, and at an alarmingly early age began casting its shadow on my future. When I was at Public School No. 87 in New York, between the ages of eleven and thirteen, my classmates used to insist that I was stuck up. Highly incensed, I would shout back: "I'm not! Only my nose is!" They naturally did not believe me, a recollection which I still find painful today. I am not a snob. Mabelle is a snob, but I am not. No one who knows and enjoys so many different kinds of people as do I, who has waded in so many pools and touched so many shores, could possibly be a snob. The carriage of one's nose is irrelevant.

At the Chase School of Art, where I studied for two years after departing P.S. 87, George Bellows nicknamed me Robin Red Nose and painted a portrait which he said emphasized my "expectant, early morning, worm-hunting look."

George Bellows became a realist painter known for his bold depictions of urban life in New York City. He has been called "the most acclaimed American artist of his generation." Today his paintings sell for millions of dollars. His painting of a teenage Webb apparently was done in art school or shortly thereafter. Richard Zanuck told the author he was "willed that painting" by Webb and it is hanging in his home.

The most a nose may do is provide an actor a cue from which he can build a stage personality to match. It is the motion picture camera, however, which allows a nose really to assert itself. The nasal possibilities of the screen are virtually unlimited. As Eliot Templeton in *The Razor's Edge*, I was able to convey a large part of that gentleman's snobbishness solely with my nose. It practically directed Mr. Belvedere in *Sitting Pretty* and *Mr. Belvedere Goes to College*.

To that extent, Mabelle has had her nose in my affairs since the day I was born.

Apart from the shared experience of parturition, Mabelle does not bear the slightest resemblance to Mr. Whistler's notorious mother. My mother is short, plump, blonde, dimpled, with what the Viennese fondly term *gemutlichyn*. It is immensely to her credit that she survived a Kentucky childhood without melting, like so many ladies of that time and place, into a mass of giggling affectations the color and consistency of butter. Mabelle is an astute person with a superb gift for sizing up characters and situations, traits which she has inherited undiluted from the Philadelphia lawyers and merchants who were her Eno and Saville ancestors. Occasionally, a gentleman of the old school finds Mabelle's Gay Nineties curves an irresistible temptation, but I venture to say that no gentleman of any school has ever pinched her more than once. Mabelle offers that expensive combination of a soubrette exterior and grande dame standards of behavior.

She has always been completely spoiled. The only one of my grandparents' four children to withstand the hazards of childhood, they denied her nothing but the one thing on which her mind and heart were set. That was a career on stage.

This ambition filled them with horror. "A girl's place is at home with her mother," they informed her unendingly. "Later with her husband." "Fiddlesticks!" replied Mabelle. Ultimately, they yielded to the extent of permitting dancing lessons, providing that pirouettes and high kicks were practiced only behind the locked door of her bedroom. She was given piano lessons as a matter of course, for that was then considered an essential facet of feminine accomplishment. At fourteen she outraged the professor in Lexington by denouncing "The Maiden's Prayer" as "silly," and declaring, "I want to play real music." Real music has figured largely in Mabelle's life, and she saw to it that it did in mine during my impressionable years.

Having established a beachhead, Mabelle proceeded to consolidate it. She won Grandfather Parmelee's consent to take lessons in elocution from a lady of local repute who favored guests at evening parties and church entertainments with recitations by her pupils. Mabelle promptly became her star, and there are still those who recall with wonder my mother's exquisitely gulping and sobbing rendition of *Curfew Shall Not Ring Tonight* at the Sayre Institute. I am happy to recommend it professionally to anybody whose taste turns toward dramatic recitation, a neglected art today.

To the growing assortment of handsomely bound, gold-tooled albums and keepsakes won for dancing and excellence at the pianoforte, Mabelle began to add prizes for elocution. And people began to say, with the proper reluctance, "Mercy! She's really almost an actress!"

If Mabelle was under the impression that the charming bounder she had married was going to be sympathetically inclined to theatrical ambition, she came in for an unpleasant jolt. Alas! The Dutch in Mr. Hollenbeck was inalterably opposed to any female pursuit which might carry a woman beyond the bedroom circuit. He saw to it that Mabelle returned from her honeymoon pregnant.

This did not depress her noticeably, but her husband's and parents' program for confinement did. They righteously felt that this period should be devoted to whipping up a Center-Door-Fancy and the cultivation of pure thoughts. When she yowled to be taken to see Modjeska, who happened to be playing a one-night stand at the Indianapolis Opera House, they pushed her firmly back onto the sofa and fed her a nourishing diet of Ella Wheeler Wilcox's *Poems*. After that she didn't ask. She

1.5. Clifton Webb and Jacob Hollenbeck, circa 1895. The John and Betsy Neylon Collection.

found it a great deal simpler to sneak out the back door after bribing the cook to reply to all inquiries that she had gone for a spiritual stroll.

As Mabelle had often been heard to remark that feet were made for dancing, not walking, this subterfuge should have deceived nobody. Such was the gullibility of the age, however, so great the disinclination to believe that anybody of gentle birth might take the stage seriously, that it did deceive everybody. Everything was fine until that injudicious slide down the banister put her in purdah. Mabelle has always sworn that the first sign of life I evidenced was a good hard kick when she was in the act of applauding the eminent Francis Wilson, and she floated home convinced that she was to be the mother of a great actor. Nobody to this day, I confide with a grave sense of responsibility, has disabused her of the notion.

My recollections of Indianapolis are unfortunately scanty, as my stay there did not last beyond the age of five. While still in infancy I held the center of the stage with gulps and burps that people found unaccountably fascinating. It is reported that my first spoken line was sensational. One day shortly after my first birthday, my grandmother was playing with me on the floor. When she suddenly stopped, I said, "Proceed!" She jumped to her feet, informed Mabelle, "The child isn't going to live!" and the two women wept tenderly on each other's bosoms. Grandmother's prediction was overly melodramatic.

My mother continued to resist her mate's insistence that she swath her personality in wet diapers. Exactly what occurred between them, I do not know. I was young and only moderately observant at the time my father vanished from our lives forever. I remember very little of him.

One afternoon my father took me secretly down the street for my first haircut. After the long tresses had been cut, we stopped in at a bar on the way home. I sat on the bar and ate pretzels and kippered herring. The solemnity of the occasion, and its possible ritual significance, escaped me. They did not escape Mabelle and Gran. With a demented shriek, Gran fainted dead away at the sight of my shorn head. Mabelle wept. My father, befuddled by drink and the violent reaction the haircut had provoked, went out to the backyard scratching his head. The day held even further reverses in store for the unhappy man for he gave a bath to a new Dalmatian he was extremely fond of, only to have the dog's spots come off at the first touch of water.

The following morning he brought me a goat as a present. I tethered the beast behind the house and fed it grass, bread-crusts, scrap-iron, and other choice morsels. It will forever occupy a favored spot in my affections, chiefly for its wise, waggish look and the manner in which it forever seemed about to deliver pithy observations of life. The promise was not fulfilled, for all it actually delivered was its dinner on the kitchen floor one night when it broke its bonds.

"Do you remember the goat?" was one of the first remarks my father made to me when we met after a lapse of many years, while I was playing a stand in Chicago. My father, long since remarried, was in that city on a business trip. He had sent a note around to my dressing room, suggesting that we have supper together after the performance. I did remember the goat, and immediately a bond was sealed between us. A trifle embarrassed by the situation, he murmured, "I hope you don't hold any resentment against me for the way I treated your mother." "Why should I?" I returned. "You were both young and impetuous fools . . . and you should have been smacked." He blinked. Then we shook hands cordially, and that was that.

His meeting with Mabelle the next day was a scene which Noel Coward should have written. She turned on the charm and even called back a ghost of that girlish lisp. He and Mabelle found each other so fascinating that I entertained grave doubts as to whether my ex-papa would make the South Western Limited that night.

Shortly after the gift of the goat, my father went out of our lives. He simply vanished. There was soon a divorce, and Mabelle and I went off to live with my grandparents. I remember nothing of him, as I have said, except his intense masculinity and the foolish events I have described.

In Webb's notes he included some insight into the breakup of his mother and father's marriage. He apparently had second thoughts about including this in his autobiography because he crossed it out. It reads as follows: "My mother continued to resist her mate's insistence that she submerge her personality in diapers. When she made the discovery that my father was giving something more than the glad eye to anything in skirts, all hell broke loose. It took the form of a separation, followed by divorce, and Mabelle and I went to live with my grandparents." This seems to indicate that Jacob and Mabelle may have been separated before Mabelle took off for New York with her child.

Webb has said more than once that he and Mabelle left for New York when he was three years old. His autobiography later states, "My stay there didn't last beyond the age of five." Still later, he states he first learned about sex at his fifth birthday party in Indianapolis. In 1940, when he was appearing at the English Theatre in Indianapolis in *The Man Who Came to Dinner*, a story in the *Indianapolis News* states, "He left his birthplace in Indianapolis at the age of ten." We know that Webb appeared with the Children's Theatre in New York at the age of seven. It seems likely he was closer to five years old when he and Mabelle headed for New York since he had memories of his Indianapolis home that would not likely make an imprint on a three-year-old.

By the time I was six, pangs of growth had consumed the fat from my bones, and in my mind I was already well-launched on a stage career. When the other children wanted to play some feeble game like mumble-dy-peg, I would counter, "Let's play Theatre." I was liberal in interpreting the rules of this game, for there were none except that I be producer, director, stage-manager, and star. It met with persistent and selfish resistance from the others, and for that reason was but rarely played.

Grandmother Parmelee was unique among my elders in encouraging my activities along this line. "Her Grace," as we all called her (her first name was Grace), was not nearly so enslaved by convention as she seemed by the reflected light of her husband's granite convictions. Secretly, she sympathized with Mabelle's unfulfilled ambitions and her hope of realizing them through me. Gran, indeed, had a frustrated yen of her own: she had wanted to be a milliner. Nothing could sound more innocent and dreary today, but in her parents' minds the vocation was

forever stigmatized by the term "little milliner," found often in sensational novels of the era. Her Grace's ambition was vehemently suppressed as
evidence of sprouting sin.

Gran must have realized that the restrictive life open to a young di-
vorcee in a small city of the 1890s would never satisfy Mabelle. She accordingly allowed Mabelle to visit New York. There Mabelle met another
dashing charmer, Mr. Green Berry Raum Jr. Mabelle fell in love with
him. Mabelle came back to Indianapolis and begged Gran's permission.
Gran granted it with a sigh.

Green Berry Raum Jr. and Mabelle were married November 24, 1897, in
New York City. In the marriage records of the State of New York, in the City of
New York, she is listed as being twenty-six years old. However she was born
in 1869. This would make her twenty-eight years old. Raum is listed as being
thirty-three years old. Webb was eight years old at this time.

My mother and new stepfather, with myself dutifully in tow, went to live
at the then very chic Fifth Avenue Hotel. The change from Indianapolis
could scarcely have been greater had we sailed off to Samarqand on a
magic carpet.

Since excessive youth prevented me from enjoying New York in this
fabulous era, I feel myself fully entitled to wax nostalgic for it. My privilege is even stronger because I remember extremely little of what I am
about to describe. Mabelle, however, has so often described it since, that
I have acquired her memories as my own by contagion.

At the beginning of the century, New York was at the zenith of its
efforts to be like the great cities of Europe, something which has not
crossed the mind of Indianapolis ever. There was an absolute frenzy
of building palaces, museums, theatres, and hotels. Now that most of
the palaces have been demolished to provide room for parking lots and
cramped flats, we can perhaps begin to appreciate the spaciousness of
the Edwardian concept of life. It was certainly an admirable showcase for
such a belle as my young and beautiful mother.

Manhattan was completely settled only as far north as 72nd Street.
Above 125th Street one was met by rocky outcroppings and squatters'
huts. Beyond that, the Harlem River was the frontier of completely
open country. As far as residential areas were concerned, the uppermost
boundary was the southern edge of Central Park. The focus was still old

1.6. Clifton Webb at eight years at Bath Beach, Long Island, 1897. The John and Betsy Neylon Collection.

Murray Hill, and the Plaza and the excellent Savoy served gourmets a remarkable five-course table d'hôte dinner for one dollar. When the St. Regis opened, the city was swept by rumors that prices there were exorbitant. In self-defense, the harried management issued a public statement that its prices were no higher than anywhere else.

The most wonderful hotel of all, needless to say, was our own Fifth Avenue Hotel, at Twenty-Third Street. It was one of the great social centers and the principal gathering place of Republican politicians in a day when Republican politicians dared congregate in public. Next door to us was the Hoffman House, justly celebrated for its food, its Hoffman House goblets, its bouquet cigars, and later on for its institution of dinner dances with Clifton Webb as the featured dancer.

Outside the window of our suite stretched the romantic vista of the gas-lit avenue, and past our panes moved a perpetual procession of victorias and hansom cabs. Day or night, the air was never quiet of the sharp clop-clop of horses' hooves upon the paving stones. Lower Fifth Avenue had the air of a small, select city-within-a-city, inhabited principally by cousins and in-laws. Couples strolled out to dine at the houses of friends a few blocks distant, wandering arm in arm through the amiable dusk. In the club windows I remember the portly gentlemen sitting like pre-Raphaelite Buddhas, with their Grover Cleveland mustaches and their heads wreathed about with smoke from big black cigars. It was, to use again the inevitable adjective, an age of passing elegance; it was also intensely stimulating, and I am glad that I was privileged to grow up amidst it.

My new stepfather was a son of General Green B. Raum, Commissioner of Pensions and Internal Revenue through many administrations. He owned some sort of secret process for treating copper. This process, carried out at a remote plant in Jersey City, required no work on his part and provided handsome revenues, permitting him to indulge his taste for champagne, ladies, and fast horses. He was a great racing man and knew the owners of all the leading stables—the Whitneys, the Goulds, Pierre Lorillard. By the normal workings of propinquity and affection, they became my mother's friends too. She discovered herself, to her boundless delight, wafted into the middle of the fastest sporting set in the country.

Evening after evening Mabelle would pin a diamond butterfly on her high-piled golden hair and be swept off to a box at the Metropolitan to her Melba or Nordica and his Brothers de Reszke. Afterwards, would more often than not come supper at Delmonico's or the Café Martin. Through this fin de siècle world Mabelle floated with the unspoiled delight of a Christmas tree angel. She reveled in the swishing silken trains, the exquisite long white gloves, the veils and frills and fluttering furbelows of the Elegant Era. She waved an ostrich feather fan and tried to regard life with the fashionable ennui of a Wilde heroine—and failed utterly. She was having the time of her life. To conceal the fact beneath an affectedly blasé exterior could not possibly have seemed more stupid.

My stepfather and I disliked each other on sight. Whether, as psychoanalysts maintain, it was owing to my childish resentment at his having usurped what I took to be my place with Mabelle, I do not know. That certainly had something to do with it. The mutual aversion had the effect of making us exceedingly polite to each other. I still find it strange to reflect that at less than six years of age I had stumbled upon a most important axiom of human relations—that only extreme and unremitting courtesy will permit two incompatible people to live under the same roof. I was a quiet and reserved child whose experience had been both limited and almost entirely with doting women. I knew nothing whatever of the sporting and drinking whirl in which my stepfather lived and was more inclined to loiter in corners like an obnoxious Little Lord Fauntleroy. He must have felt reason to have as little use for me as I had for him.

The result of the abrupt transplantation was that I was wretchedly lonely. My principal companion was a dog. I also secured a trapeze, which I had forced my parents to buy at Spaulding's after a visit to the circus. It was screwed into the ceiling of my room at the Fifth Avenue Hotel, and on it I spent hours of delirious delight, hanging by my knees and swinging like a demon. I practiced an act with my patiently suffering dog, holding him on the bar beside me, then flinging him across the room to land on the bed while I finished "pratt in style."

My stepfather (whom I called "G. B." in revolt against the "Dad" he favored) was an extraordinarily distinguished-looking man. He dressed for the occasion even when no occasion was in sight—usually in a top hat, stiff white cuffs, high stiff collar, and the elaborately folded cravat then in fashion. I remember once being appalled at his announcement that his father, the General, changed his socks four times a day. He prided himself immensely on his manners and on being a "ladies' man." He was a great believer in appearances and would not permit Mabelle to drink beer because it made her giggle.

Later on, when I was advancing on my teens and he considered me sufficiently elderly to benefit by worldly counsel, he informed me: "It doesn't matter how much you drink, Webb, providing you get drunk like a gentleman." Unlike many parents, he was kind enough to illustrate by his own actions what he meant.

I don't believe G. B. was ever sober after five-thirty in the afternoon. After falling into bed perfectly stinking some night, he would arise in the morning, pat some bay rum on his face, and appear fresh as a daisy, smelling of bay rum, glycol-thymolin, and the fanciest British boot polish. After five-thirty he would come home slightly more debonair, still smelling of expensive cigars and the fanciest French brandy, fully prepared to be charming to my mother and any other ladies who might be about the premises. I often saw him carry on a long and flattering conversation, hand around cups of tea, and finally see some lady to the door with magnificent, if exaggerated, courtesy. Then, as soon as the door closed, he would fall down senseless on the rug.

Fortunately, my education was not confined to these homegrown exercises in gentlemanliness, for I was enrolled in a school run for small children by some Catholic sisters. Mabelle's twinges of Presbyterian conscience at this step were assuaged by considerations of geography and fashion. The school was near the hotel and attended by all the nicest children in the neighborhood. I loved it. The rich drama of the liturgy moved me profoundly. I recall the clean, cool smell of the corridors, the nuns' soft, musical voices and the incredible innocence of their faces framed by the starched, white coifs.

One winter's day, in honor of some saint whose name I never did know, we children knelt on the altar steps while our throats were blessed by the priest. This was designed as a preventative against colds, sore throats, and diphtheria, provided that one had reached the required degree of faith. I had a great deal of faith, unquestionably bolstered by the realization that a blessing done with two crossed, lighted candles held against my quivering Adam's apple was immeasurably less painful than having the doctor stick his steel-handled mirror down my throat and order me to pronounce disgusting monosyllables. Unfortunately, however, the weather at the time was terrible, and I trusted the efficacy of my unknown saint to such an extent that I neglected to wear my overshoes. I awoke next morning with a very sore throat.

Mabelle was in favor of summoning the doctor immediately. Hoarsely but vehemently, I protested. I tried to make her understand that I was committed to the saint and his supernatural cure, and that the arrival of Dr. Murdock with bag and instruments would cause me grave embarrassment in the hereafter.

Mabelle referred the problem to the good Sisters. One of them came around to the hotel and sat by my bed, and assured me that Saint Who-ever-it-Was and my Guardian Angel—a very important member of the hierarchy with whom I was just getting acquainted—would not take it amiss if Dr. Murdock acted as intermediary between earth and heaven.

My Catholic education ended soon thereafter, when we moved uptown to an apartment overlooking the Museum of Natural History. So, I am afraid, did this limbo of extreme youth and idle memory, of which I have been writing. The things of that period which have lodged in my recollection are an odd lot, mostly trivial and unsubstantial and seeming ever more so when pickled in ink, but I suppose that they are also the things which have made me what I am.

In the apartment above ours on West Seventy-seventh Street lived a little girl named Jeanette Chamberlain, with whom I sometimes played and whose labored practicing on the piano I endured with more equanimity than I can now believe possible. Jeanette's father was an Englishman of the illustrious Chamberlain family, and she was accordingly a stupefyingly well brought-up child, if a little on the dull side. Weekly attendance at Constantine's Dancing Class was part of her curriculum, and one afternoon (while Mabelle was visiting G. B.'s father in Washington) Gran agreed that I might go along with Jeanette and her governess to one of Mr. Constantine's sessions.

I cannot say that I was impressed by the row of prim little girls in starched white dresses and long black collars, nor by the opposing row of small boys in Buster Brown collars. Mr. Constantine was instructing in a watery version of the polka, but the steps were too tame for my taste, depraved as it has been by the trapeze. I went off into a corner by myself and was doing some kicks and twirls when another visitor arrived. This was a tall gentleman who looked the class over and finally became interested in what was transpiring in my corner. "Who's that?" he asked Mr. Constantine.

"I don't know. He came with Miss Jeanette."

"Is he a stage child?"

"I don't know."

The stranger came over to me. "Hello, son," he said, "What's your name?'

"Webb," I replied guilelessly.

"How would you like to go on the stage?"

"I'd love it," I said.

"Where's your mother?"

"In Washington."

"Do you think she'd allow you to go on the stage?" he asked.

"The important thing," I answered, "is that she couldn't possibly stop me!"

He took down our address and vanished.

A few days passed, during which (although you could not have forced me to agree) the stars doubtless wheeled in their normal courses, Memnon kept singing up the Nile. Then a telegram was delivered at General Raum's house in Washington, D.C. Its prose was completely unembroidered.

COME HOME AT ONCE . . . WEBB IS GOING ON THE STAGE.

CHAPTER 2

First Vision of a Name in Lights

A critic once said of me: "Mr. Webb wears a top hat as if he was born in one." Like all statements by critics, that one is somewhat exaggerated. Only my career was born in a top hat.

Webb frequently refers to "Gran" (Mabelle's mother) as though she were living with them in New York City. Obviously, she did spend some time there, but he never indicates how long she stayed. The 1900 census of Manhattan shows the Raums living at 101 Seventy-seventh Street with son Webb and Mabelle's widowed mother, Grace. Ten years later they were at 214 West Eighty-third Street, except there is a separate entry for Mr. Raum with an address at the Alexander Cummings Hotel on Reed Street.

When the tall visitor to the dancing class dropped in to see Gran the next day, he turned out to be Mr. Malcolm Douglas, manager of the New Amsterdam Theatre. He was about to produce a series of matinees by and for children at Carnegie Lyceum, known then as the Children's Theatre, and had fallen upon me during his search for a boy to play the role of the dude, Cholly Boutonniere, in a revival of Palmer Cox's *Brownies*. It called for a youth who could sing and dance, abilities which had eluded Mr. Douglas until desperation took him to Constantine's dancing class.

My stepfather, as expected, strove to prevent what he considered a fatal social gaffe. Mabelle and Gran were resolutely on my side. A Parmelee aunt in Granada, Mississippi, informed of my impending debut, wrote Mabelle a note which began, "You are sending my nephew and your son straight to perdition." It was a most diverting situation while it lasted, but even then I never felt the issue in any particular doubt.

I still own the impeccable, miniature, glossy topper which Young's, the famous hatter of the period, made for me. Fortified by that, a white waistcoat over a straw-stuffed false belly, tails, a monocle, and a brass-headed cane, I sang and danced my one number in *Brownies:*

> Miss Virginia,
> Can I win ya'
> Tell me, honey,
> Tell me, do . . .

The play was feeble beyond description and an immense success. G. B. refused to attend, although on his insistence I was billed as Master Webb Raum. Most gratifying of all was a note from Palmer Cox saying that I was the first actor to play Cholly Boutonniere as he had conceived him, a magnanimity not often found on the part of dramatists.

While I was strutting my stuff as Cholly, a rather obscure manager–playwright, Alexander Hume Ford, came backstage after the matinee and asked to speak to Mabelle. He explained that the following season he wanted to present a program of children's matinees—a ghastly form of entertainment which has happily since vanished—featuring *Oliver Twist*, the tower scene from *King John*, and various short plays from his own pen.

When he asked Mabelle if she would permit me to pursue a career behind the footlights, I noticed that a glazed chintz expression beclouded her eyes. She realized that there would be more than a little hell to pay if G. B. heard of such a notion. She told Mr. Ford as much. There was a pregnant pause during which I feared that my elders would ruin my career irreparably. Since I had no intention of allowing such a calamity to come about, I ended matters by informing both of them that I accepted the kind offer and would assist in concealing it from Mr. Raum.

In a fine spirit of compromise I agreed that I would submit to various tutors during the interim. It was an unhappy experiment. A succession of odd gentlemen used to arrive at our house bursting with optimism and erudition, only to depart after a few weeks' contact with me. It was discovered that I had a definite resistance to formal education.

When rehearsals began, my stepfather, not unnaturally noticing the sudden gaiety that filled the air, suspected that something unpleasant was happening. We informed him that I was to become a professional actor. "If this nonsense doesn't stop," G. B. declared, "that boy will be selling boot laces on the street corner before he is twenty-one!"

The following season, in the highest of spirits, I made my debut at the Children's Theatre as Oliver Twist. I played the role with boundless enthusiasm and very little skill, ingredients which resulted in highly favorable notices. From there I went on to being Prince Arthur in the tower scene from *King John*, during which I made dowagers' bosoms heave in pretty unison as I begged Huburt, with the utmost restraint and courtesy, not to "burn out mine eyes." This was followed by a heartbreaking performance in *The Master of Carleton Hall*. My role therein was a Southern youth who has discovered the disgraceful skeleton in the family cupboard—the fact that his father fought with the damn Yankees. I played the foolish boy with such abandon, so many sobs and tears, that it was suggested that I add to my repertoire by doing *Little Lord Fauntleroy*. I resisted the suggestion with indignation, a point which I wish entered on the record to my credit.

Throughout this period I received a great deal of favorable mention in the press and, as the ultimate accolade, was honored by having my head read by the then-eminent phrenologist, Mrs. Fowler. She forecast such amazing success for me that I have been obscurely dissatisfied with even the best notices ever since. In the fine afterglow of Mrs. Fowlers' forecast, I took it as only my due when, after the Children's Theatre closed, Mr. Ford persuaded Mabelle to allow me to play *The Master* at a few of the less conspicuous vaudeville houses on the Proctor Circuit.

It was during that engagement that I ran afoul of the Gerry Society. This imbecile organization had been founded by well-meaning, fashionable people to prevent the exploitation of children on the stage and sent watchers to all the theatres to see that nobody under sixteen years of age was supporting either a parent or himself by singing or dancing in public. The law was quite explicit: no singing or dancing! Nobody minded how arduous a part a child enacted just so long as he didn't break into a musical number. Unfortunately, however, Mr. Ford had written a song for me to sing to my baby sister in *The Master*, a touching bit of sentimentality designed to stop the matinee ladies from munching on their chocolates for at least three minutes. The Gerry Society, horrified by this innocuous lullaby, entered a formal protest. The result was that the music was eliminated. I was made to recite the lyrics, which I disliked intensely and did in such an insufferable ponging manner that my baby sister frequently was moved to tears of rage.

This was also the first occasion at which I learned that there are such things as stage tricks. At one point in *The Master* I had a long speech followed by a rush into my daddy's arms. The elderly ham who played my Daddy—and rather badly, as I remember—was supposed to kneel downstage with his back to the audience during my speech. One pleasant afternoon it dawned on me that something had been changed. I discovered myself delivering my tear-jerking comments with my back to the audience while poor daddy was upstage, mugging like hell at the delighted ladies. I gave the situation a good deal of perplexed thought as I ate dinner. When we came to the scene that night, Daddy started to pull the same trick. It was injudicious of him, for I stopped dead. After an appreciable pause I declared in a loud, ringing tone, "When you come downstage where you belong I shall continue the scene."

To my great delight the audience broke into laughter and applause. Daddy paled beneath his hoary makeup. As I showed no inclination to continue on his terms, he got up from his knees and, snorting like Faffner, took his proper position near the footlights. Having accomplished my purpose, I delivered my endless and affectionate speech with an even more sugary Southern accent than usual.

The Master was my first exposure to the Westphalian breed of actor, but not my last. As a result of the youth at which I learned my lesson, however, I have generally been prepared when anybody began to slice it thick. Years later I played with a diminutive red-headed star who had acquired the odious habit of mumbling her feed lines. It is well known that if an audience does not hear the question, it will not laugh at the answer. Each time she pulled this stratagem on me, I inquired in bell–like tones, "What did you say, dear?" She was infuriated, but after we had played the game for a few nights the audibility of her feed lines improved remarkably.

In movies there are ill-guided actors who will try to pull the same ancient technique. Some of them have even thought up new ones, such as the "Shifting Weight Gambit" attempted by one of America's leading stars in a recent picture. It results, when successfully executed, in the victim finding that the back of his head is to the camera. Quite aware of what was happening, I pretended to blow my lines. I went further and engaged in subtle conversation with the director. "I know that I have unusually handsome ears," I said to him, "but I don't think they interest the public." When this failed to remove the back of my skull from public view, I had a private session with the cameraman. He was kind and understanding. Whenever the pattern began to repeat itself, an apologetic

2.1. Clifton Webb at age eleven as the young father of our country. The John and Betsy Neylon Collection.

but firm voice would issue from behind the camera. "Sorry," it would say, "but we can't shoot this scene if you keep shifting your weight out of your marks and your lights."

And in my fancy I would for a moment be transported, not without amusement, back to Carleton Hall and dear old daddy and the matinee ladies who munched chocolates. The education of an actor is not acquired from books.

During his days at the Children's Theatre at the Carnegie Lyceum, there appeared a photo of a young "Webb Raum, Leading Man" in the *Brooklyn Eagle*. The article was headed, "Child Actors in Grown-Up Plays." The *New York Times* ran a review on March 16, 1902, of the plays at the Children's Theatre. It said, "Yesterday afternoon was signalized by the return of Master Webb Raum, whose successful vaudeville performances last Autumn in *The Master of Carlton* [sic] *Hall* was cut short by scarlet fever and diphtheria. His appearance yesterday in *Rags of Royalty* had him acting the double part of a boy King and his gamin counterpart with unwarranted exaggeration." He also played in *Washington's Birthday*, representing the Father of his country at the age of eleven.

2.2. Clifton Webb as Sid Sawyer in *Huckleberry Finn*. The John and Betsy Neylon Collection.

While I was thus in the elementary stages of a theatrical education, my stepfather was otherwise occupied. His talent for picking winners having left him, he was rapidly becoming the bookmakers' pet. Day after day Mabelle would return white-faced and unhappy from a calamitous matinee appearance at the Sheepshead Bay Racetrack. Suddenly a jewel or two would mysteriously be seen no more. The atmosphere around the apartment became strained and tense, but it was not Mabelle's fault. It was an essential part of her code and temperament that our home should be a gay place, an interesting place touched with success. She repeatedly cautioned me that I should neither talk to others about my own home life, nor inquire about theirs. This undoubtedly contributed to the impression that I was unfriendly and stuck-up, but I am glad that I followed her advice then and have ever since.

Life was drifting along in this mildly disorganized manner when an offer came from Klaw and Erlanger. They were going to produce *Huckleberry Finn* and wished me to play Sid Sawyer, the tattletale kid. By this time I was sufficiently experienced to override G. B.'s vehement opposition with very little trouble. I threw my schoolbooks out the window into West Seventy-seventh Street the day rehearsals began. *Huckleberry Finn* staggered along for five weeks in Philadelphia without perceptible success.

G. B.'s obvious disinterest in our whereabouts began to cause Mabelle deep concern. One Saturday night, a week before we closed in Philadelphia, she informed me with only the vaguest explanation that we were going to take a midnight train to New York. The trip was entirely shrouded in mystery. Upon arriving at the apartment we discovered that the safety latch had been set on the front door. After a great deal of bell ringing and pounding, the haughty Mr. Raum opened the door. He was costumed only in embarrassment. Embarrassment unfortunately, is a transparent emotion and therefore an inadequate garment.

This shock was followed by the appearance of a rather sporty young brunette who had obviously been playing Delilah to his Samson. Instead of a pair of scissors, she carried a satin slipper. Mabelle was temporarily speechless, but not so I. When I asked the young lady what she was doing in our apartment, she instructed me in no uncertain terms, brandishing the slipper, that if I came any closer she would dash out my brains.

It was not until years later that I learned that the night's discovery had not startled Mabelle so violently as one might have thought. At least one thoughtful friend had given her the name and address of the young lady currently receiving G. B.'s attentions. We spent what remained of the night at Gran's apartment nearby, and next morning went to Philadelphia to finish the run. When we returned to New York a week later, Mr. Raum had prudently seen fit to depart on a business trip.

I find myself, as I write this, laboring under the strong tendency to turn Green Berry Raum Jr. into a villain, probably because there have been so few villains in my life. If I extended myself at all, I am sure I could make him out a great deal worse. Perhaps he was not a villain, but only a son-of-a-bitch. The distinction is considerable, and not flattering to villains. Anybody who has lived extensively must have met a great many delightful sons-of-bitches.

It is not known how much Webb knew about his stepfather's background. Green Berry Raum Jr. was the son of General Green Berry Raum. General Raum was an author, lawyer, Civil War brigadier general and businessman. President Benjamin Harrison appointed him Commissioner of Pensions. He quickly had trouble separating his private business from his political life. He appointed his son (Webb's stepfather) to a newly created position in charge of appointments and promotions. Young Raum's actions in such a potentially lucrative position were extremely questionable. The Democratic majority declared that General Raum had prostituted his office for private gain and political advantage. There were charges of employees betting on horses, having bureau romances, and borrowing money. General Raum finished his term of office but never again held a high office or enjoyed his former status in the Republican Party.

Shortly after the close of *Huckleberry Finn* my professional career suffered a severe setback. In it I was entirely blameless. I suddenly and annoyingly began to grow. Like some rank species of weed I became taller and taller, and in a vain effort to cover my humiliation donned long trousers. Mabelle approached Marc Klaw for a new part that I might play. "Feed him whiskey," replied Klaw, "or else make up your mind to wait ten years until he catches up with himself."

After a good deal of reflection we adopted a compromise somewhere between the two. I was dispatched to Public School 87, which was conveniently located down the block, and to the acute surprise of everybody concerned, took to it very well. I did admirably in all my studies but arithmetic. I have ever since considered arithmetic a superfluous facet of education.

What I chiefly recall from my public school period is the principal, Mr. Boyer, who spent an inordinate amount of his time preaching cleanliness. While I was not by nature hostile to soap and water, I was nevertheless powerfully impressed by a story which Mr. Boyer related on every occasion he visited our classroom. It concerned a boy who was covered with gold paint to appear in a pageant and subsequently had the misfortune to die because all his pores had been filled. I spent the periods properly devoted to arithmetic in staring at the boys who sat ahead of me, noticing the dark rings about nearly every neck and speculating on whether or not they would be dead by three o'clock. When they thrived persistently and, indeed, even waxed stronger, I concluded that academic knowledge was largely fallacious.

Having been most unfairly banished from theatrical pursuits, I diverted myself in other ways. One of them was falling in love. I had learned about sex from a pretty little girl at my fifth birthday party, while still living in innocent Indianapolis, but it did not discernibly influence my feelings. Gladys Taliaferro, the object of my affection, was a soft-spoken Southern child who lived with her parents, Colonel and Mrs. Taliaferro, in a charming apartment on West Seventy-eighth Street. Her father, grotesquely cadaverous, with silky white hair that extended to his absurdly high collar, was the typical Southern colonel. I can remember nothing about the early phases of this attachment except that the Colonel and his

2.3. Mabelle Parmelee, circa 1900. The John and Betsy Neylon Collection.

lady regarded us with an indulgent amusement which I found entirely out of keeping with my emotions.

Life at home was meanwhile in an undulant condition, as G. B. strove desperately to follow the lines on the new leaf he daily promised to turn over. Without in any way realizing it, he furthered my career immensely by giving one Abe Hammerstein a job in his office. Abe happened to be the son of one of the greatest impresarios of all time, Oscar Hammerstein. Through Abe, Mabelle met Oscar I. They took a great shine to one another and he affectionately nicknamed her "Blondie."

Nearly everybody connected with Oscar I, including his three sons, Willie, Arthur, and Abe, was deadly afraid of him. At the sound of his gigantic feet approaching, faces would lose their expression and conversation smother. His most casual entrance (the inevitable outsized cigar in one corner of his mouth and a silk hat clinging improbably to the side of his head) brought the entire company to its feet, frozen at attention—all except Mabelle. She invariably answered his deadpan, sardonic remarks by bursting into howls of laughter.

I think the secret of Mabelle's success with Oscar lay in his rather pathetic longing for somebody who didn't treat him like a god. He was most generous, and every Monday evening would see us gaily installed in a box at Hammerstein's Victoria, then the city's leading vaudeville house. My stock went up immensely with Gladys Taliaferro when I was in a position to invite her to see the stars of the day.

Oscar had at this time just realized his dream of years—to be impresario of an opera company. The first few weeks of his Manhattan Opera Company were not a marked success and met with the fiercest opposition from the rival Metropolitan. It was not until he produced *Carmen* with an extraordinary singer, Bressler-Gianoli as the gypsy cigarette girl, that his venture took on vitality. Seated in the box which Oscar had given us, *Carmen* was the first opera I had ever seen. I at once determined that I would be a great opera singer myself, but did not confide my resolve to Mabelle during the first intermission as I was tempted to. I felt that my career had caused quite enough trouble already and, furthermore, was perfectly confident, in my guileless youth, of accomplishing whatever I wanted by my own unaided efforts.

After two years of formal education, school and I went our separate paths for the last time and forever. At graduation time it was found, to my own consternation and Mabelle's, that I was the *Abou Ben Adhem* of the class in all subjects save algebra. This prestige seemed to me to demand something special at graduation exercises. Being known as "that young fellow who has been on the stage," I felt that my farewell appearance before my classmates should leave them with no uncertain impression of my histrionic abilities.

Mabelle was all for a song and dance act, but I reminded her of what had transpired at the previous commencement when I was put down for a number. Mabelle had taken her place at the piano, everything was going according to rehearsal, and I was spreading my personality by extravagant kicks and bounds in all directions when the music suddenly ceased in mid-chorus. Mabelle had become so fascinated by my prodigious cavorting that she had lost her place in the music. There she sat, crimson of countenance and close to tears of shame. "Start over again, Mother dear," I directed composedly, and so we did.

This time however, I told Mabelle reluctantly that I was taking no more chances on her conduct. She was to sit with the other parents and dress and try to look like a mother—something which was contrary to all her instincts—while I delivered *Spartacus to the Romans at Capua* from McGuffey's Fifth Reader.

On the appointed day I arose in the assembly hall, made a bow, and started off in the approved dramatic manner. Halfway through I forgot a line and turned for aid to the young man who was holding the book. I found him staring at me in a daze, so shaken by the eloquence of my recitation that he had let my speech flutter to the floor. Again I was forced to start from the beginning while Mabelle looked as if she had swallowed the family canary.

So it was that I departed academic pursuits forever, a leave-taking which has never occasioned any particular regret on my part.

That autumn, as our joint finances were dismal and G. B. was more often absent than with us, I decided that I should become the family breadwinner. I answered an obscure advertisement and almost overnight found myself an office boy in a curb broker's office in that section of New York whimsically known as "Downtown," a region of skyscrapers and little sun of which I knew nothing. I was stationed in a smudgy window under instructions to signal certain cabalistic signs to the buyers and sellers in the street, according to directions relayed by a clerk who stood behind me. For this legerdemain I was to receive fifteen dollars a week.

Unfortunately, for both the firm's customers and my own financial future, I soon showed an extraordinary ability at getting the signs mixed. With an elegant gesture I turned bears to bulls, profits to losses, sales from short to long. When the confusion became intolerable, I was removed to the comparative security of a desk job. Why the firm put up with me at all is something I cannot understand. I suspect that because the months of my employment were just before Christmas, kindhearted Mr. Gallagher did not want to discharge the only support of a widowed mother (as I had described myself piteously on my application blank) at the season of peace and goodwill. Indeed, I think he rather liked me for my eagerness, although more than once he remarked in a troubled manner, "You're not suited to this, kid." From the expression on his face I knew that he was wondering, without success, what on earth I *was* suited for.

I was a particular enigma to the sweet, big Irish girl who managed the office. On Saturdays the office boys were expected to toil over the week's sales books. One Saturday I asked if I might have the afternoon off.

"What for?"

"Mme Nellie Melba is singing at the opera," I explained. "I am very anxious to hear her."

"What does she sing?"

"*Otello*," I said.

"What's that?" said Miss Ryan blankly.

But catching the look of ineffable wistfulness and longing which I manufactured to support my wish, she said, "Okay, kid—skidoo."

When the Curb exchange closed on the day before Christmas, Mr. Gallagher came in rather plastered. To each of the assembled staff he gravely handed an envelope containing either a five- or ten-dollar gold piece. As he handed me mine—I was in the five-dollar class—he mumbled helplessly, "You're a nice kid."

The pathetic air in which he had said this, and the gold piece itself, set my conscience pricking. After his New Year hangover had been soothed, I bearded Mr. Gallagher and told him frankly, "I don't like to take your money when I can't do your work."

"You don't like it here, do you?" he asked.

"No," I said, then added with equal honesty, "But I do like all of *you*."

That marked the end of my financial career. Even in those formative years I had little inclination to waste my energies on jobs which could obviously lead me nowhere along the path which I had resolved to follow—and that path, I already knew with absolute certainty, did not at any point pass through the chasms of Downtown.

Mabelle not only agreed, but abetted me. She had by this time entirely transferred her own longing for a theatrical career to me and resolutely refused to settle for anything less glorious than a vision of my name in lights.

Our future could scarcely have been more obscure and unsettled than it was that wretched January, but she cheerfully dismissed Wall Street and its environs with a wave of her pretty hand. "Thank God that's over," she said. "We won't try *that* again."

CHAPTER 3

Art and Opera

My first and last gambol with the Bulls and Bears having proved a wretched failure, I began to look about for another occupation. The theatre was unfortunately impossible. Until my skinny legs showed less tendency to wobble and my voice could be trusted to remain on one pitch for the duration of a complete breath, I could not aspire to any better part than the front legs of a giraffe in a circus.

In the meantime there was the matter of my further education. Neither Mabelle nor I entertained any serious thought of high school, for it was clear to both of us that any future I might have did not depend upon algebra and economics. Encouraged by Mabelle in the belief that to be a success in the theatre one should know something of the sister arts, I hied myself to the Art Students' League in West Fifty-seventh Street. Barely in my teens, but already six feet tall, I enrolled there as a student.

I spent my first week in the Antique Class. I defiled sheet after sheet of beautiful soft, white paper with sketches of the Hermes, the Venus de Milo, and unrelated scraps of less illustrious anatomies, all of which was presented to me in disgustingly grimy plaster of Paris. Not unnaturally, this palled on me. Gladys Taliaferro, not to be outdone in artistic aspiration, had in the meantime joined the New York School of Art—commonly known as "The Chase School"—and urged me to enter the Illustration Class in which she was working. I had a sneaking impression that she wanted to keep a closer eye on me. Delighted at the compliment, I bade farewell to Venus and the League and presently found myself seated beside Gladys, sketching a model who was clothed in everything thought best of in the Fashionable Young Thing of the period—complete with high button boots, ruffled parasol, and towering pompadour crowned with a baker's dozen hair-puffs.

"Isn't she lovely?" Gladys breathed enthusiastically in my ear.

"Not that I can notice," I replied. I found no fault with the model's costume, but her face failed to win me. The more I tried to draw it, indeed, the more intense became my dislike. Why, I reflected, should I be the instrument of perpetuating *that* for posterity?"

Striving with the best of faith to enable Art to improve on Nature, I lent my portrait features modeled after the style popularized by Charles Dana Gibson. Gladys was more than a little apprehensive of this flagrant departure from rule, but I scoffed at her anxiety in what I felt was the best man-of-the-world manner. I had not the slightest doubt but that on criticism day my instructor, Kenneth Hayes Miller, would recognize that I had created a masterpiece and would trumpet my genius to the world.

With highest hope I watched his approach. Finally he positioned himself before my drawing, squinted from behind his pince-nez, and drew a heavy crayoned cross through my masterpiece. "Paint what you see," he said into his beard, and passed on amid the sycophantic titters of the other students.

The experience convinced me immediately that the Illustration Class did not suit my talents. I had recently read *Trilby*, and what I longed for in the realm of Art was something closer to the vie de Boheme so piquantly depicted by the Messrs. DuMaurier and Puccini. In quest of this I investigated other corridors of the school and was ultimately rewarded by coming upon a door labeled "Men's Life Class." I opened it and found my quivering nose greeted by a cacophony of odors in which cheap tobacco, turpentine, dust, and human sweat commingled. Through clouds of smoke I made out twenty or more men sitting or standing at easels around the model's throne, zealously committing to canvas the mottled and Rubenesque bulges of a nude female.

Here, I decided at once, was the place for me. Inquiry of the monitor revealed that as a student at the school I was entitled to enter the Life Class if I fancied to do so. "Of course," he added, "on your first day you'll have to set 'em up for the boys."

"Of course," I agreed, without the faintest idea what this obligation meant. It was fortunate for the effect I intended that my voice began with a squeak and ended with a froglike croak, but the monitor kindly overlooked this. He explained that according to custom immemorial, a new member stood the class to beer and sandwiches.

That evening I informed Mabelle that I had joined the Life Class and required three dollars. The words, "Life Class" passed over her head, but a demand for three dollars called for explanation in view of the rickety state of our bank balance. I indulged in some roundabout verbosity, however, and she kicked through handsomely.

Next morning I handed the money to the monitor and took my place hastily, hoping to escape notice. The men around me, several of whom affected shaggy beards, were all much older than I. The conversation was highly spiced, the smoke stung my eyes, and trying to trace the model's voluptuous curves—so different from the barren plaster of Paris—caused me considerable inner confusion. At the luncheon recess the monitor announced that a new member had joined the class and was going to set 'em up. This welcome news was greeted with cheers and shouts of "Speech! Speech!" Suddenly I felt myself lifted bodily by innumerable hands and placed embarrassingly close to the smiling and unabashedly naked model.

Absolute panic gripped me. I felt myself redden from nose to toe, and for the first time in my life I resolutely wished that I were dead—or better yet had never been born.

This was my first experience with an emotion which has never left me. On the stage my ad libs are fluent, but pathological terror overcomes me at the thought of having to rise before an assembly of people without footlights between us, and to start cold: "Ladies and Gentlemen . . ." One night at Reisenweber's, where it was the habit of the master of ceremonies to pick out people in the room and ask them to "say something," I saw the spotlight moving towards me. I ducked down and under the tables and made my way out the door.

Such flight, however, was not possible from the eminence from which I surveyed the Life Class. After a most dreadful pause I heard a voice, scarcely recognizable as my own, tremulously announcing: "I feel like a damned fool!"

This was the best and certainly the most truthful public address I have ever delivered. If I should ever get an Oscar, I shall repeat it, confident of its success. It brought a laugh and a rather surprising amount of applause. From the midst of the turmoil I heard a deep, Middle Western voice drawl: "Don't worry kid. Come and sit by me. I'll look out for you."

That was my introduction to George Bellows, and the beginning of a friendship which was to play a large part in my education. George completely fulfilled my concept of what an artist should be—breezy, happy-go-lucky, adventurous, hearty, and enormously talented. He was serious about nothing except art, and on this he concentrated fiercely all the energies of a vigorous mind and body. In retrospect, I know that I gained more from companionship with him than from anything else the Chase School had to offer me.

Bellows taught me by vehement word and by constant example the habit of work. His scorn for the idler and the dilettante was scathing, and his vocabulary on this topic might have furnished James M. Cain with some choice epithets. In his company it was possible for even the most callow adolescent to develop neurotic or trumpery ideas about life or art.

My portfolio, which I religiously carried home each evening, ultimately piqued Mabelle's curiosity. She asked to see what I was doing. With an air I trusted was suitably nonchalant, I spread several sheets before her gaze. "My God!" she screamed, "Don't tell me you've been drawing naked women?" It required all my persuasion to convince her that the sort of model engaged for the Men's Life Class was not such as would provoke unchaste thoughts, nor tempt me from the trail blazed by Sir Galahad.

My friendship with Bellows continued through the two years I spent in art school, and up to his untimely death. To me he combined the offices of older brother and young uncle at a time in my life when I sorely needed someone in at least one of these capacities. Occasionally he would invite me to go out on the town with him. Innocent, indeed, were our roisterings, for we had very little money; what we did both have was the infinitely more precious gift for being easily entertained. Mabelle and he hit if off wonderfully from the very first time he came to the apartment—economy had driven us to a smaller, cheaper place on Broadway—and sampled our *specialte de maison*, corned beef and cabbage, Indiana style. When George later became engaged to Emma Story, whom he had met and courted at the Art School, he brought her over to partake of this delicacy and to pry its secret from Mabelle.

From time to time George would desert the Life Class for a term at Portraiture, and I followed loyally and literally at his heels. Under the guidance of that splendid artist and uncompromising teacher, Robert Henri, Bellows's powers began to give further promise of the achievements which were ultimately his. Even I began to sprout. In my second year I somewhat unaccountably won an Honorable Mention at the school's annual show. That same year I took first prize for the most original costume at the Students' Ball . . . an honor in which Mabelle shared, for she literally forced me to make up as Eddie Foy singing his current song hit, *I'm a Poor Unhappy Maid.*

I'm a poor unhappy maid
On the shelf for years I've stayed
My poor heart it itches
To mend someone's britches
I'm a poor unhappy maid

Spurred by these scattered laurels, I began to consider abandoning my theatrical ambition in favor of becoming America's premier artist.

As a mild step in this direction I imitated George to the extent of acquiring a large bulldog pipe. Lacking courage to practice smoking the diabolical instrument at home or school, I produced it one evening in the Taliaferro's parlor, while paying a call upon Gladys.

She had taken my desertion of the Illustrated Class rather poorly, until I had subtly led her to believe that the sophistication I was acquiring in an exclusively male atmosphere would do something to bridge the three years gap in our ages. Gladys, if the truth be known, was developing serious if premature intentions of becoming the first Mrs. Webb Raum. I felt that my pipe would not only accrue me prestige in the Colonel's eyes, but would make his daughter realize that I was a man of serious mien who would stand for no nonsense.

When I took the briar from my pocket and fondled it negligently before asking permission to smoke, I thought I was making headway. Impressively, I produced my Old English Plug Cut—a variety of weed which I did not at the time realize was smoked only by superannuated veterans. I lit up and proceeded to puff like Siegfried's dragon when the steam valves at the Met are working full blast. Gladys seemed gratifyingly impressed—at least for ten minutes. Then things began to drift curiously out of focus.

"What," inquired Gladys, "can be the matter with you, Webb? Why, you look so green!"

I wove to the window just in time.

Later that evening, extended limply on the divan as Gladys assuaged my head with damp towels, I tardily joined the rest of male humanity in discovering that a woman may be better conquered by weakness than by strength.

Bellows shared a studio with two other artists in the Lincoln Arcade, an enormous arcade at Broadway and Sixty-seventh Street devoted to the arts. Its decor and surroundings were on the grubby side, but it had, among too many other things, a piano. George's love of music had led him to the point of feeling that singing was a vital part of his progress as a painter. There one day, I met a girl named Grace Inman, who was studying voice and whom George was not disinclined to impress with his own vocal gifts. Undistinguished as these latter were, I think he thought Grace more likely to appreciate his romantic rendition of "Rose in the Bud" than his portraits of sinewy pugilists.

In his usual generous mood, George thought he would be helpful. "Robin, here," he remarked, "chirps."

"Chirp," said Grace.

I did. My voice, just past the cracking stage, gave vague promise of becoming a baritone. Grace liked it enough to offer to recommend me to her teacher, Paul Savage, who was one of the best in New York.

"I haven't any money," I confessed ruefully, but I was a dweller in that enchanted Bohemia where anything might happen. Grace brushed my remark graciously aside and a week or so later sent me a note that Mr. Savage would see me at his studio in Carnegie Hall the next morning.

After hearing several songs, Savage offered to take me as a pupil. Again I confessed my temporary impoverishment. "Never mind," he said, "I'll give you lessons now, and you can pay me back later."

Paul Savage's faith in me had a decisive effect in shaping my still nascent career. Painting passed from consuming interest to relaxation. Singing took its place. I spent less and less time at Art School—I soon left it entirely—and more in practicing and going to hear good music.

Webb studied with at least two well-known artists, William Chase and Robert Henri. When he was thirteen his paintings were exhibited.

This last was quite easy. In addition to the entree which Oscar Hammerstein had given us at the Manhattan, Mabelle had acquired passes for the Metropolitan. She and I made excellent use of them. We had practically no money to devote to pleasure or anything else, for Mr. Raum had decided to depart for the Klondike (for what reason I still have only the sketchiest idea) and the promised remittances did not materialize. The dinner jacket I was rapidly outgrowing, however, was still passable in a crowd.

"For God's sake bend your knees and keep your hands in your pockets!" Mabelle would instruct me; "Then nobody will see that your trousers and sleeves are too short."

I like to think that we made a rather piquant pair as we sallied forth under these straitened circumstances. Mabelle still possessed the treasured remnants of a once well-stocked, smart wardrobe. These, fortified by her talent with scissors, needle, thread, and a few safety pins, enabled her to sail into the Met's first nights with radiant self-assurance.

Looking back, I strongly suspect that she got a tremendous kick from her innocent game of make believe, of showing herself as fine as the finest in the fabled Diamond Horseshoe. Such guile is one of Mabelle's most delightful traits. Once long afterwards, when we were affluent and Molyneaux was designing her clothes (his pet name for her is "My Stylish Stout"), she went with me to one of Valentina's Russian Easter parties wearing a hat which I had never seen before but which looked vaguely familiar.

Valentina, from her chosen vantage point at the head of the stairs, was casting a critical eye on each piece of approaching millinery. "Darling," she murmured against Mabelle's cheek, "it's simply wonderful to see you. Who made your hat?"

"A little woman I discovered," said Mabelle.

"If anyone asks you where you got it," Valentina said, "please say you got it from me."

"Of course, darling," Mabelle purred. Out of sight and earshot, my mother favored me with a meaningful wink. "Not bad," she said, "for the bow off a fruit basket and some of the year-before-last's Paris violets."

With the same bravura spirit we enjoyed our gala evenings. We dressed punctiliously and took a cab to the Opera House. Mabelle would invariably order me to perform a singular operation which she called, "sitting light," apparently under the impression that by so doing the taximeter would register less. As we drew up to the blazing marquee she would hiss, "Don't you dare treat me like a mother!" And in we swirled.

During the entr'acte we usually managed, with becoming naiveté and delight, to run across a number of old friends. If we failed to wind up with a bid to supper and the offer of a lift home, we would slip unobtrusively—and with the greatest indignation—into the bowels of a subway.

At the Manhattan, Mabelle was in her element. As we ordinarily sat in the front row, her blonde vivacity immediately drew the attention and admiration of the Italian male members of the cast. When they rolled their dark liquid eyes and sang expressively to her, she would nudge me and giggle. Oscar found it all intensely amusing, particularly the tenor Bassi, who once took Mabelle for a drive in Central Park in a rented Victoria. The unfortunate man did not know a single word of English, but by means of his ubiquitous Berlitz book they carried on what must have been a peculiarly circumscribed conversation.

We frequently went to rehearsals, and I exerted my utmost efforts in maneuvering to snatch backstage glimpses of the ravishing Mary Garden. When Ben Ali Haggin's portrait of her at *Thaïs* was exhibited, I made a copy, which I hung proudly in my bedroom.

Among Mabelle's old friends in New York were Mr. and Mrs. Alfred Barnes, whose son, Emerson, and daughter, Rose, were companions of mine. The Barnes family was utterly unmusical. They had a pianola, of course, but when the three of us pumped long and arduously at its entrails, it was with far more enthusiasm for the *Merry Widow Waltz* and selections from *The Red Mill* than for any classical numbers. Emerson remarked frankly and frequently that he could not understand why I was wasting my time on what he derisively called "that grand opera."

His sentiments in no way deterred me. Under the inspiration of Paul Savage I was taking music as seriously as I knew how. I remember sitting through the piano rehearsals of Strauss's *Elektra*, score in hand, marking the phrasing. On the afternoon of the dress rehearsal of *Pelleas and Melisande* I boasted to Emerson that I was going. Debussy's score meant nothing to him, but Mary Garden, whose recent *Salome* had set up a howl that had exploded on the sacred front pages of the *Time* and *Herald*, did. At the notion of seeing Miss Garden, his eyes sparkled.

"Come along . . . I'll get you in," I offered. When the doorman at the Manhattan addressed me as "Mr. Raum," I could see that Emerson was becoming increasingly impressed. True to his lights, he concealed it by mumbling as we went down the aisle, "If only she was going to sing *The Merry Widow.*"

Mary and Debussy—severally or together—never made a more complete and sudden conquest. The witchery of the music and the loveliness of Mary's *Melisande* very nearly altered the course of Emerson Barnes's life. He sat rapt, lifted out of himself. When it was over, he moved as if in a dream. On the way out he bought tickets to the next opening and from that moment on was a devoted opera lover. The study of music became the major and enduring interest in his life.

Of such petty triumphs are the peaks of a boy's life built.

There was a line in *Sitting Pretty* which I like to think is as true of Clifton Webb as of Mr. Belvedere. When Mrs. King remarks to her babysitter with entirely understandable exasperation, "Is there anything you haven't been?" Belvedere replies, "Yes, Mrs. King. I have never been an idler or a parasite."

It was, I believe, my capacity for hard work and concentration which primarily caused Paul Savage to take such an interest in me. He used to commend me on the quality which he respected most and insisted upon in his pupils—application. I fear that it is a quality all too often lacking in the younger generation in the theatre today.

I mention the point at this juncture because this was the time in my life when Orville Harrold came to New York from Muncie, Indiana. He was a young man with high hopes of becoming an opera singer, and someone gave him a letter of introduction addressed to Mabelle and told him to visit his fellow Hoosiers.

Orville Harrold was born in Cowan, Indiana, just south of Muncie. He grew up in Muncie and was married there. Webb does not mention if there was any Indiana connection between Harrold and Mabelle. Presumably, when Harrold decided to move to New York, someone told him to visit fellow Hoosiers Mabelle and Clifton in the hope they might be able to further his career. In addition to performing in his hearse, Harrold was good enough to sing at the Chicago World's Fair as a teenager. The New York Metropolitan Opera lists him performing at least 160 times from 1919 to 1921.

Back in Muncie, Orville had worked for an undertaker. Driving the hearse, he had sung *La Donna e mobile* so extravagantly that some of the mourners had suggested that the caroling hearse-driver was wasting his talents and should be storming Hammerstein's and the Met. Mabelle heard him sing the afternoon he arrived at our apartment. The next morning she was at Oscar's office, torturing his ears with praises of the new American tenor whom she had discovered.

"Looks like it's some black-eyed boy you're stuck on, Blondie," he commented—and would have none of it.

Mabelle was indeed fond of him, but a great deal more than that was involved. She urged Orville to study, swearing that she would keep at Oscar until he had a hearing. She did keep at Oscar, but Orville did not keep at studying. He went on the road with a quartet, playing the second-string vaudeville houses.

A year passed during which we saw or heard nothing of Orville Harrold. Then, without warning, he turned up at our apartment one afternoon. Mabelle's inclination was to have no more of him, but he begged forgiveness so naively and touchingly that he won her over completely.

His quartet was appearing in *Wine, Women, and Song* at the Circle Theatre. When the show closed they went back to vaudeville and secured a booking at Hammerstein's Victoria. Mabelle badgered Oscar into coming down from his office to hear Orville. When he did, he turned to her and demanded: "Why didn't you tell me about him before?"

"He's the one I've been telling you about for a year," Mabelle said.

"I hear he's been living with a pony dancer, drinking his head off," Oscar grumbled through the inevitable cigar.

"What the hell does that matter if he can sing?" Mabelle retorted.

Oscar was too astute not to concede that point. "You have a voice," he told Orville, "but you have nothing up here." He tapped a finger on his forehead. "You must study, study, study!" And for a full year Orville did. Hammerstein financed him while he learned French and Italian, mise-en-scène, and a number of the leading tenor roles. When Oscar thought his new tenor was ready, he one Sunday afternoon invited the foremost music critics to a private audition. Mabelle and I attended.

Orville sang *Vesti la giubba* and the tenor aria from *Manon*. He sang them so magnificently that the critics were swept off their feet by "Oscar's discovery." They saw that here was a really great native tenor. Everybody present that afternoon was swept off his feet—except Orville. When Mabelle and I went backstage, his first remark to us was, "Say, could you hear me?"

Orville Harrold opened at the Manhattan that season in *Pagliacci*. The house was jammed. All standing room was sold out. Orville Harrold was an immediate and spectacular success. His dressing room was piled to the baroque ceiling with wreaths from all the Italian societies, with bouquets sent by the women who had fallen for his melting eyes and his coal black hair and his glorious, golden voice.

The tributes apparently meant nothing at all to him. "Don't you want them?" Mabelle asked helplessly when Orville was for walking out after the performance, leaving the sea of flowers and cards and telegrams to be swept into the dust bin.

"You take them, if you want," Orville answered. He left.

When Hammerstein's London Opera House was opened, Orville Harrold was the star. London went mad for him. But in London, too, he was extraordinarily indifferent to his success and the demands of a great career.

He rapidly lost his powers and his prestige. He came back to New York and sang in *Naughty Marietta*. After that—a very short time after that—he became an almost forgotten name.

3.1. Orville Harrold in *Faust*, circa 1919–21. The Library of Congress.

It may be that Orville Harrold suffered from some obscure will to-wards self-destruction. I have no idea where he is today, or if he is even alive, but I have thought of him often over the years. I suspect that his failure was something far more tragic than any psychic perversity. Some-body whose name I cannot recollect once wrote that every artist has a fore-destined appointment with himself—and that it is very rare that any artist keeps this appointment. It is a teasing truth for one to ponder. The hour of the appointment is not disclosed in advance, nor the place designated—but one thing is certain. Talent is not the only password. Without the application of which Paul Savage spoke so often in his high little studio over Fifty-seventh Street, it is certain that you will not be at the appointed place at the appointed time.

According to Charles A. Hooey in an article in *Music Web International*, Harr-old sang too often and in roles too heavy for him. In short order his voice began to show strain. His popularity waned and his career as a great tenor was soon over. He might have been pushed too much, too soon, but Harrold must bear some of the blame. He may have squandered his great gift. He became an itinerant musician, playing in vaudeville, and even appeared in two Broadway musicals in the 1920s. He died October 23, 1933, at age fifty-six.

CHAPTER 4

Making Progress and Moving Up

Our stock of saleable objects, principally Mabelle's jewels, was running low. It was vitally necessary that I begin earning some money.

I was now seventeen and for a year—my second studying with Paul Savage—I had been working on a number of the great dramatic baritone roles: Scarpia, Escarmillo, etc., with even a chromatic fling at Pagliacci. If I was to be a singing actor, it appeared, I should by all means get going.

At Paul Savage's suggestion I went down to the office of the Aborn Brothers' Opera Company. I asked for and was given an audition. I saw my name—Webb Raum, baritone, and address—entered on a card. I was also given the stock promise which every young actor soon learns to loathe: "If anything turns up, we'll let you know."

I knew perfectly well that the chances were overwhelmingly against anything turning up. Stronger than that knowledge, however, was another: that I belonged to and in the theatre, and that some day, through one door or another, I would find my way into it. My only concern was in leaving no doorbell unpushed and in being ready to insert a stubborn foot the moment any door, even the most unlikely, should open so much as a crack.

The accusation of being unduly lucky has often been leveled at me. I have always rejected it, and do so again. For in order for a ripened plum to fall into one's lap, it is necessary that one's lap be waiting for the plum and otherwise unoccupied at the moment of harvest. The stars in heaven cast a pretty light, but their combinations have nothing to do with the comings and goings of the most elusive femme fatale on this planet, Opportunity.

I have always said "yes" because it has never occurred to me that I could not do anything I set out to do. It is an attitude I endorse completely, although it does matter to whom and to what one says "yes"—and the manner in which the monosyllable is spoken. You can always say "yes" and change your mind afterward to "no," but "no" once spoken is irrevocable. The irrevocable, in the theatre as elsewhere, is to be sternly resisted. When I was asked, "Can you play a man of ninety?" I at once replied, "Yes . . . of course." I thereupon played old man Rockefeller. I have boundless faith that God and Darryl Zanuck will prevent me from ever being typed.

Having indulged in this rather elaborate qualification, I must confess that it was actually less than a week after I put my name down at the Aborn Brothers' office that I was called on the telephone and asked if I would leave at once for Washington, to take over a part in *The Bohemian Girl* in which one of the Aborn companies was touring.

When I did not immediately replay, the voice at the other end of the wire said persuasively, "We'll pay you thirty-five a week and traveling expenses."

"I'll go," I said. Honesty balanced with effrontery, however, to the extent of my admitting that *The Bohemian Girl* and I did not enjoy so much as a nodding acquaintance. I had never seen either the score or the libretto. In view of this I thought it fit to inquire when I was expected to go on, and was told that the actor whom I was to replace would leave at the end of the week. That gave me exactly four days in which to learn the role.

Mabelle packed me and saw me off. I do not know whether it testifies to her confidence or her foolishness that she never once even implied the slightest doubt of my success. Whichever, it was extremely comforting and may well have helped work the miracle. Six days of watching performances, one rehearsal, and I went on. I was presumably at least acceptable, for I finished the tour with *The Bohemian Girl*. She survived eight weeks before sinking to an asthmatic death.

Having inadvertently gained a reputation as a quick study, I was suitably rewarded. My next job was a hurry call to hie myself to Boston to sing Laertes to Mabel Garrison's *Mignon*. Again it was a role which I had never studied, only this time the good brothers Aborn rang me up on a Friday morning. "I'll take the one o'clock today," I promised, "and I'll be ready to go on Monday night if you will send someone to Grand Central with the score and give me an accompanist to work with when I get to Boston."

All the way up the Connecticut shore that April afternoon I pored over *Mignon* and mumbled Laertes lines. Through Saturday, Sunday, and most

4.1. Clifton Webb at age nineteen. The John and Betsy Neylon Collection.

of Monday, George Siemon—Mabel Garrison's husband and a superb pianist—coached me. I remember hearing the cries of the newsboys that afternoon, drifting up from the street: "*Titanic* sunk! Many lives lost!"

It was Mabel Garrison's debut as Felina in *Mignon*, and, consequently, she and George were particularly keen about having all the details perfect. Having a completely green Laertes thrust into her salon must have been remarkably unpleasant, but both she and George were charming to me. We opened Monday evening. On Tuesday morning the press was kind. On Tuesday afternoon I asked Milton Aborn for more money. On Wednesday morning he raised my salary five dollars.

Ten minutes after I returned to New York I pushed Mabelle into a chair and shut the door. "Get a divorce," I said. "Get rid of Raum. Get rid of every goddamn piece of furniture and everything connected with him. From now on we're on our own!"

I handed her twenty dollars from my week's salary. "Well, if I divorce him at least I'll know I'm really a grass widow," she sighed. "The way things have been the last few years, with no word from him, I haven't known if I was married or not . . ."

The spring opera season was drawing to a close, but the Aborn brothers decided to put on Humperdink's *Hansel and Gretel* for a short run at the Broadway Theatre. Two men had been engaged to sing the Witch—alternately, as the music is excessively difficult and the role makes tremendous demands on a singer's strength. Four days before the opening one Witch caught a cold. It resulted in another urgent phone call to me.

I said my customary "yes," then rang Paul Savage. He promised to teach me the part between rehearsals. His sister, Ruth Savage, who was his accompanist, worked tirelessly day and night as I committed the score to memory.

When the wardrobe mistress handed me my costume, I found myself gazing upon a limp, colorless rag suspiciously reminiscent of a filthy Mother Hubbard. My nose mounted sixty degrees above its usual zenith. I spread the nauseating thing before Mabelle. "You can't go on in that!" she howled. "I wouldn't dream of letting you!"

When I came home after rehearsal I found my parent up to her neck in shredded bed sheets, and the pots in our miniature kitchen overflowing with Diamond Dyes in every imaginable shade of red, orange, green and brown. Out of this unholy mess Mabelle evolved a long, floating, russet garment that looked something like the Disney Witch which Walt thought up years later to unnerve poor Snow White. My makeup for each performance required a full hour and a half, as I even painted my long fingers to resemble talons.

My first appearance was at the Monday matinee. The other witch went on that night, but it turned out to be not only his first but his last performance. In the morning Milton Aborn asked me if I would sing every performance from then on. The press had been extremely flattering to me, and to Mabelle's intense delight every critic mentioned my costume.

"I'll sing the part," I said to him. "But I think I should have more money."

He demurred, more as a matter of principle than from conviction. I held firm. "All right," he said, "I'll give you ten dollars more." That made roughly fifty dollars a week for ten performances.

We played two weeks in New York and two in Washington, D.C., in the hottest May weather ever recorded in the District. My makeup ran in chromatic rivulets down my nose, and my painted talons dripped about my toes. It did not trouble me at all. For fifty dollars every Saturday night and the knowledge that I was a hit, I would willingly have played one-night stands in hell.

Webb was tutored in French, German, and Italian and took to the piano so well that he was composing concertos at age sixteen. As mentioned previously, he made his opera debut at age twenty-two in *Mignon*, playing the important comedy part of Laertes. He also appeared in *La Tosca, Tales of Hoffman, La Boheme,* and *Madame Butterfly.* He and Mabelle went up and down the eastern coast for two years.

I was billed as Webb Raum, but as Mabelle's divorce proceedings got under way we both felt the time had come to drop my stepfather's name forever. I had always loathed it. The name Webb I liked. The sensible thing seemed to be to keep it as a surname and find another that went well with it.

I found a pencil and paper and started to write down every name we could think of, from Abraham to Zachariah. We in due course arrived at the C's—Charles, Charlemagne, Clayton, Clinton—none of them appealed to me. I wanted something with rhythm. For no particular reason I wrote down Clifton Webb. Clifton Webb . . . pum-tee-pum . . . Clifton Webb.

"I think that does it," I said.

"How right you are, dear," Mabelle said. "It will look very nice in lights."

The selection must have been a happy one, for everybody accepted it at once. I cannot recall anybody ever calling either of us Raum again. Mabelle became Mrs. Webb—and Mr. Raum became a memory that seemed less with each passing year.

I must indulge in a moment of irony at Mr. Raum's expense, before discarding him entirely. A few months before my twenty-first birthday I was headlining the Palace Theatre in a dance act with Mae Murray. We had been engaged for a week, but so pleasant was the audience's response that we were held over seven more. I was feeling peculiarly pleased with myself, for Mae and I were the first dance team to play the Palace continuously for more than two weeks.

One evening I was on my way to the theatre with my Boston bull on a leash. As I crossed Broadway at Forty-sixth Street, the dog decided to pause at a convenient hydrant. There was a man, obviously drunken, standing by the curb. Reeling slightly, he leaned over to pat the animal. "Hello, Sporty," he mumbled thickly.

The man was G. B., my stepfather, but in the shadow of the building he did not recognize me.

I looked up at the Palace. There—in lights and letters three feet high—burned the glittering legend "Mae Murray and Clifton Webb." I looked back to the curb. Indeed, I thought with a pride which I am afraid is wholly reprehensible, "So you're the son-of-a-bitch who said I'd be selling cigarettes on this corner of Broadway when I was twenty-one!"

"I've taught you all I can," Paul Savage said one day. "What do I do next?" I answered. It was summer now, and there had been no emergency calls from the Messrs. Aborn for several weeks.

"One of the world's greatest singers is here in New York," Paul told me. "Victor Maurel. He created Falstaff, and Iago in *Otello* at La Scala. No one has ever touched him in those roles. I hear he's forming an opera company. You might go to him."

"I certainly shall," I said. I found the Maurels, Monsieur and Madame—she was the business half of the firm—occupying an enormous brownstone monstrosity on Seventy-Fourth Street, just off Eighth Avenue. Maurel must have been seventy, but he was still extremely handsome, tall and magnificently built—and reeking of perfume. He heard me sing and nodded condescendingly. "Very good," he said. "Very in-ter-es-ting. So . . . you wish to become a singer, *n'est-ce-pas?*"

"I am a singer," I reproved him icily.

He moved to one side and surveyed me minutely, remarking that I had a face—and a nose, as I have already recounted—for comedy. I was becoming painfully accustomed to this impression. When I had met Mario Sanmarco and sung for her the prologue to *Pagliacci*, she had tapped my nose and said to my intense displeasure, "Funny face . . . funny boy."

Maurel, however, agreed to take me as a pupil. "Madame will arrange everything," he announced. "Be here tomorrow morning promptly at nine. Au revoir." With a wave of his long white hand, he took his way upstairs.

The terms laid down by Mme. Maurel placed this molding of my operatic career unreservedly in the maestro's hands. I would spend the entire day, six days a week, under his roof in pursuit of French and Italian diction, operatic traditions, mise-en-scène, and singing. The two last, Maurel himself would teach me. In return I signed an agreement to pay 20 percent of whatever I earned by singing as long as I was under M. Maurel's direction. The agreement signed, I was without further preliminary plunged into feverish activity.

In October of 1914 Victor Maurel had Webb arrested for lack of payment. Webb claimed that Mabelle took all he earned. He was allowed to put up two hundred dollars borrowed from a friend for bail.

It transpired that the founding of Maurel's projected opera company depended upon the support of Tito Ricordi, the renowned music publisher of Milan, who was expected shortly in New York. I was promised a part in it, of course, as were several other of Maurel's students. One of the latter deserves particular mention. She was an ample girl blessed with soprano ambitions and snappy brown eyes, at the time named Esther Cobb. Later she was to achieve a certain degree of notoriety as Cobina Wright.

After devoting a day and a half to sizing me up, Esther presumably decided that I was worth cultivating. She waylaid me one afternoon as I left the studio and announced that if I would walk a block with her she should give me the lowdown on Maurel's establishment and those connected with it. I graciously accepted and the intelligence was delivered to me as promised, in a singularly high-pitched voice. Monsieur was a bottom-pincher, although Esther thought it unlikely that I would be subjected to his attentions. Madame was a penny-pincher and kept an acute eye on her mate's philandering. Madame, indeed, a gaunt Frenchwoman who affected a rusty ill-adjusted wig and whose gigantic mouth was stretched tight over a display of gigantic porcelain teeth, was, according to my informant, no less a personage than the mysterious veiled woman in *L'Affaire Dreyfus*.

I believe Miss Cobb's respect for me was increased by my skeptical reception of these scraps of information. Then—as later, when she had achieved greater reputation—she was torn between the desire to astound and the hope of meeting an antagonist whom she could not disconnect.

Eventually Ricordi arrived and was enthroned in the studio to hear a carefully picked few of us display our talents. Esther and I performed a scene from *Tales of Hoffman*, she as the doll and I as the grotesque little man who winds her up. I think we acquitted ourselves rather creditably, and on the strength of it I arrived at the studio ten minutes early the next morning.

So, indeed, did all the other hopefuls. I at once noticed an unexpectedly chilly atmosphere about the old brownstone. Monsieur was indisposed and did not descend from the superior regions at all. Madame's eyes were ringed with immense dark circles. There was neither sign nor mention of Signor Ricordi. All too obviously, the future of M. Maurel's Opera Company lay well behind it.

I seized upon Madame and told her quite frankly that I could no longer afford to trail along in the insubstantial wake of her husband. I informed her that if M. Maurel could not secure me an engagement, I would have to go out and find one myself—and with no 20 percent commission.

Madame understood my situation to the point of tears. "Alas," she wept, "who knows better?" She was *desole*, and the maestro even more so, she assured me. But I must not lose hope. Though the blackguard Ricordi had refused to back the company, there was a producer at the moment seriously considering a musical for which she herself had written the book. If I would just wait.

I waited, principally because I had nothing better at hand. To my acute surprise a producer actually did take Mme. Maurel's play, *The Purple Road*, and fresh intimations of riches and success lightened the gloom of the morgue-like house. *The Purple Road* centered around Napoleon—to be played by Maurel, of course—and a considerable assortment of ladies of the demi-monde. Maurel descended like the archangel to the ground floor and contact with the rest of us. Mme. de Gersac became terrifyingly arch as she coached me in the comedy part of de Vestris, the dancing-master, and Madame became tenser and more anxious than before, an occurrence which I had not previously thought possible.

Esther Cobb, who was given no part at all, flounced from West Seventy-second Street and chez Maurel with the most extreme indignation. She made it quite clear that she would never again lower her standards by crossing the western frontier of Fifth Avenue.

Rehearsals of *The Purple Road* began. Janet Beecher was engaged to play Josephine, and Valli-Valli, one of the other ladies. It was announced that we would try out the show at Atlantic City and then (D. V.) come into the Casino Theatre. Our innocent hearts were veritably bursting with hope.

Only one thing did I find mildly puzzling: at rehearsals, Maurel went through his part merely humming the numbers. When I remarked upon this, it was explained that he was saving his voice, the glorious basso which had made history at La Scala and which I had longed so long to hear. "Wait till the opening," said Madame.

The opening came. The Boardwalk Theatre was jammed with holiday vacationers and people who had come down from New York to look over the show. Backstage we had all succumbed to rumors that *The Purple Road* was terrific.

I stationed myself in the wings, waiting for my cue and admiring Maurel's magnificent entrance. Breathless, I awaited his first number. And then—then I knew why he had never let his voice out. There was no longer any voice there. It was utterly gone—dwindled to a husky whisper which was inaudible beyond the fifth row.

It would have been ludicrous if it hadn't been tinged with tragedy—and possibly disastrous for the rest of the company. Somehow we managed to get through the three acts. Afterward, over the cheapest procurable supper, instead of the cold pheasant and oysters of which we had dreamed, we held an indignation meeting. I was personally in favor of packing up and taking the first train back to New York. The idea was fortunately overruled by the others, led by Janet.

For when we showed up at rehearsal next day the backers of the play, aware that the great Maurel was the only fly in their rich ointment, agreed that a graceful retirement should be arranged for him. Amidst the most heart-wringing pathos Maurel consented, and Harrison Broadbank was imported to sing the lead. The show was closed down, we returned to rehearsal, and after Broadbank had been pronounced ready, swept on to New York. After a gala first night everybody knew that we had a hit and were set for a long run.

The Purple Road did good business all winter, and I confess that on countless occasions during its run at the Casino Theatre I paused in the backstage alley to gaze at the lurid three-sheets which plastered the bricks. At the top of them were the names of the stars "in *The Purple Road*, with the following cast . . ." At the very bottom, almost imperceptible to anybody but myself, was the name Clifton Webb. I also confess that on these occasions I said to myself: "Someday that name is going to be on top."

When spring arrived, we departed on a tour of the eastern cities. It was in Boston that there occurred the odd chain of circumstances of which I was only dimly aware at the time, but which I am certain affected my life and career profoundly. I do not sincerely know if I would have conducted myself as I did, were those circumstances to repeat themselves. I prefer never to speculate on matters involving moral judgments. At the time I did not believe in moral judgments, and now that I am older I leave them to God and drama critics.

After the Boston opening of *The Purple Road*, Mabelle and I were dining at Locke-Ober's when all heads swiveled at the entrance of an improbably distinguished-looking man. He was well over six feet tall, had the build of an ox, and from his shoulders depended a jet cape of a style long since antique. This, combined with a Van Dyke beard, a gold-headed cane, and a massive silver watch-chain across his belly, gave him the look of a high-ranking grand duke. I saw Mabelle's face light up. Then I recognized the man as the mysterious Mr. Richardson, who had paid a great deal of attention to Mabelle when we were in Atlantic City during *l'affaire* Maurel, and whom I had seen from time to time lurking about the Casino Theatre in New York.

"Mabelle, dear," I whispered, "I think we are being followed." I was so surprised at the deep blush with which she answered me, that I said no more.

During the run in Boston, Mabelle went around a good deal with Mr. Richardson, but she seldom mentioned him to me. The principal reason was the rude delight I took in calling him R. Rembrandt because his beard was not quite a Van Dyke. I found it quite impossible to regard anybody who looked like him as anything but an impractical joke.

On the first morning of our second week, the girl who portrayed Mme. Sans-Gene became acutely ill. The manager thereupon became acutely distraught.

"I can get an actress up from New York," he lamented, "but what actress could learn the whole part in an hour?"

"Let Mabelle try it," I said. "She learns things incredibly fast."

"Learn it?" bellowed Mabelle. "I've watched every performance for months—give me a cocked hat and I'll go on as Napoleon in fifteen minutes!"

"You will not," said Harrison Broadbank, stepping from the wings at a singularly unfortunate moment. "I won't play with an amateur."

"An amateur?" cried Mabelle.

"I will accept full responsibility," I said haughtily. Harrison Broadbank grunted and departed. "Let her try it," I said to the manager. "By tomorrow night the new actress will have learned her lines."

I was completely astonished at what happened next. Mabelle bit her lip and looked quite ill. "Of course, I'd like to help you out," she said weakly. "I'd really love to . . . if it weren't for my dinner engagement tonight."

"My dear Mrs. Webb," said the manager, "Surely the most important thing is to keep the play running."

"Is it?" echoed Mabelle. "It seems to me that the most important thing is to keep my word. I told Mr. Richardson that I would dine with him."

"Get out of here," I said to the manager. "I will talk with Mabelle alone." He went. Mabelle seated herself on the end of a trunk. "Why can't you postpone this damn dinner with Rembrandt?" I asked.

"I suppose I could," she agreed.

"You know you've always wanted to be an actress."

"Yes, I always have," she said.

"Then . . ."

"Then there are other things in life besides acting," Mabelle interrupted. "I like to act . . . but I have other aims too."

I realized for the first time, if incompletely, that this was not to be any ordinary dinner.

"I agree with you completely," I said. "But I want you to realize one thing—I've taken full responsibility. If anything goes wrong tonight, we'll be laughed out of town. Bookings aren't easy to come by, Mabelle."

"Very well, Webb . . . I'll play it," Mabelle said quietly. Throughout that day she went over her scenes with Broadbank and me. She tried repeatedly to phone Mr. Richardson, but he was out with business associates. As we left the hotel in the evening, she scribbled him a note. I slipped over to the hotel florist and asked for three dozen unusually long-stemmed yellow roses to celebrate my mother's debut. The florist looked at me most curiously. "I'm extremely sorry," he said. "Every flower you see in this shop has been paid for. We're sending them up to a private dining room."

"Bought by Mr. Rembrandt?" I asked.

"By a Mr. Richardson," said the florist.

I was in an agony of apprehension when the curtain arose that night. When Mme. Sans-Gene entered for her first long scene with me, I choked with embarrassment. My emotions were both needless and not shared by Mme. Sans-Gene. She played the part to perfection and to Harrison Broadbank's sincere delight. After that night, indeed, there was no talk of sending to New York for a replacement.

But after the last curtain-call that night, I hurried with the utmost speed to Mabelle's dressing room. There, for the first time, I noticed how red were her eyes. It was not until after the last member of the company had departed and the echoes of their congratulations died away that Mabelle began to cry. During the five minutes she wept I was speechless, so terribly incongruous was the scene. Her dressing room had been miraculously converted into a veritable bower of blossoms, and in a dingy vase on the floor were the unusually long-stemmed roses. They had ended up with Mabelle after all.

We walked back to the hotel in silence. I could think of nothing at all to say. I did not want to say anything. Mabelle mounted directly to her bedroom. I remained below for a while, on what pretext I cannot recall. While I was sitting there, the manager of the hotel approached me.

"You were a friend of Mr. Richardson, I think . . ." he murmured.

"Mr. Richardson?" I echoed.

"He went quite berserk tonight," said the manager sadly. "You should see our private dining room. It's an absolute shambles."

"Tell me what you mean," I said.

"At nine o'clock . . . I don't know what could have come over him. With his gold-headed cane he broke the mirrors and lights. He tore the draperies from the walls. He threw a Wedgwood china service into the street . . ."

"I don't believe it!" I exclaimed.

"Then," said the manager, shaking his head, "he handed me his check for two thousand dollars. He was very correct about it all. He apologized for his intemperance. He instructed me that he was required to leave for Europe at once, and to forward any mail."

"Incredible . . ."

"Indeed," said the manager with the same mournful smile. "I found this in the wreckage." He opened his hand. In it lay an exquisite diamond feminine ring. "I shall forward it along, of course," he said. "I can't imagine what could have happened."

Mabelle and I never mentioned Richardson's name again. He never wrote to her. But for the remainder of our Boston run, each night the flowers in Mabelle's dressing room were miraculously renewed.

By one of those whimsical coincidences in which the gods delight, Mabelle's other break was also in Boston—although sans Mr. Richardson.

When we played Jerome Kern's *Love O' Mike* there during an influenza epidemic, and everybody was wandering around with sacks of asafetida around their necks, the girl who played the soubrette maid to George Hassell's immensely funny fat butler came down with the flu. Mabelle stepped into the part just three hours before curtain time. She and Hassell could not possibly have been a more comical combination. As they did a kidding dance together, he would vainly try to throw her off with his ad-libs. One night, in the middle of a rather complicated dance routine, he suddenly shot at her: "Where did you learn all you know?"

"Haven't you heard?" replied Mabelle. "I was twenty years with the circus and never lost a spangle!" And with a Frenchy flirt of her black taffeta skirt, off she went laughing.

Love O' Mike opened at the Shubert Theater on January 15, 1917. In the cast was Peggy Wood, who would later team with Webb in *Blithe Spirit.* In her autobiography, Wood gives us a look at what has been described as Webb's "wicked sense of humor": "When we were in *Love O' Mike,* Clifton Webb used to terrify me by saying under his breath in the middle of a scene, 'Charlie Dillingham just came in at the back of the house,' or 'Hearst is here with Diamond Jim.' How he could be conscious of exterior distractions and not be put off his stride is something I could never make out."

Webb's new dancing partner for this musical was Gloria Goodwin. The *New York Times* said that there is "some exuberant dancing by Clifton Webb and Gloria Goodwin." Music was by Jerome Kern with lyrics by Harry B. Smith.

During the run of *Love O' Mike,* the rector of St. George's Episcopal Church in New York publicly objected to Webb's dancing, calling modern dance nothing more than "jungle antics." This prompted Webb to counterattack, running an ad in several New York papers. Webb's ad is as follows: "Dr. Reiland says patronizingly that while he does not dance, he is musician and psychologist enough to know that the 'music accompanying some of the modern dances has a real effect on the moral substance of those habitually swayed by it.' Now I can state just as appropriately that while I am not a preacher, I am philosopher and psychologist enough to appreciate that the noises and other antics accompanying the pulpit outpourings of Billy Sunday have a real effect on the moral substance of those habitually swayed by them. I claim that they are injurious to the artistic sensibilities of people who attend the meetings of the wealthy revivalist. If Dr. Reiland's artistic nature is marred by the so-called 'jungle antics' of a few isolated dancers, let him avoid them as I am sure the artistic dancers will avoid Billy Sunday."

CHAPTER 5

Dancing into Xanadu

Several times during our run at the Casino, Valli Valli told me that I should take up modern dancing. Until *The Purple Road* closed, I had taken the suggestion as only a rather nice compliment. The dance craze swept the country that summer of 1913. Cabarets were springing up everywhere, particularly on the roofs of Broadway hotels, and dance teams were drawing bigger crowds than many successful plays. Maurice and Walton, the Castles at the Cafe Martin, and Joan Sawyer and Carlo Sebastien at the New York Roof were the headliners.

When, as it must to all plays, closing night came for the by now deeply rutted *Purple Road*, I drifted over to the New York Roof to see the much discussed Turkey Trot. After watching Sebastien and Sawyer's gyrations for a turn or two, I invited one of the girls at our table to try it with me. This was actually the first time that I had ever danced on a ballroom floor, and I found the sensation quite pleasurable.

A few moments after we returned to our table the headwaiter appeared at my elbow, discreetly murmuring that a lady would like to speak to me. Thoroughly delighted, I followed him through the maze of tables to the edge of the floor, where a man was sitting with one of the most ravishing blondes I had ever seen. The girl introduced herself as Bonnie Glass and her companion as Al Davis. She explained that she was dancing at Murray's Roman Gardens and was looking for a partner.

"I just saw you in *The Purple Road*," Bonnie said. "I saw you dance just now. Would you like a job?"

"Yes," I said, pursuing my infallible formula. Although my plans for the future were something less than nebulous, I did not disclose this to Miss Glass. Simulating a pose of thoughtful reflection, I wondered whether even I had sufficient effrontery to carry this one off.

"Do you do the Tango?" she inquired.

I allowed a discreet elevation of my right eyebrow and a drop of my left shoulder to convey the sentiment at which my truthful nature balked—that the tango and I were indeed old and intimate friends.

"The Maxixe?" she said.

"But of course," I said.

They looked at each other and Al Davis made a gesture which might conceivably have been a nod.

"What's your salary?" Bonnie asked.

I had heard it rumored that Hal Ford, the leading man in *The Purple Road*, received $150 a week. This seemed to me an altogether satisfactory figure.

"One hundred and fifty dollars a week," I said.

"Okay," Bonnie said. "Drop by the Gardens tomorrow for a tryout."

In exactly that fashion did I become a dancer.

A critic from this period termed Webb's introduction to ballroom dancing a "sheer fluke." However, many professional ballroom teams began their careers in this informal manner. Webb was already a dancer, but he was not a ballroom dancer. He learned the basics of ballroom dancing from Bonnie Glass and then relied on his native talent to transform himself into the consummate ballroom dancer he became. Webb and Glass delighted audiences for the entire 1913–1914 seasons. His slim physique and suave personality contributed to their impact as a team.

Weeks later, when Bonnie and I had become great friends, she said to me, "Tell me the truth. When I asked you about the Maxixe, had you ever danced it?"

"No," I said.

"Neither had I," Bonnie said, with a burst of that infectious laughter which was one of her most wonderful traits. She was a warm, impulsive, and generous person. I supposed that I fell in love with her, as nearly every other normal male did, and she treated me half the time as a small boy, the other half a sophisticated family friend on whose sage counsel she might safely lean. It was unquestionably in this role that she saw me one night years later, when we met at Castles by the Sea in Long Beach. We hired a double chair for a peaceful hour's ride up and down the boardwalk.

5.1. Bonnie Glass in 1914. The George Grantham Bain Collection.

"Do you know a guy named Ben Ali Haggin?" she asked suddenly, lifting her eyes from a particularly dreamy gaze at the sea.

"Of course," I said. "As a matter of fact, I'm a great admirer of his work."

Ben Ali Haggin was a well-known portrait painter and stage designer. He staged and designed costumes for many Ziegfeld productions. In 1914 Haggin inherited almost twenty million dollars from the estate of his grandfather, James B. Haggin. He and Bonnie Glass (real name: Helen Roche) were married in 1916. They had one son together but were separated in 1922 and eventually divorced, with Bonnie getting ten thousand dollars a year.

"He wants to marry me," Bonnie said. "He must be kind of nuts. He thinks I have a cute belly."

"Don't flatter yourself, darling," I said. "It's just that all you girls go around imitating Irene Castle . . . standing with your tails pulled in."

"Go to hell," Bonnie said, and back went her eyes dreamily to the sea.

Murray's Roman Gardens was something entirely new in my experience—as indeed it must have been to anybody who hadn't been there. An enormous place on Forty-second Street just off Eighth Avenue, it was presently very popular with the sporting crowd and the demi-monde. When I arrived in the afternoon for my tryout, it was deserted and dark, and the potted palms and pseudo-Roman columns festooned with artificial grapevines contributed to a general funereal atmosphere. The pianist, a home-rolled cigarette drooping limply from his lips, bore the aspect of one recently bereaved. He plunged mechanically through his numbers, and for an hour and a half Bonnie and I rehearsed a waltz which she knew.

She was such an exquisite dancer that only the most insensitive clod could have failed to follow beautifully.

"That's swell," she said finally. "Be here tonight at eleven thirty."

"Wearing what?" I said.

"White tie and tails, of course," Bonnie said.

"Naturally," I said. "How very stupid of me."

When I went home and announced to Mabelle that I was going on at Murray's that night, she demanded, "To do what?"

"The modern dance," I replied.

"My God!" said Mabelle.

I then brought up the small matter of the requisite white tie and tails. All I possessed was an excessively ancient dinner jacket. It was already nearly six o'clock. With a wild cry of distraction Mabelle dashed out to buy me a shirt, collar and white cravat. I began mentally running over our male acquaintances. Unfortunately, all the ones I could think of were either large and portly or miniature and dapper. Among our set the Gold Mean seemed to have been neglected. The likeliest, I concluded, was the son of some next-door neighbors, who had a reputation for going out a great deal. I descended on his sister, alarmed her into resolute action, and together we foraged her brother's closet. I carried off a coat which fitted not too badly across the shoulder, although it was oddly loose in front. So, too, was the matching white waistcoat, for both had been made for a man weighing forty pounds more than I.

Mabelle had meanwhile returned from the haberdasher's with a shirt, a grotesquely high collar, and a white tie. From the size of the latter, she apparently labored under the delusion that I was going to present an imitation of Lew Dockstader. When all was done, the waistcoat defied Mabelle's safety pins and protruded two inches below the edge of the coat. I blush to think of how far I was removed from sartorial perfection, but at least there were two tails unmistakably depending from my back—and when I turkey trotted before Mabelle's cheval glass, they flew out with inspiring effect.

Bonnie surveyed me hastily and smiled without comment; nor did Al Davis, who was something of a fashion plate, criticize my attire. A few nights later, however, he said to me casually, "How do you like the cut of this coat?" I assured him that I thought it splendid. "I have a very good tailor," he said, handing me a card. "Wetzel. I'll give you a card to him, if you like."

I took the hint, which I shall always remember as a model of courteous subtlety, and entrusted myself to Mr. Wetzel's magic hand. He made me a tail coat and trousers of midnight blue broadcloth, and I introduced the style at Murray's. Black cloth, as Mr. Wetzel explained, looks grey under spotlights.

Murray's fascinated me. Its unbridled lushness represented a world which I had never seen before, and which rather frightened me. It was the last word in that mingling of show business, wealth, and the sporting world which made Broadway the magnificent thing it was in those days, when penny arcades still belonged to Coney Island. My eyes popped and my ears were on stems. I was overcome with a desire not to miss anything around me. Many of the names I heard bandied about were unknown to me, but one could not doubt that they belonged to personalities. There were always a number of men-about-town in attendance, gentlemen of breeding and wealth who descended upon Broadway for late-hour entertainment. If there were ladies with them, they were never wives. It was predominantly a champagne-drinking crowd, free spenders who were out for a good time and prepared to pay handsomely for it.

One of Murray's regular patrons was Diamond Jim Brady. He drank no champagne—only quart after quart of orange juice. It was an unforgettable spectacle to watch that great hulk of a bon vivant turkey trot with one of the Dolly sisters; he would clasp her to his paunch as he plunged ahead, one jeweled hand beating time meticulously on her bottom. Barney Baruch's brother, Sailing Baruch, was another frequent customer and a great one for dancing. For these were the halcyon days of cabaret dance contests and prizes—silver cups, magnums of champagne, and armfuls of American beauties to the winners who came from all over America to compete.

The crowds could only be satisfied by a diet of frequent and dashing innovations of technique. Bonnie and I found a little fellow who danced the tango and paid him to teach it to us. "For the love of Mike, Cliffy, we've got to be different," Bonnie would say as we rehearsed.

"All right. How?"

"Think up something."

"Okay . . . let's tango without holding on."

We did it one night and met with a wretched reception. A great deal of spying went on between the various dance teams. We went often to see the Castles, then appearing in a basement establishment opposite the Time building. It was a little later that Bessie Marbury took them under her management. Their routines were extraordinarily buoyant and gay—the two most important attributes of good dancing. Style in dancing, as in everything else in life, is immensely more important than technique. The Castles had it. Under Bessie's fine hand they went on in succession to those atrociously named palaces of art, Castle House, Castles-in-the-Air, and Castles-by-the-Sea.

One evening a waiter handed me a note. "Yours is the poetry of motion," it read. "Do you teach?"

Unfavorably impressed by the diction, I scribbled a reply: "No."

I confess, however, that it started a train of thought. This was accelerated by a series of further inquiries, all in delightful feminine hands: "Have you a studio?" "Do you teach?" and others somewhat less discreet. The first person to whom I had the temerity to mention this notion was Lillian George, a photographer who was taking some dandified portraits of me. She found it not at all fantastic—indeed, she suggested that we step downstairs to have a look at a vacant studio in her building, 5 West Fifty-eighth Street. I gazed upon a big room with a good floor, two bedrooms, a bath, and a kitchenette. I found it altogether charming. I paid the first month's rent on the spot and went home to tell Mabelle that she must prepare to move.

Mabelle was thoroughly aghast.

"How do you propose to get pupils?" she demanded.

"I shall have some cards engraved," I replied. "They will be displayed on the tables at Murray's. The eager throngs will be directed to phone my secretary for terms and an appointment."

"Phone your what?" she gurgled.

"My secretary," I said. "You are now my secretary. I baptize you Miss Parmelee."

"My God! said Mabelle. "I've never heard of such a thing!"

In the space of forty-five seconds, however, she assumed the personality of the secretary ideal—poised, exact, brisk, with just sufficient snootiness to provoke social climbers to a frenzy of anticipation.

I wrote out a card.

Clifton Webb, Esquire, will accept a few pupils at his new studios 5 West 58th Street.
Private Lessons...Five dollars the hour.
Two in a class...Seven dollars the hour.
Evening sessions arranged by appointment.
Kindly call Miss Parmelee, Secretary.

I left this with a stationer and ordered five hundred engraved copies. I hired a Victrola on the installment plan. I bought a number of records. Concurrently, I found myself financially embarrassed. The situation was further aggravated when Bonnie decided that she would go to Chicago for a while. Faced with the prospect of immediate bankruptcy, I did something which I had never done even in my lean and jobless years—I asked a friend for a loan. He obliged with a check for one hundred dollars.

Rather surprisingly, word of my venture spread at Murray's even before the cards had been distributed. Miss Parmelee's phone began ringing with delightful persistence.

Mabelle made the sordid arrangements in her own matchless fashion. First it was five dollars a lesson. Then it was ten, then fifteen. We were in the turmoil of moving when I wandered in one afternoon on a telephone conversation which appalled me.

"Certainly," Miss Parmelee was saying in the crisp accent of her role. "First I'll have to look at Mr. Webb's engagement book. Tuesday? . . . No. Wednesday? . . . No. Ah . . . Thursday at eleven. I'm afraid that's the first convenient hour. Yes . . . would you spell it please? Thank you. . . of course you wish private lessons? That will be twenty-five dollars."

"Twenty-five dollars!" I exclaimed. "Have you lost your reason?"

"Certainly not. If the Castles get twenty-five, why the hell shouldn't you?"

"That woman will never appear," I said.

"My poor innocent," Mabelle said. "You don't know much about women. She'll be here on the dot. Do you think she'll pass up a chance to tell her friends that she's taking lessons from that wonderful Mr. Webb who charges twenty-five dollars an hour?"

Mabelle was quite right. I can only conclude that it requires a snob to grasp the true artistry of snob appeal. "From now on, my dear," she commanded, "Miss Parmelee will handle the business."

I acquiesced graciously.

As my secretary's hijacking methods had made the engraved cards worse than useless, I never picked them up from the stationer's. She kept no records whatever, and I am happy that I never knew at what point conscience checked her piracy. Perhaps it never did. Business boomed, however, and very soon I had paid back my debt and become full owner of the Victrola. Miss Parmelee developed the habit of going to the bank several times each week. It was reported, whether accurately I do not know, that a vice president developed the habit of smiling at her approvingly.

Among my clients I encountered that insatiable craving for novelty which so often seems to afflict the very wealthy.

"Mr. Webb, do you teach the Twinkle?" said a large fat lady as I propelled her about the room.

"The Twinkle?" I said. I did not know the Twinkle. "Oh, yes . . . the Twinkle."

"Exactly," the fat lady said. "The Twinkle."

"I'm afraid that I must refuse to teach you the Twinkle," I said. "It is a step which I find dreadfully vulgar."

"Do excuse me," the fat lady mumbled apologetically.

She was, however, despite her gross, an extremely lucrative customer whom I did not want to lose, for she had displayed a happy facility for going on paying me twenty-five dollars a lesson indefinitely. The next time she turned up at the studio, I honored her with my most ingratiating smile. "I have been thinking about the Twinkle all week," I said. "You will be glad to learn that I have refined it. The Twinkle is no longer vulgar." For the balance of the period I taught her the various steps which I had improvised and a smattering of others so obscure that it would require several more lessons before she had the vaguest conception of what it was all about.

From the Twinkle, I proceeded to learn and distort the Scissors, the Cortez, and the Grapevine. By the time I was finished, each of these, essentially simple enough to be within the grasp of a moderately clever ape, required from two to four hours of arduous instruction. I invariably whispered admiringly during the second hour, "I have never seen anybody who learns as quickly as you, my dear."

Not all our pupils were women. We instituted a series of evening classes at which I danced with the ladies and Miss Parmelee with the gentlemen. The famous Fox Sisters once appeared en masse, appearing precisely as rendered on the label of their revolting patent hair tonic. As the autumn social season began to flower, calls started coming in for me to dance at parties in private homes. For these Miss Parmelee instituted a new scale of fees, graduated according to the social and financial ratings of the hostess. She also insisted that a car be provided to fetch me and bring me home and that I enter the home by the front door. My illusions of grandeur became infinite.

Once at a dinner given by Mrs. C. B. Alexander, captain of the Old Guard, I was confronted by a notorious and pop-eyed stuffed shirt. "What are you doing here?" he demanded.

"Exactly what you're doing," I replied, lifting my cocktail elegantly.

"Do you realize that no professional entertainer has ever before been asked to this house?" he said indignantly.

"Indeed?" I said. "What a great deal they must have missed."

The management of Delmonico's asked me to organize a series of tea dances. At these it was my custom to dance first with the most glittering society girl, then with any of the other guests who wished me as a partner. Our opening was immensely chic. Among the guests was Lou Tellegen, a leading matinee idol and a remarkably bad actor. He lifted his trouser leg and revealed to my astonished eye a gold anklet. I noticed that it matched exactly a gold anklet on the lady sitting beside him at the table. She was the Baroness de Meyer. Baron de Meyer was with them.

I came to know the Baroness and her patient Baron quite well that winter. Lou Tellegen was almost always with them. Once I invited him to go with me to the premiere of *Mme Sans Gene*, when Geraldine Farrar created the part in this country.

Characteristically, Lou completely failed to grasp Farrar's extraordinary genius. When the curtain descended, his only comment was, "Hmmm—that's a very intelligent woman."

A number of years afterward, I had the opportunity to remind Tellegen of that remark. I was a guest at a dinner given by Geraldine Farrar, after which we were all supposed to go to see Grant Mitchell in *It Pays to Advertise*. Geraldine had taken two boxes for the performance, but we were still at the dinner table when curtain time approached. She instructed her butler, to my complete astonishment, to phone the theatre that the curtain should be held until her arrival. They did. The moment our party appeared in the boxes, the curtain went up. Any recollection of the performance, however, has been effaced by the news that greeted us when we stepped out into Broadway—the street was filled with newsboys shouting extras, filled with the shocking news of the sinking of the *Lusitania*.

A great deal subdued, we passed on to Bustanby's Domino Grill to dance. There, across the floor, sat Lou Tellegen with a woman no man could conceivably have taken out except for pity or obligation.

When she disappeared into the powder room I went over and invited Lou to join our considerably brighter party. I introduced him to Geraldine when he came over. Eventually the two of them wound up in Hollywood making pictures together. Stories began making the usual rounds. I could not resist the temptation of asking Gerry's fabled mother about Tellegen and the woman he had once found merely "so intelligent."

"Are they going to be married?" I inquired.

"Geraldine wouldn't marry Mohammet!" said Mrs. Farrar icily.

Geraldine Farrar and Lou Tellegen were married in 1916. They divorced in 1923.

I made the acquaintance of another of the screen's illustrious lovers that winter. Bonnie, having floated in her unpredictable manner back from Chicago, was in need of a new partner. She asked me to go with her to look for a likely young man. It was the custom at that time for cafes to retain young men to dance with ladies whose escorts were unwilling. They were not gigolos—they were purely professional dance partners, and a fairly reputable group of persons. At one of the clubs Bonnie and I noticed a remarkably handsome, dark young man named Rudolph. His specialty was the tango. He wanted the job Bonnie offered him, but was not shy in telling us that he had no money to buy the clothes he would require as her partner. Bonnie offered to pay for them. I, remembering a similar service rendered in a moment of need, sent him to my tailor. They opened shortly afterwards at the Colonial. It is a matter of record that Bonnie and Mr. Valentino were a wild success.

In the years which ensued I ran into Valentino from time to time. Once we went to a matinee of *Charlot's Revue* together, and I recall a rather disorganized party at which he wandered about repeating over and over, "For God's sake . . . I've got to have some bicarbonate of soda!" I did not see him after that until he was dead.

Andre Charlot was a French theatrical impresario who is best remembered for the musical revues he produced in London circa 1912 to 1937. The opening of his *Charlot's Revue* in 1924 on Broadway was a major event. Charlot

5.2. Rudolph Valentino with Alice Terry in the famous tango scene from *The Four Horsemen of the Apocalypse* (1921). Courtesy of The Academy of Motion Picture Arts and Sciences.

introduced such British talent as Gertrude Lawrence, Beatrice Lillie, and Jack Buchanan to American audiences. In 1937 he went to Hollywood and spent his declining years as an actor, mostly in B movies.

Mabelle and Marilyn Miller and I drove from Long Island, where we were passing the summer, to the funeral parlor where the "Great Lover" lay amidst unparalleled *pompes funebres*. When we were escorted to the coffin, I could not believe my eyes. The man was completely wasted away. His face seemed grotesquely small, his hands like the talons of some small savage bird. With an exquisite unfitness, the hair which in life had been worn in the manner of patent leather, was piled high in a pompadour. Most macabre of all was the funeral, at which I ushered. For perhaps the first time in his fantastic life, Valentino had a scene stolen from him—by Pola Negri, who provoked audible cries of horror when she was led like a blind crone down the middle aisle, an impenetrable black veil landing at her feet.

One of the nicest things about Bonnie Glass was her willingness to do people favors. She related to me one day that Mae Murray had said she would like to have me dance with her. I had known Mae at Murray's, where she was known, for obscure reasons, as "the Brinkley Girl" and was being courted by Jay O'Brien. Although I had not been particularly fond of her, she danced admirably. When Mae called me with the news that she had a chance to go on at the Palace and would like me as her partner, I replied that there was nothing I would like better. In those days the Palace was the Xanadu dreamed upon by every vaudeville actor. For the chance to play there, indeed, no performer would have thought twice about committing murder, arson, and aggravated mayhem.

Webb's dark features and cool demeanor were the perfect match for Murray's blonde, graceful appearance. Part of Mae Murray's appeal was her rather eccentric habits. She danced with a long scarf tied around her neck and struck artistic looking poses.

A 1914 program from the *Folies Marigny* described the floor show: "The house lights dimmed and white spotlights were thrown onto the four corners of the dance floor. For the opening number four female dancers entered, performing to a tango rhythm. Through song they invited four men (planted in the balcony) to accompany them in the dance. All eight couples then whirled through the spirited ensemble number. Several variety acts followed. The finale was the ballroom routine of Murray and Webb. They opened with a *Brazilian maxixe*, followed by the *Barcarole Waltz*, Murray's version of the hesitation waltz, closed with a number called the *Cinquante-Cinquante*, a variation of the Castles' *Half and Half*. For an encore they performed the *Pavlova Gavotte*, a dance inspired by the Russian ballerina, and adopted widely by exhibition ballroom teams."

Murray used her fame as a ballroom dancer to make the transition to silent motion pictures, where she became a star.

I left the business end of the deal to Mae, at her own suggestion, but with an understanding that billing and salary were to be shared equally. On the Saturday afternoon before our opening I was, as usual, at Delmonico's. Baron de Meyer was there too. He remarked that he had just strolled by the Palace and had seen men putting up posters announcing next week's attraction. "Have you seen them?" he asked. I said that I had not. "I recommend that you do," said the Baron with his slight stutter. "Mae Murray's n-name is gigantic. Yours, on the contrary, cannot be m-made out without a m-monocle."

I called Mabelle at once and sent her off to reconnoiter. She marched into Delmonico's with blazing eyes an hour later. Since the lady is my mother, I will not repeat the language she employed. De Meyer's report, it seemed, was painfully exact. Little Mae—she of the bee-stung lip and the kissing-papa-goodnight countenance—had pulled an extremely fast one.

We had arranged a last rehearsal at my studio that evening, preparatory to trying out our act at a Bronx theatre on Sunday. Mae's conduct caused me to alter my plans. I did not show up for the rehearsal at all, and did not even go home until long after midnight. Early the next morning Mae telephoned to remind me that we were to appear at the matinee that afternoon. Mabelle told her that I would not appear and promptly hung up. She then called the United Booking Office to inform the Palace management that Mr. Webb would not appear on Monday, as he had no intention of "assisting" Miss Murray or anybody else. At this point I began to suffer severest qualms.

"Does Clifton Webb realize what he's doing?" asked the telephone.

"Certainly," said Mabelle.

"But you can't do this . . ."

"We are doing it."

"Uh . . . give me ten minutes," said the telephone.

"You may have as long as you like," said Mabelle.

In less than ten minutes the United Booking Office was back on the wire. Everything, they assured us, would be all right.

"How do we know?" Mabelle demanded.

"Look," pleaded the tired voice, "If I give you my word as a gentleman that those posters will be down and new ones up by Monday, will you promise me that Mr. Webb will appear?"

"How do I know that you're a gentleman?" said Mabelle.

At noon we arrived at the Wadsworth Theatre in the Bronx. Mae was there, red eyed and remarkably quiet, attended by the faithful Jay O'Brien. Mabelle and I maintained an attitude of rigid dignity.

The act passed off very well. "Isn't it going wonderfully?" she whispered in my ear as we tangoed.

"Indeed," I answered icily.

Bright the next morn, Mabelle posted herself opposite the Palace. At half-past the new ones were up—MAE MURRAY and CLIFTON WEBB. At noon I packed up my makeup and tails for the matinee. We headlined the Palace bill for eight weeks. During the entire engagement Mae was sweetness incarnate. The battle of the billing was never mentioned. Since that painful weekend, however, I have entrusted the matter of billing neither to chance nor to anybody else.

The experience marked the beginning of a new relationship between Mabelle and me. She became my business manager, a position she still fills with the utmost competence. There have been times when our ideas have differed, others when I have disagreed with her on principle. Never, however, has she been wrong in the long run. A good deal of her success has been the result of persistent refusal to "yes" me.

In 1916 Webb won a role in Cole Porter's first Broadway show, *See America First*, which failed to win critical or audience favor. "I played a cowboy and an autumn flower," remembered Webb. "Others had roles not so believable." Despite the failure of Porter's initial try at Broadway, Webb developed a long and close relationship with Porter.

Now in his late twenties, Webb was still known as a dancer but was beginning to get parts in which he had dialogue. He decided that in order to better prepare himself for speaking roles, he should go see the man he considered to be the master of dialogue, John Barrymore.

When I was playing a rather cretinous juvenile in *Listen Lester*, and John Barrymore was playing *Redemption*, Jeanne Eagels and I used to attend nearly every one of his Thursday matinees. We reserved the same front row seats. In one scene he was required to cry, 'Christ!' with extraordinary fervor. It impressed me so inordinately that under the influence of Barrymore's Tolstoy I would exert myself to the limit each night in *Listen Lester*, attempting to fill my frivolous lines with Christ-like overtones. One evening I remember especially. Until the first intermission, I was convinced my performance was quite fine. Then an usher knocked on my dressing room door. "Mr. Webb," he said, "your mother is out front. She asked me to remind you that you are not playing *Redemption* this evening."

It was in *Listen Lester* that Webb first won a secure place for himself in the musical theatre. He became one of its most suave and sophisticated performers as well as a marvelous dancer during the next two decades. Strangely, he only briefly mentions his appearance in *Listen Lester*. In fact, he barely mentions any of his early stage appearances. A complete list of Webb's stage appearances as well as his filmography appear as appendices at the end of this book.

5.3. Clifton Webb as he appeared with Gertrude (Gertie) Vanderbilt in *Listen Lester* (1918). The David L. Smith Collection.

Webb's debut film is said to have occurred in 1920. However, he and his dance partner Bonnie Glass appeared in a film in 1917 that was simply entitled *National Red Cross Pageant*. This featured many greats of the stage, including Ethel Barrymore, John Barrymore, and Lionel Barrymore. Webb's great future friend, Jeanne Eagels, also appeared in this film. Webb and Glass were featured as dancers in a segment called *The Pavane, French episode.*

Webb's early foray into films had no impact on his career. He certainly was not impressed with this film work. He said he forgot about making them until old friend Ina Claire reminded him in 1962. Webb said, "I'm fairly egotistical about recalling anything connected with my career, and I'm flabbergasted that I forgot those silent pictures I did. Here for years, I've been saying my first picture was *Laura.*"

In 1921 Maurice Chevalier and comedian Saint-Grenier opened the first fashionable nightclub ever started in Paris. The European tradition had not included nightclubs as part of Paris entertaining. Society entertained at home.

5.4. The Dolly Sisters, circa 1923–25. The David L. Smith Collection.

However, Chevalier apparently sought to change this. He was not as successful as he had hoped and in 1922 he sold Les Acacias to Edward Molyneaux and his young assistant and social overseer, Elsa Maxwell. The dashing Captain Molyneaux was a hero of World War I. He wore an eye patch as the result of the loss of an eye in the war. He had become an international success as a *couturier* to the rich and famous.

Webb had met Elsa Maxwell in New York. She decided that Clifton Webb and Jenny Dolly, of the famous Dolly Sisters, were the perfect act to open the club. Molyneaux and Maxwell redesigned the club to look like a Southern plantation. Molyneaux created a new gown for Jenny Dolly every night. For the opening, he designed a slinky cloth of gold with the cape covered with real gardenias, which Jenny would pluck out and toss to the men as she danced around with Webb.

Webb had two little black boys who waltzed around with him, holding two baskets filled with corsages which he handed out to the ladies as he danced. The club was a smash hit. When Webb and Jenny Dolly came to the closing night of their act at Les Acacias, Webb convinced Rosie Dolly to escape to Paris from the private yacht of some wealthy friends and join him and her sister.

5.5. Clifton Webb and Mary Hay in their "eccentric dancing act." Russell Ball photo.

Webb devised and choreographed a dance for the three of them. It came to be known as the Pony Trot. Webb inspirationally charioteered the two around the black-carpeted dance floor. The Pony Trot became a staple of the Dolly Sisters act and was one of their trademark dances.

Unfortunately Les Acacias lost money because, as Maxwell put it, "Molyneaux and I were too busy having a good time to check incoming revenue against outgoing expenses." They sold Les Acasias to American dancer Harry Pilcer.

Webb began to tire of his early stage roles. He was frequently cast as "a plaything of society." He decided to try to get away from these kinds of roles and stay with dancing for a while. He partnered with Mary Hay, the wife of actor Richard Barthelmess. When Webb and Hay opened a new nightclub (Ciro's), they were a big hit. Their dancing, without departing from rhythmic perfection, had odd quirks that made them a highly amusing pair.

5.6. Marilyn Miller and Clifton Webb aboard the *Majestic* (1925). The David L. Smith Collection.

Richard Barthelmess was unhappy with his wife's teaming with Webb. She said that he was jealous at first, but when she convinced him that Webb was not interested in women, he calmed down. In 1925 Hay and Webb accepted an invitation from Harry Pilcer, who now owned Les Acacias, to dance there again. Webb, with the ever-present Mabelle, sailed on the *Majestic* with Mary Pickford's brother Jack and his wife, Ziegfeld star Marilyn Miller.

Webb said, "On the boat was Marilyn, who was then married to Jack Pickford, the Dolly sisters were going back . . . Mary (Pickford) and Mrs. Dwight Wiman." Wiman was Dwight Deere Wiman, the grandson of John Deere, the Illinois farming implements millionaire. He became an actor/playwright and a producer who was involved in several productions that featured Webb. It was Wiman who was the backer for *The Little Show* and who signed Webb and Fred Allen for that production.

Regarding the voyage, Webb said, "I assure you that if they could have stopped the *Majestic* in mid-ocean, they would have put us off. We went to London first. Then we went to Paris."

While Webb and Mary Hay were dancing together abroad, she and Bar-thelmess decided to separate. Webb said when the news broke, the press began to play up the story that he was the cause of the breakup.

Webb amusingly recalled, "After the news came out, we were followed on the streets, and automatically I was the villain. Everybody thought that I came between them. This divinely happy couple had allowed this little housewife to be lured away from her husband. Dick [Barthelmess] and I roared about this. I continued to play the heavy . . . [and] it was in all the papers. I broke up this happy home. Dick continued through the years to be my greatest friend and laughingly referred to me as 'Corre' [co-respondent]."

Webb and Mary Hay were a great success in Europe. On their return to the United States. Mabelle was questioned about her son and Mary Hay. Mabelle told the press, "My son and Mary Hay! It is perfectly ridiculous! Why, he is in Great Neck weekending with Dick Barthelmess now. So you see, he hasn't broken up any home. Yes Clifton and Mary danced together for two months abroad and were a great hit. But as far as romance, that is absurd. My son will never marry. I am his best pal."

None of Webb's Broadway shows up to this time could be considered "hits." Webb finally managed to hit the jackpot when he and his partner Mary Hay were cast in a Marilyn Miller production with music by Jerome Kern. The show was *Sunny*. It opened September 22, 1925, and ran for a pleasing 517 performances.

CHAPTER 6

To Europe in Search of Adventure

"I like house-broken people," said Elsie de Wolfe the first time I met her. Whether the remark is of any particular profundity or not, nobody can doubt that it is striking.

Elsie and her great friend Anne Morgan, urged by Baron de Meyer, had turned up at one of Delmonico's matinees early in the season for the express purpose of examining my doubtful talents. The "Triumvirate" had recently returned from a lengthy sojourn at the Villa Trianon outside Paris and had discovered, to Elsie's intense dismay, that they were frightfully out of step with the times. The other two were somewhat less concerned, for Anne Morgan was too stately to be interested in the dance craze, and Bessie Marbury altogether too fat. Elsie, however, could never endure being less than ten steps ahead of the rest of humanity. By some perhaps less than Divine providence, I found myself selected as the instrument by which she hoped to make up for the time lost abroad.

Upon being introduced to me at Delmonico's, Elsie came directly to the point. She would require, I was told briskly, that I come to her house to teach her the newest thing in the tango. Her schedule was very full, but she believed she could sandwich me between her masseuse at ten and an important client at eleven-thirty. I would kindly telephone her secretary promptly at nine the next morning.

"I also have a secretary," I replied. "She makes all my appointments. You'll have to call her."

The next day her secretary, who was certainly not her mother, phoned my own Miss Parmelee. I shortly found myself committed to perfecting the energetic Miss de Wolfe in the one-step, the tango, the maxixe, and my reliable old standby, the twinkle. Mabelle had settled for the customary twenty-five dollars an hour.

"Why didn't you get more?" I said.

"Damn it, I tried!" Mabelle said.

At the time, Elsie shared with Elizabeth Marbury an exquisitely decorated house on East Fifty-fifth Street. Friends from childhood, they had shocked the innocent era by establishing themselves as New York's first "bachelor girls" in a house on East Seventeenth Street which had once belonged to Washington Irving. It quickly became a gathering spot for fascinating people.

This was in no way the result of luck, but rather of the formidable rules which Elsie laid down. She insisted that everybody should bring something to the community. "It's very important," she frequently used to say somewhat sententiously, "to remember that a person must always drag his own weight. You can be rich and dull . . . or poor and amusing. But whatever you are, you have to make your contribution. No one rides free; . . . it's never morals; it's manners that count." It has been said of Elsie, Lady Mendl, that she prefers a witty contortionist to a dreary duke. This is unfortunately only partly true. If the duke is decorative and sufficiently ducal in demeanor, he can be as dreary as many of them are without losing his place on Elsie's guest list.

The friends had progressed a long way from the early Seventeenth Street days by the time I met them. Elsie had graduated from actress to decorator, a profession which she veritably created in America. Bessie was an extremely successful and busy literary agent, with offices in London and Paris as well as New York. Our acquaintance developed rapidly, and for years, whenever I was in New York, I had a regular date for Sunday lunch and mahjong with Bessie. She was an inspired conversationalist. She would sit in her especially designed armchair and entertain me, with a rare sense of fitness, by allowing me to talk about myself. I know nobody with whom I would rather discuss myself.

Through Elsie, my circle of friends branched out in a terrifyingly social manner. Particular among them was Mrs. Laurence Keene, a leader of real society long before Cafe Society had ever been heard of, who introduced me to all the greats of the musical world. Our friendship was looked on askance in certain circles. It was, in fact, when I discovered myself referred to in Cholly Knickerbocker's column as "Mrs. Keene's dancing knight of the carpet" that I knew that I had arrived at some sort of distinction, however questionable.

One summer Mrs. Keene rented a charming villa at Long Beach, then one of the most fashionable resorts. On a Sunday when I was motoring down there with Bessie Marbury, we learned that Sarah Bernhardt was staying at the Long Beach Hotel. We immediately conspired to slip quietly off after lunch, without a word to the others. We mounted to the great lady's suite in the elevator and were admitted by a manservant who looked long since embalmed. The windows overlooked the board-walk and the Atlantic, but on a throne chair placed with its back to the scenery was installed Bernhardt, surrounded by yellowed palms. She was dressed in something more engulfing than flowing, her hair was an arsenical green from dye, her hands grimy, and rouge from her lips had melted down over her teeth. She could not possibly have removed her makeup for a week.

For all that, one had the awesome sensation which can come only from the presence of greatness. She began to speak, and before I knew a moment had passed, it was after six. She and Bessie conversed in French which almost completely escaped my untutored ears. It mattered not at all: that voice—those vibrant gestures—I was emotionally exhausted when we left.

During the eight weeks Mae Murray and I played the Palace, my schedule was unreasonably arduous. I had to dash from the studio to the theatre in time to dress for the matinee. I had to change from tails to cutaway and arrive panting at Delmonico's for the tea hour, then back to the theatre and tails for the evening show, and finally, greatly battered, on to the Follies Marigny, where Mae and I were dancing at supper.

Abruptly, one warm day in May, my energy ebbed. The Palace engagement was finished, but the Shuberts had asked me to dance in an Al Jolson musical they were constructing for the Winter Garden in the fall.

That news failed to impress me at all. It is well enough to appear blasé when the occasion demands, but here, I realized with an unpleasant emotion, I was treating an offer to return to the theatre as though it were merely a free ride on the Coney Island Ferris wheel.

It was in this melancholy state of fatigue that I was wandering up Fifth Avenue when I halted to stare at the array of posters blossoming outside the American Express Company office. I had no intention of stopping—it was something quite beyond my will. I looked with growing feeling on the chromatic castles, stretches of white sand labeled Ostende-Plage and dotted with quaint seaside machines, ultramarine lakes framed by Alps, edelweiss and goats and beribboned yodelers—Europe!

In that instant I knew what I wanted. I went into the office. A clerk told me that the S.S. *Vaterland* was sailing in three days. There was a cabin I might have. I wrote out a check, received a ticket and a sack of bright gummed labels, and went home whistling "The International Rag."

Mabelle reeled under the shock of my announcement. When she stopped reeling, she declared that for once I had made an intelligent decision without having been goaded into it.

I filled a valise with what I guilelessly believed the well-dressed young man should affect on shipboard, particularly notable for an immense, floppy, tweed hat which covered my face as far as my lower teeth. I looked rather like an understudy for William Gillette in the role of Sherlock Holmes. Without further ado, I caught the ship.

The *Vaterland* was a mammoth seagoing hotel, furnished in the most florid Teutonic manner. The humblest functionaries wore bemedalled uniforms, and the promenades were a jungle-like vista of Kaiser Wilhelm mustaches. Bonnie Glass's name appeared on the passenger list, and I lost no time in searching her out. She introduced me to the boxing champion Freddie Welsh, to Julian Eltinge, Pauline Frederick—and, to the exclusion of all others, to a ravishing blonde sprite with eyes which could change in a splintered second from the tigerish to the angelic, whose voice was husky and whose sense of humor was absolutely cockeyed. This was Jeanne Eagels.

I mention her only in passing now. She will presently receive her due.

Freddie Welsh won the world's lightweight boxing championship in 1914. A Briton, he was a very intelligent man who finagled successfully to prolong his title by only fighting people who had to knock him out to claim the championship.

It was said of Julian Eltinge that he was "the greatest female impersonator on the American Stage, no one before or after has been able to rival him." His personal life was shrouded in mystery due to his desire to stop any gossip about his possible homosexuality. He made several movies, some as a female and some as a straight person. He died in 1938. His will stated, "I declare that I am a bachelor," and left everything to his mother.

Dorothy Parker was quite taken with Eltinge. In an article for *Vanity Fair* in 1916 she wrote the following poem:

> My heart is simply melting
> at the thought of Julian Eltinge;
> his alter ego, Vesta Tilley too.
> Since our language is so dexterous,
> let us call him ambi-sexterous.
> Why hasn't this occurred before to you?

Pauline Frederick was a well-known stage star when Clifton Webb met her. She was in her thirties when she began making films. She specialized in playing commanding and authoritative women.

My plans for the trip included an initial visit to London to buy the clothes which I would need for the Winter Garden show. I asked an Englishman on board who were the best tailors in London. He advised Anderson and Shepherd. When I enquired concerning a hotel, he replied with classic understatement, "Claridge's is fairly nice."

London fulfilled my most extravagant dreams. The sun, by special dispensation from the sour British heavens, shone. The parks blossomed with elegant strolling couples. I started at once making the rounds of the theatres. The style of the leading English actors impressed me tremendously. Nijinsky and Karsavina were the stars of the Diaghilev Ballet Russe at Covent Garden. Nijinsky was astonishing.

I did not meet Nijinsky until a dinner party the following year in New York, while he was doing *Tyl Eulenspiegel* at the Met. He was an extraordinary man, very small, with a sallow, greenish cast to his complexion and secretive Slavic eyes. He spoke no English at all. When the cocktails were passed at this occasion, he reached for one only to have Mme. Nijinsky cry out so violently that he drew his hand convulsively back from the tray. I gave him my drink. He bolted it and threw me a pathetically grateful glance. The same thing happened when he was about to take a cigarette. At his wife's furious reaction, he dropped the cigarette as if it had been an adder. I remember thinking: This is going to end very badly.

I had left the United States with a folder of American Express checks representing a sum that would have supported me amply for a year in New York. As a tactical measure, however, Mabelle and I had arranged a private code; if, for instance, I cabled "Firmanite," it signified "Please send funds immediately." After several weeks in London and a number of visits to enticing Messrs. Anderson and Shepherd, I realized the necessity of "Firmaniting." Mabelle responded handsomely. Discarding my huge tweed hat with no further concern, I packed my new English clothes in my new English luggage and set out to cross the Channel in search of further adventure.

In Paris I selected a small unpretentious hotel, for memory of the bill I had contracted at Claridge's was still painful. On my first Sunday in France I went out to the Villa Trianon at Versailles, the house which

Elsie de Wolfe and Bessie Marbury had bought some years before. Notwithstanding the tales I had heard of it, I was more impressed than I had expected. Elsie had remodeled and decorated with surpassing elegance and affection. It furnished her background in the grand tradition, but with none of the idle pomposity she loathed.

On that particular afternoon, Elsie was giving one of her usual Sunday shindigs. The guests represented the top layer of the international creme, there was superlative food, and an excellent jazz orchestra had been engaged to play for dancing.

Elsie herself was a little handicapped by her inability to tell one tempo from the next. "For God's sake, what are they playing?" she would whisper in my ear.

"It's a waltz, dear." So we would waltz, with little concern for the rhythm. Had I pronounced it a fox-trot, she would have trotted to the waltz tempo quite as cheerfully.

Everybody, it seemed, had come to dance. The Duke of Manchester arrived with his patent leather pumps in a neat paper parcel. Donning them in full view of everybody, he snapped the elastic bands which held them in place with the most consummate self-possession. Royalty was represented by the Spanish Infante Don Luis Ferdinand and by a rather untidy but amiable lady on the weather side of sixty who, somebody said, was the Grand Duchess Anastasia.

The Grand Duchess, posted near the top of the sweeping marble stairway, beckoned to me. Since I had never been exposed to the ways of the Romanoffs in my sheltered upbringing, I looked to Elsie for help. "Go along, darling," said Elsie. "She wants to dance with you."

"But suppose I do not wish to dance with her?"

"One does not question the whim of a Grand Duchess," said Elsie with some severity.

Unfortunately, her Imperial Highness suffered from a tendency to overwork her royal prerogative. I asserted myself as a son of the Republic. When she approached, I turned on my heel and simulated acute interest in somebody at the furthest end of the room. This was not a difficult piece of acting, for at the furthest corner of the room was stationed Lady Duff Gordon, the famous Lucille who dressed Florence Walton and many other artists I admired. She had a flaming head of red hair and an intriguing cast in one eye, and the waltz was her passion. She waltzed with excruciating languor, punctuated at intervals by improper suggestions whispered into the ear of her partner. "Don't you just adore the waltz?" I would whisper back sternly upon these occasions.

Harry Lehr, the man who had taught the *haute monde* of Newport how not to be stuffy, was a prominent guest at Elsie's party. His snobbery was exceeded only by his wit, a combination of virtues which placed him in the highest social demand. Lehr was one of the four men from whom Somerset Maugham built the character of Elliott Templeton in *The Razor's Edge*, and my recollection of him served me admirably when it later fell to my lot to play Templeton in the motion picture.

In the meantime, which was an excessively gay time and a time orchestrated principally by the explosions of champagne corks, I "firminated" repeatedly.

So went it, until the fine late summer afternoon when I lunched with a party at the apartment of Don Luis Ferdinand. While we were toying with our salads, the prince was summoned to the telephone. He returned shaken. He announced that the heir to the Austrian throne had been assassinated at Sarajevo. I confess that the event concerned me as little as it did most other people of that innocent age. I was under the impression that Austrian grand dukes were in ample supply.

"How extremely unfortunate," I murmured correctly to the Infante.

"It will probably mean war," he said.

"War?" said a lady down the table, transfixing a frayed anchovy with a tiny golden fork. "My dear Don Luis, you have obviously taken too much wine."

The anchovy vanished down her jeweled gorge, and with it all further talk of such improbable topics as war.

With August at hand, and concurrently the start of rehearsals for the Shubert show and the end of my excursion, I plunged myself into a frenzy of shopping. I purchased lingerie, fripperies, and four feather boas for Gran. Idly counting the American Express checks which remained, I discovered that I did not have remotely enough to pay for my clothes ordered in London. I naturally "firmanited" vigorously.

Nothing happened.

I "firminated" again. Nothing happened. Unfortified by the knowledge that guests at nice hotels may sign checks for their meals, I subsisted for four days on bread and red wine. I became a familiar figure about the *place de l' Opera*, which is the home not only of art but the American Express office. Ultimately, Mabelle relented. I dashed to London, was handed my elegant new wardrobe with Anderson and Shepherd's blessing, and left aboard *The Lusitania* at Southampton. On the day we sailed, Germany invaded Belgium.

Webb's recollection that he sailed the day Germany invaded Belgium is at odds with the facts. The passenger manifest shows that Webb arrived in New York on July 10, 1914, from Liverpool aboard the *Lusitania*. Germany invaded Belgium on August 2, 1914. England declared war on Germany August 4, 1914.

England's declaration of war was wirelessed to us. As we were a British ship and a target for the U-boats rumored to be prowling the Atlantic under specific orders to torpedo the great *Cunarder*, the trip was the most subdued I have ever made. Gay paper hats were to be seen on the heads of only the most jaded or drunken shipboard revelers, and nobody felt happy until we steamed up the Narrows into sight of the Manhattan skyline.

When I strolled into the Shubert office a few days later, I was conducted with a vast show of secrecy into an inner chamber. The door was closed behind me.

"Are you," I was asked, "obliged by the grace of God to dance with Mae Murray."

"Certainly not," I replied.

"Wonderful. We want you. We don't want her."

"You may consider us divorced," I said.

The partner produced by the Shuberts was an English girl named Eileen Molyneux. I had seen her in a London revue, and my impression had been excellent. She was extremely beautiful and a talented dancer. She was particularly wonderfully dressed. Her clothes, she told me, had been designed by her cousin, Edward Molyneux. He had been working for the siren of the waltz, Lucille of the red hair and improper tongue, until entering the British army at the outbreak of the war.

The show, *Dancing Around*, went into rehearsal—ten weeks of rehearsal, in those pre-Equity and pre-air-conditioning days. Fortunately, the company got on with each other remarkably well, for ten of us were crammed into an insufferably airless little dressing niche at the Winter Garden, where our wretchedness was somewhat tempered by the frequent visits of Al Jolson.

Although Jolson was sometimes difficult to work with, he apparently had a genuine affection for Clifton Webb. In one of Webb's autograph books (found in his estate collection) Jolson wrote this note to Webb:

If they all were as easy to get along with as you . . . enough said!
Yours truly, Al Jolson.

The show opened well and a long run was indicated. Meanwhile, business at my studio continued briskly. The war in Europe, for reasons which I must leave to sociologists, fanned the dance craze to even wilder flames. New dance clubs opened at every hand, and a sea of new faces thronged New York. One of them was Elsa Maxwell, whom I met the first time she came prospecting in Manhattan. Miss Maxwell had changed very little, except (after the customary pattern) for the impact of success upon her waistline.

Succumbing once again to the delusion that my energies were boundless, I was engaged to open the new grill at the Knickerbocker Hotel on New Year's Eve. For this event, Eileen and I worked out a special number whimsically called "The Tipperary Trot." Four days after trying it out at a party given by Bessie Marbury atop the Strand Roof, I came down with bronchitis and was obliged to drop out of *Dancing Around*. This worried me negligibly, as my part was confined to a few scattered dances. The thirty-first of December arrived; however, my throat was still very sore and my fever at 103. This worried me a great deal, for my role on the Knickerbocker Roof was more impressive.

Resisting all of Mabelle's well-intentioned threats, I dressed and dashed off to the Knickerbocker. Eileen and I trotted like mad. I went straight home and back to bed. Next day the press reported, in exaggerated style, our brilliant opening. This being New Year's day, I had a special matinee at the Winter Garden. When I arrived, I found the manager awaiting me. He handed me a notice. It informed me that my services, as of that moment, were superfluous.

Strangely elated, I rolled the notice into a small, perfect sphere. I handed it back to the manager. "I want you to give this to Mr. Shubert with my compliments," I said. "I trust that he will know what to do with it."

This ends the six chapters Webb wrote. The following chapters use material gleaned from notes left with the autobiography plus independent research.

CHAPTER 7

In Love with Jeanne Eagels

Noel Coward said, "Of all the actresses I have ever seen, there was never one quite like Jeanne Eagels." Her fame as an actress inspired people like director-writer Joe Mankiewicz to reference her in this famous bit of dialogue voiced by George Sanders in *All about Eve* (1950): "Margo, as you know, I have lived in the theatre as a Trappist Monk lives in his faith. I have no other world, no other life . . . and once in a great while I experience that moment of revelation for which all true believers wait and pray. You were one. Jeanne Eagels another."

Clifton Webb says in his notes, "I came uncomfortably close to being married on two occasions. One woman I fell in love with was Jeanne Eagels, the famous actress. She and I discussed marriage in 1921 and were ready to take the fatal step." The other woman was Gladys Taliaferro, the girl he met in art school and with whom he kept in contact during most of his young life. Webb said, "Gladys, a hometown girl with whom I grew up, was the second charmer. She and I perhaps would have hit it off . . . but she knew nothing about the theatre and at that time it was my whole life."

The magazine section of the *Syracuse Herald*, Sunday, July 17, 1921, had this headline: "Clifton Webb, Versatile Young Dancer, Smiles at the Rich and Distinguished Admirers of Pretty and Talented Jeanne Eagels and Goes Off with Her to Europe to Marry Her." The story goes on to say: "When Miss Eagels sailed to Europe a few days ago, Mr. Webb and his mother were on the same ship. The marriage, Broadway informed and informers say may occur in Paris or Madrid according to Miss Eagels's fancy." The marriage of course, did not happen. Webb said, "I talked it over with Mother. She gave me some advice: 'If you feel that way, wait a little while. You know what happens to most people who marry in haste.'"

7.1. Jeanne Eagels. Courtesy of Strauss-Peyton photographers.

It appears that this proposed union with Eagels might have been a plot in which Webb agreed to play along with the talk that he and Eagels were about to be married. In reality, Eagels was to meet another older man in Europe. The fact is that Webb and Eagels spent little or no time with each other on this trip. Eagels sailed back to the United States aboard the *Adriatic* on July 20, 1921. Mabelle returned on the same ship.

Webb stayed in Europe for at least two and a half seasons, working for impresario Charles B. Cochran. Webb did not return to New York until January 17, 1923, aboard the *Olympic* from Southampton.

Once he returned in 1923, he went to see Eagels in her new smash success, the play *Rain* by Somerset Maugham. Eagels welcomed him happily and introduced him to, as Webb described him, "a very handsome, clean cut, and muscular creature in her dressing room named Ted Coy." (The Coy-Eagels relationship did not begin until mid-1925. *Rain* opened in November of 1922.)

Webb had no idea who he was. He said, "You see, not being a college man and not being a football player, I did not know him as he was a great gentleman in his field." Coy was an outstanding football player for Yale and had become a national sensation. Eagels said, "You know he wants to marry me." Shaken, Webb said, "That's lovely . . . goody for your side." Eagels then said, "The son of a bitch is married."

7.2. Clifton Webb and his mother, Mabelle, in St. Mark's Square in Venice, circa 1921.
The John and Betsy Neylon Collection.

Webb saw *Rain* many times, standing in the wings, sitting in Eagels's dressing room. *Rain* ran on Broadway at the Maxine Elliott Theatre, and Ted Coy was there in the orchestra every night. Clifton Webb was smoldering in the wings.

Webb said he met Eagels in Paris in 1914 when he was just twenty-five years old. This is possible since Eagels sailed for Europe on May 18, 1914. She returned July 31, 1914. Webb was in Europe until July 10, 1914. This means they probably met some time in June 1914. At this time Eagels was a total unknown. Since Eagels had no money, she evidently was either being escorted by the "elderly gentleman" to whom Webb refers below or using his money.

"The great thing about Jeanne was our intense love for one another. We were too much alike. She had a great sense of humor, and anybody

7.3. Jeanne Eagels as Sadie Thompson in *Rain*. The David L. Smith Collection.

who has a sense of humor endears themselves to me immediately. She was protected by this elderly gentleman who had sent her abroad. She had that husky kind of voice combined with her cock-eyed sense of humor.

"We went to a party given for [actress] Gaby Deslys and everybody came dripping in jewels, but Jeanne always did the reverse. She came in a beautiful organdy dress . . . having no jewels . . . she loved the reverse scene. She defied convention. She defied the mold. She created her own mold."

After seeing her in *Rain*, Webb had this reaction: "Sadie Thompson was described as a frowsy blonde whose flesh dripped over her high button shoes, but Jeanne was fragile, and in order to create the impression of this voluptuous woman she put on this voice and immediately gave you the picture of this raucous woman."

Rain had an amazing run on Broadway of 648 performances. Jeanne Eagels missed very few performances, a testament to her stamina. The original production ran from November 1922 to June 1924. After an equity strike closed it down, it came back and ran from September 1924 to early November 1926. Eagels was the star in this entire run. After the last Broadway closing, she took the production on the road for more than two years. Thus, she kept the production active for some five years in all.

Ward Morehouse, in his book *Matinee Tomorrow*, interviewed Kathryne Kennedy, a supporting actress with Eagels in *Rain* (and Eagels understudy), who said of her, "I sincerely doubt if Jeanne Eagels really knew, in spite of her pretensions, that she was a great actress. She was. Many times backstage I'd be waiting for my entrance cue, and suddenly Jeanne would start to build a scene, and we would look up from our books at once. Some damn thing . . . some power . . . something would take hold of your heart, your senses, as you listened to her, and you'd thrill to the sound of her."

Clifton Webb was obviously caught up in the magic that she possessed, both offstage and on. He was disappointed with her infatuation with Ted Coy, thinking she deserved better. Describing Coy, he said: "He had never met an actress before in his life. He was married. As a matter of fact, we went up to his house one night . . . his wife was away . . . charming apartment. He gave us a party. I thought this was wrong because the man was not cut out for that kind of life. He was not cut out for the demanding personality she was. He was never cut out to be the husband of a star. He had been a great hero in his own name. This took something away from him and you could see the deterioration. I think his background impressed her. In the first place, he was very handsome. She saw that she could upset his placid life and that intrigued her. One moment a saint, the next a tigress. She could turn at the snap of a finger. If she had not died when she did, I think she could have gained a great deal from psychiatry. She was a definite neurotic."

Eagels had bouts with alcohol, and these were exacerbated when she was out of work. She began her career as a child actress and said, "Once I had begun I could not be stopped. I was ill when I was not on the stage. It seemed to me I couldn't breathe in any other atmosphere." Her situation was not helped by the fact that after Coy became her husband he also became a boozer. She divorced him after claiming he broke her jaw and she was subjected to other physical abuse.

When she was touring with *Her Cardboard Lover*, she was a no-show both in Milwaukee and St. Louis. She claimed she was suffering from ptomaine poisoning, but eyewitnesses placed her in Chicago on a boozing binge. As a result, she was given an eighteen-month suspension by Actor's Equity. Clifton Webb knew the suspension would be disastrous for her.

Webb recalled, "The most awful thing . . . the most tragic thing that happened to her was when Equity kept her from working." Webb was playing in the first *Little Show* in 1929 when Eagels was on suspension.

"I had a house above Washington [Connecticut]. She would come down for the weekend. Everybody just sat around drinking. I had two dressing rooms in the theatre. She would come up to my dressing room . . . one flight up. There was a fire door, and it looked right down to the stage. She used to come in—dropped in all the time—and laugh and say, 'See that door, Cliffy? When I play here I'll get a slide and just slide down to the stage.'"

When Eagels was offered a Paramount film called *The Laughing Lady*, she was very pleased to do it. Eagels made just nine movies; only two were sound. Her performance in *The Letter* (1929) garnered her an Oscar nomination for best actress. She lost to Mary Pickford in what has been described as an early example of cronyism in the Academy. Early meetings of the Academy were held at Pickfair. In Gary Carey's biography, *Doug and Mary*, the author states, "It gives the impression that the Academy was handing out its statuettes on a political or social basis." Eagels died before knowing that Mary Pickford had won the Oscar.

Webb said, "It is not pleasant for a person to be kept out of work for a year—it's being sent to Purgatory." As shooting time neared for *The Laughing Lady*, Eagels came down with conjunctivitis. (Actually, she had eye surgery for ulcers in her eyes, a not uncommon ailment with actors who were blinded every night by Klieg lights) She was sent to the hospital and many assumed she had gone on another drinking bout. Sam Harris, her manager, tried to convince everyone she did not have a drop to drink. Webb said, "If she'd been dying of something, they'd still have said she was drunk." Walter Wanger sent her a notice in which he said that he did not think they could hold up production.

A frustrated Webb said, "All this coming on top of her Equity trouble!" When she came out of the hospital, she went to her place and locked herself in alone and began to drink. Webb described the scene.

"Her secretary couldn't get to her. No one could get to her. This went on for about three days. Finally they broke into the house and got her to New York to her apartment. They sent for a doctor and he came and gave her one of his famous cocktails. He also arranged for her to come and have an irrigation. So, at the appointed hour, in her nightdress and a fur coat, she went to the doctor's office. He was out, and an assistant, not knowing that he had already given her this 'cocktail' a few hours earlier, gave her another. The next thing the assistant heard a 'boom,' and she had dropped dead."

No definitive cause of death was ever determined. The chief medical examiner stated she had died from alcoholic psychosis. Two doctors said an autopsy showed traces of chloral hydrate. Eight months later a final autopsy showed she had traces of heroin. According to *Time* magazine, the hospital where she died was a private psychotherapeutic sanitarium. Her physician, Dr. Edward S. Cowles, was a neurologist, psychiatrist, and the proprietor of the hospital. Dr. Cowles was not a member of any local or state medical society, nor the American Medical Association. The AMA did not accept the sanitarium for its register of hospitals. Dr. Cowles said, "I had treated Miss Eagels for almost ten years and never knew of her taking any drugs. Any story that drugs caused her death or contributed to her death is false."

Jeanne Eagels died on October 3, 1929. She was thirty-nine years old. At that time, Clifton Webb was playing at the Music Box Theatre in the first *Little Show*. A stagehand came to Webb's dressing room and said that he had seen on the Times Square board that Jeanne Eagels had dropped dead. Webb questioned the report. "I'm not kidding, and I called the *Times* and they said it was true!" said the young man. Webb couldn't believe what he heard. He decided to verify the tragedy.

"I called the doctor and got him. He said, 'Yes, it was a very unfortunate accident.' This was on a Thursday night, I remember because very often the night before matinees I would stay in town and take a suite at the Algonquin. Mabelle was in town. I phoned her and naturally she was speechless. We wanted to talk to someone, anyone, so we wound up by seeing Tallulah Bankhead, who was now living at the Elysee, and Beatrice Lillie. We talked about this. The next day I had a matinee. Friday she was laid out at Campbell's. Sam Harris took care of everything."

Webb and Mabelle went to see her.

"There she was lying with a pompadour. So my mother called an attendant and asked for a comb, and she took it and dressed her hair. Jeanne wore her hair in ringlets. Mabelle took flowers and put them in her hand. So we did all we could. The funeral was the next morning at eleven. She was buried in Kansas City, Missouri (the place of her birth), and some years later when I played there, I called on her mother. She took me out to her grave. I saw on it Jeanne Eagles (which was her birth name) and I said, 'Julia, Jeanne would turn in her grave if she saw her name spelled that way—she'd spit in your eye.'"

Clifton Webb never believed Jeanne Eagels died of alcoholism or drugs.

"The point is this: Jeanne Eagels never drank a lot. She couldn't drink a lot. One drink and she'd be off. It was only when she played in *Rain*, beginning about the second year—and then in the show she would drink champagne. The rain never dried up, and everybody felt this constant wet and dank. She played that show for four years. She was the first lady of the theatre. No, there has never been anybody quite like her. Her range was extraordinary. She knew her job well."

Webb fondly remembered their times together.

"We would prowl the streets late at night—she had to have her chili concarne—joints of all types. She loved to cook chili, would open a can of chili and say, 'God damn it, let's get down to it.' She had a beautiful apartment in town—exquisite taste. She dressed beautifully, very chic. We had a standing joke. 'Cliffy let's walk down the Avenue properly dressed.' That was the point–'for the occasion.' You see, we never went anywhere without one another, and people would say, 'God damn it, if you aren't married, you should be.'"

Webb said she called him "Cliffy" (as did Marilyn Miller later) and he called her "Mrs. Dubinsky." This was in reference to Eagels first marriage, during which she claimed to have given birth to a child that died in infancy. Webb said being addressed as "Mrs. Dubinsky" used to "burn her up." She would say, "Son of a bitch, don't call me that!"

Despite his declaration that he wanted to marry Eagels at one time, he later had different thoughts about such a union.

"We had a very romantic affair, but marriage would have been fatal— we were very much alike. The moment she knew she had me, she would not have wanted me, and with me the same way. We were very sensible about it."

At one time when Eagels had been touring, she returned to New York, called Webb, and wanted him to come over. Webb was very tired and told her he had to get some rest. But Eagels was adamant. "Cliffy come up, it will be very quiet, and you will have a rest." Webb knew her husband would be there but he reluctantly agreed. He arrived and there was no one there. Eagels had a main house and a cottage. On this particular Sunday she had rented the cottage to Fay Bainter. When Webb could not get in the house, he wandered over to Bainter's cottage.

"Fay said to have dinner with them. I didn't want to do it. I said I was expecting Jeanne, but Fay said, 'Don't be silly.' Well about 9:30 I was sitting where I could see Jeanne's house and I saw the headlights of her car. I said to Fay, 'I think I'd better go over.' I went over and she was like a tigress. I kidded her along. Her husband, Ted, always tried to keep things going, watching this creature, trying to see which way she's going. She brought the servants up with her and I said, 'Jeanne I'm desperately tired. I have to go to bed.' The next morning I went down to the kitchen kind of early, and there were Jeanne and Ted in the kitchen in dressing gowns, and she said, 'See that son of a bitch, he's filled with gin—he's hitting the bottle.' With that she took a big sock of liquor. Then she wanted to know if I wanted to know what happened on the trip and said, 'Why he tried to break my arm!' I said, 'Jeanne don't air your dirty linen in public. I came here for a rest. This is all very embarrassing. Why can't we have a nice day?' Then I said, 'I think I'll go and get dressed.' So I went up and got dressed. When I came down she was sitting in the living room. She said to me, 'Get out.' I said, 'OK.' So I went upstairs and packed my bag. I phoned Mabelle. I said, 'Well dear, you have a surprise. I have been put out.' She said, 'What have you done?' I said, 'I have done nothing, but I'll be home."

In a couple of days, Webb's phone rang. "Is that you Cliffy?" Webb hung up. This went on for some time. Noel Coward came to have dinner with Webb one night when suddenly Eagels stormed into the house. She said, "You son of a bitch. Why didn't you knock him down? You could have protected me!" Webb said, "We started to laugh, and then we were back again to where we started. She used healthy profanity, but she used it beautifully."

Several actresses have tried their hand at portraying Somerset Maugham's Sadie Thompson. Gloria Swanson did a silent film version in 1928. Joan Crawford (1932) and Rita Hayworth (1953) made feeble attempts in sound films. In 1944 there was even a musical version entitled *Sadie Thompson.* June Havoc was praised for her performance, but several reviewers couldn't forget Jeanne Eagels corrosive Sadie of 1922. Crawford was particularly apprehensive about playing the role and asked comedian Walter Catlett for suggestions about interpretation. Catlett replied, "Listen, fishcake, when Jeanne Eagels died, *Rain* died with her."

In 1949 Webb expressed in a lengthy and candid essay his view of why he never married. This essay was never published. It was found among the notes for his proposed autobiography.

"The career of a roving actor is not precisely the kind of existence a wife longs for. There are few women who can endure the constant moving from place to place, the inherent restlessness of the people who are always on the *qui vive* to entertain. Mabelle is one; Grace Moore was another; so is Mary Garden. Bea Lillie is a fourth.

"These are people who live gracefully and freely, who distill all the fun out of life that is possible for one to have. They are individuals who light up a house or an apartment with a sparkle that leaves it cold and dead when they go away. They are women, too, who are not afraid to put their cards on the table—to play whatever game they play with men out in the open.

"Perhaps it is this candid kind of feminine, independent personality which has given me a secret fear of any other kind. It sometimes seems to me that a wife must continually plot against her husband, in a cosmic conspiracy of the sexes. It is precisely the insidious things that forge a bachelor out of the heat of argument. I dare say there are thousands of husbands that are devout bachelors at heart in the country today. They are bound irrevocably to their 'better halves' by vows of religion or—in some cases, more securely—by the drastic community property laws.

"I have discovered in my life that boredom can kill as subtly and thoroughly as does a dose of cyanide. It creeps up upon its victim over a score of years and strikes him down before he knows it. How many husbands have I seen who are walking cadavers with their proud wives by their side? The possessive, the clinging, the assertive, the slavish, the domineering women are always in evidence. When such become wives, they appear to devote much of their time to taking over the souls of their husbands. 'Don't you think, darling, it would be better if you didn't do that?' should be the motto graven on the escutcheon of every couple in that category.

"On the other hand, a bachelor is likely to become self-centered and crotchety. Both these accusations have been directed at me—though I refuse to admit them. I believe that the reason I have remained single so long is that there are few women who can hold their own with Mabelle, even at her present age of eighty.

"At one party she was able to corral the late King George for the duration. At another, dancing with the basso Ezio Pinza, Mother left the room in exact rhythm to the music and slammed the door on the beat. Ezio called me up the next day to compliment her on her rhythmic talents. What sitting-knitting sister or wife could keep up with such a pace?

"A man wants adventure, humor, gaiety in whatever woman decorates his life. He wants someone to pay him attention, to grace his table, to enliven his friendships. I suppose it is because I am so demanding—and marriage must be give-and-take—that I have avoided it for so long. The French are clever, after all; they insist that their wives shall remain mistresses, that the essential mystery of a woman shall not be entirely stripped away by the wedding ceremony.

"Finally, there is the problem of making a choice. In a world filled with more women then men, in a world I have seen a great deal of—my crossing the Atlantic last year was my forty-eighth—I am doubtful of my ability to know what I need in the way of a woman in my life. I have no legitimate reason for wanting one, not even the usual excuse of being able to file a joint income tax return.

"It seems that when I have come to the point of dramatically delivering two speeches—'Marry me, darling, I adore you!' and 'Go find an apartment, Mother, and live by yourself'—I have never had the courage to say either. Or the cruelty.

"I find it hard to believe in Mabelle's energy and vitality. At her age she has three gray hairs—which distresses her—all her own teeth, reads without glasses, and can out-dance a twenty-year-old. I often ask myself: 'What woman can compete with her?' If this sounds like an apron-strings complex, it is not. It is merely that I take a dispassionate view of my mother and I find myself very fond of her as a friend and companion.

"An acquaintance listened to one of my panegyrics on Mabelle the other day. When I had concluded, he said quietly, 'What will you do, Clifton, when Mabelle dies?'

"It hit me like a blow in the face. 'I don't want to think about it,' I said. But it will happen as it happens to all of us. When it does, it is very likely that I will find my particular lady and bestow upon her the intriguing title of Mrs. Clifton Webb."

Judging from this lengthy analysis of his attitude toward women and marriage, Clifton Webb often thought about it. While in his mind there were a number of reasons to avoid such a union, the overwhelming argument against marriage seemed to have been the unbearable thought of turning his mother out. He never had the courage or the cruelty to do it.

On November 8, 1928, Webb found himself opening at the Alvin Theater on Broadway in *Treasure Girl* opposite the legendary Gertrude Lawrence. Webb and Mary Hay charmed the audience with their eccentric dancing. The failure of the book dragged down some of George and Ira Gershwin's great songs. It was in this show that Webb and Mary Hay introduced the durable Gershwin standard, "I've Got a Crush on You." They both sang this song, but at a faster tempo and not the slow version that has become known since. Webb and Hay were also fortunate to sing two other Gershwin songs in this production: "K-ra-zy for You" and "What Causes That?" (both of which were heard in the 1992 Gershwin Broadway production *Crazy for You*). Brooks Atkinson called them "the brightest pair in this production." This show had a mere sixty-eight performances. After the show closed, Webb and Hay moved to the Palace for a vaudeville stint. They adapted one of Gershwin's songs from *Treasure Girl*, changing it from "Where's the Boy?" to "Where's the Girl?" and made it an integral part of their act.

Clifton Webb enjoyed the company of women. In 1929, when Jeanne Eagels died, Webb was playing in the first *The Little Show*. His leading lady was Libby Holman, who became his best friend after Eagels death. Webb was already known as a sleek and stylish dancer. This production gave him a chance to show that he was a first-rate actor and comedian. In addition to Webb and Holman, comedian Fred Allen was cast as the third star. *The Little Show* was a revue. It grew out of a series of Sunday night concerts. A battery of writers and composers contributed to the show, which was framed by Howard Dietz and Arthur Schwartz. It was smart, sophisticated, and entertaining. The songs were first rate with several showstoppers.

In his autobiography, Howard Dietz said that he and Schwartz thought they had finished the score. However, Clifton Webb was not satisfied. Dietz recalled, "He wanted a number that was more perverse, a number he could deliver all alone in full-dress suit and spotlight. He said it should be a lyric with suave romantic frustration." Apparently, Webb was big enough at this time to demand such a thing. Dietz said he knew that Webb "craved parts that were virile and sensuous. He was not virile and sensuous offstage, but onstage he knew what moods would work for him."

In response to Webb's request, Dietz and Schwartz wrote "I Guess I'll Have to Change My Plan." Pleased with the new song, Webb stepped into the spotlight and intoned:

> I guess I'll have to change my plan
> I should have realized there'd be another man
> Why did I buy those blue pajamas
> Before the big affair began?

It became known as "The Blue Pajamas Song" and was a huge hit. Holman also had a hit with "Can't We Be Friends?" "Moanin' Low" was the third hit of the production. When it was time to go to work on "Moanin' Low," Webb had a few ideas. Dietz said it became a sensational showstopper in the form of "a musical playlet staged by Webb for Libby Holman and himself."

The staging of "Moanin' Low" gave Webb not only a shot at comedy, but also a chance to play against type. It was in this song that he got to dance as well as play a pimp—a "sweetback" as it was known in Harlem. Webb put on tan makeup, a gaudy suit, and exaggerated sideburns. Holman and Webb rehearsed the number in secret for days before finally showing it to the producers. In the number, Webb performs a frenzied dance, using "snake-hip" movements taught to him by Buddy Bradley, a famous black dance instructor. He makes love to Holman, practically raping her. Then, after he discovers she has concealed money from him, he chokes her, leaving her for dead. After he leaves, Holman recovers and crawls to the door. She begins singing "Moanin' Low" in a deep, throaty obbligato.

The producers were startled. They liked it, but said they thought it should be "toned down." Webb immediately called Noel Coward. Webb and Holman did the scene for him. Coward said, "If even a soupcon is changed, the producers would be quite, quite mad." Thanks to Coward's sage advice, the producers relented and the number was played as rehearsed. There were two more *Little Shows*, but the first one was the best. It gave considerable boost to Webb's career and made Libby Holman an overnight sensation.

In The Playbill for *Present Laughter*, there is a humorous story about an event that occurred during the run of *The Little Show*. A group of Webb's friends decided they would try to break him up on stage. Algonquinites Marc Connelly, Alexander Wolcott, Franklin P. Adams, Harpo Marx, Beatrice Lillie, and Frank Sullivan bought out the entire front row of the theatre. They made their way to their seats, each with an armful of props, and waited for Webb's first entrance. When Webb appeared, the entire front row had mustached faces. When Webb made his second entrance, the front row wore goatees. On his third entrance they all sported huge black beards. Webb never batted an eye. Finally, in desperation, Frank Sullivan began pitching pennies on stage. Bea Lillie followed. Then everyone in the front row was pitching pennies. Webb continued to rise above the disturbance, picking up pennies while he danced. Finally, Fred Allen could stand it no longer. Gratefully, he remarked that the money would tide them all over until payday.

The producers of *The Little Show* decided to do a follow-up without the services of Webb, Allen, and Holman. Max Gordon looked upon this as an opportunity. He promptly signed all three, and then got Howard

Dietz and Arthur Schwartz to write the bulk of the songs for a new show he called *Three's a Crowd*. The second *Little Show* ran for only sixty-three performances in 1930. In 1933, the *Third Little Show* was produced (again without Webb, Allen, or Holman) and did poorly. Conversely, *Three's a Crowd* became a huge hit. It opened October 15, 1930, at the Selwyn Theater in New York.

It was an important show for Webb. It was an even bigger hit than *The Little Show*. Lyricist Howard Dietz and composer Arthur Schwartz produced a fine score. Libby Holman sang "Body and Soul" while Webb danced. She also sang the hit song "Something to Remember You By" to a young sailor played by twenty-three-year-old Fred MacMurray. *Three's a Crowd* became a major moneymaker in the height of the Great Depression.

"Body and Soul," by Johnny Green, was reprised in the second part of the show, with Webb and Tamara Geva providing a dance interpretation that proved to be the highlight of the evening. Tamara Geva had attended the Kirov School of Ballet in Leningrad. In 1923, at the age of fifteen, she married George Balanchine. They left Russia in 1925. She then joined Sergei Diaghilev's Ballet Russe in Paris. A couple of years later, she arrived in America with the Chauve Souris Company. *Three's a Crowd* was her second Broadway show.

Although Webb's teaming with Tamara Geva provided some exciting dancing, he also danced with Amy Revere in a romantic waltz sequence. Revere was a ballet-trained dancer and appeared in at least two editions of the *Earl Carroll Vanities*. Webb and Revere's waltz, "The Moment I Saw You," came at the close of act 1. Webb's charm, coupled with Revere's graceful dancing, led one reviewer to say, "The days of the Castles and the other kings and queens of ballroom dances were recalled and most pleasantly."

Webb's masterful dancing in this revue showed his command of the dance in the variety of routines he presented. With these two shows back to back, Webb seemed to be at the top of his game as a dancer.

One rather risqué skit came when Webb was interrupted in his bath by Tamara Geva, who recognizes him only when he pulls out the plug, as she peers over the rim.

It seems Clifton Webb was forever trying to be the peacemaker or at least working to help people understand each other. At a party at Danny Kaye's house, Tallulah Bankhead, for no apparent reason other than to shock people, decided to hone in on Sylvia Fine's mother. Fine was Danny Kaye's wife. After a fight with Tallulah, Fine said, "I will never have

7.4. Clifton Webb, Libby Holman, and Fred Allen in *Three's a Crowd*. Billy Rose Theatre Division, The New York Public Library for the Performing Arts, Astor, Lenox and Tilden Foundations.

her in my house again." Webb said, "You must be more tolerant of Tallulah. That's just her way." Fine replied, "I don't like her anyway, Clifton." Webb reiterated, "You must be more forgiving." Fine said, "I would be if she had her human moments, but if she has them, they're not apparent. She has them in private." Tallulah raised hackles and knocked a good many conventions off their pedestals throughout her tempestuous life. Webb remained her defender and close friend to the end.

Any one who came to New York during the 1930–31 seasons had to see at least three shows: *Grand Hotel*, *Green Pastures*, and *Three's a Crowd*. When Gloria Swanson visited New York in the early spring of 1931, she said, "The only musical I was dying to see was *Three's a Crowd*, which starred Libby Holman, Fred Allen, and my outrageous darling Clifton Webb."

Three's a Crowd was one of the few shows of that time to actually make money. Before the 1931 season was over, most actors were begging for work. Even the powerful Shubert brothers were in financial straits. While the show did well in New York, the road show was not nearly as successful. Drastic cuts were made in salaries. Libby Holman, who had been making fifteen hundred dollars a week, was reduced to fifty dollars a week. The show was finally forced to close in late February 1932.

In April of 1932, Webb, Alexander Wolcott, and Noel Coward sailed together for London on the *Europia*. Webb recalled that the sailing was a prime example of "prewar luxury life afloat." Webb described the scene aboard the ship.

"During the entire trip over, they sat from morning until night in the salon playing backgammon and Russian banque. Luncheon was served as they played, and people walked by and looked at them and made rude remarks about them.

"One evening at dinner we were sitting in the Ritz dining room on the ship. I said, 'Just look at us—three children of the Ritz.' I saw a funny look come into Noel's eyes, so I quickly said, 'That's a good title for a song.' He said, 'I know it. I'm going to use it.' He did just that later on in a revue called *Words and Music* in London. The first night we arrived, we dined at the Ivy restaurant in London: Noel, Gladys Colthrop, who designs all of his sets and costumes, Woolcott, and Noel's secretary, who addressed him as 'Master.' At first, I thought she was kidding, then I realized she was quite serious.

"We went to see Noel's *Cavalcade*, and we had the Royal box. It was very impressive. After the first act, powdered footmen came in and served us brandy in a little antechamber in back of the box. I had a tremendous urge to use the royal toilet, which I did. At the end of the play, when the audience realized that Noel was there, they all stood up and applauded. He bowed from right to left from the box, and I suddenly caught Alec Woolcott bowing too. Why, I don't know."

Webb now was very well known in theatrical circles. His fame was to the point where he was even lampooned in other shows. In late 1932, Bert Lahr was the star of *George White's Music Hall Varieties*. In his book *Notes on a Cowardly Lion*, Bert Lahr's son John writes, "White wanted Lahr to do something he had never done before . . . a satire on the popular English matinee idol, Clifton Webb, whose sophisticated and genteel dance routines seemed an unlikely target for Lahr." Apparently, John Lahr was under the impression that Webb was English, which was a rather common assumption at that time.

The Webb take-off, *Chanson by Clifton Duckfeet*, was a stretch for Bert Lahr. He was forced to be elegant instead of bumbling, controlled instead of excessive. Lahr met the challenge and produced a perfect caricature of Webb's clipped, precise personality. In the sketch, Lahr appeared, as

Webb often did, from behind the curtain at center stage. He was dressed in tuxedo pants, a white bolero jacket, and top hat. A gold watch chain stretched across his waist. He spoke delicately and lisped in an attempt to mimic Webb's clipped, precise monotone. The spotlight caught him with his legs tight together and his hand nonchalantly in his left pocket. He took a cigarette, fingered it, then threw it away as he began to sing:

> Til midnight we chatted . . . romantic the scene!
> Adventure? Well, rather . . . my spirits ran high.
> The French are so friendly . . . if you know what I mean.

He then went into a delicate soft shoe, swiveling his hips and emitting delighted gasps at his steps.

At the end of the sketch Lahr struck Webb's confident pose, but the sound of a Bronx cheer filled the air. Lahr did a disdainful double take and made a hasty retreat through the center curtain.

Not to be outdone, Bobby Clark and Webb's great friend Bea Lillie provided one of the highlights of a rather dismal revue called *Walk a Little Faster*. It appeared on Broadway in late 1932 and closed March 18, 1933. Clark and Lillie did a spoof of Tamara Geva and Webb doing the "Alone Together" dance from *Flying Colors*. Thus Clifton Webb had the singular honor of being the butt of both Bert Lahr and Bobby Clark in two concurrently running revues. Webb was now an established star and much in demand. In 1933 Brooks Atkinson said, "It is almost impossible to produce a smart revue without putting Clifton Webb in it somewhere."

Noel Coward was playing next door to *Three's a Crowd* in his own play, *Private Lives*. One day Coward came to Webb's dressing room. "Now, don't tell anyone, but I would like to tell you the story of my new show." He began to tell Webb the story of *Cavalcade*.

Cavalcade was a spectacular pageant of English history seen through the eyes of different generations of the same family. It opened in 1931 at the Theatre Royal, Drury Lane. It has seldom been performed on stage since it requires a cast of almost three hundred plus one hundred extras. Fox studios, with a British cast, filmed it in 1933. It won a best picture Oscar plus two others for art direction (William S. Darling) and best director (Frank Lloyd).

The next morning, both Webb and Coward were invited to spend the weekend at Cobina Wright's home in Sands Point, New York. They got in Webb's car and began their journey. On the way Coward again began talking about *Cavalcade*. Webb said, "Without having one word on paper he knew the entire show, even to the day he would open. He knew how many musicians he wanted—every little detail. He was very definite about his casting."

When they arrived at Cobina Wright's house, they discovered that Lawrence Tibbett was there.

"Somebody else was playing the piano; Lawrence was singing beautifully, I must say, all the tenor arias which I loved to do. It was very nice. I was very agreeable. About four in the morning we were taken to our various rooms. Next morning about eleven o'clock people began to drop in. Cobina kept it so quiet that everybody in Long Island knew Noel Coward was there, and suddenly everybody began dropping in. Cobina, a great party girl, said we should go out for lunch. We drove for miles to this very quiet lunch consisting of 182 people—very quiet. We got home about 4:00 p.m. and had just about settled down for a little siesta when more people arrived. 'Darling how divine . . . too, too divine.' So we dragged ourselves out of our respective beds, combed our hair, more people arrived, more drinks were served, more conversation, more questions asked. Naturally, Noel and myself couldn't sit still like lumps. You have to enter into things and make people think you are enjoying it. This is very wearing. Then some people thought it would be ducky to take a dip—icy cold water—January at Sands Point. So then you begin to get your second wind. I said to Cobina, 'When is it going to be just us?' She laughed merrily. More people arrived. 'Oh, you must stay, take potluck.' Potluck consisted of an enormous dinner. Everything was very gay, very amusing.

"After dinner there were charades. There were all sorts of games. Larry decided to sing. Noel did a few light numbers. I was very retiring. By that time I was quite speechless. This went on till all hours, and the rooms had to be shifted about. I moved in with Larry, Noel with Mr. Wright. We finally dragged our bodies and went to our respective places where we were supposed to sleep. It seemed that Mr. Wright snored and it seemed that Mr. Coward disliked companions who snored. He stood it as long as he could, and about six o'clock in the morning, not having had a wink of sleep, he got up, packed his bag, sneaked out in the snow, and walked, not having any idea where he was walking. He finally took a milk train to New York. I had a good night. Larry didn't snore. The awful part was that someone was missing the next day, and this missing person was Mr. Coward."

Coward's version of this event differs somewhat from Webb's. Coward said when they arrived, Cobina Wright showed him directly to his room.

The bathroom had a communicating door to the room Webb was to occupy. Coward's recollection can be found in William Marchant's book, *The Privilege of His Company*.

Coward finally left the house, making sure no one saw him leave, and was picked up by a truck that took him to a railway station. Two years later a short story by Coward appeared dealing with the activities of this weekend. Cobina Wright vowed she would never forgive Coward. However, they later made up and Cobina again invited Coward to her house, stating that the war had changed everything and it was impossible to entertain in that grand style.

"And so I went," said Coward, "And it will perhaps not come as a surprise to you, as it did to me . . . exactly the same house party was still going on!"

Webb maintained he didn't know what happened to Coward until quite some time after the party. Webb and Lawrence Tibbett both had shows to do the last night of the party and both were pretty well done in.

Webb said, "Larry was doing *Peter Ibbettsen* that night and I was doing *Three's a Crowd*. We walked on the beach. We stood on our heads. We rolled over and breathed deeply. We took our eggs with Worcestershire. We did everything. We turned in together about three o'clock in the afternoon. While I could get by with my show, he had to sing an operatic performance that night. All I know is that I and the aromatic spirits of ammonia walked together and with every step, I'd say, 'Thank God, that's one step nearer the end.'"

In the first chapter of this book, Webb describes his experience in 1925 at the Bal des Quat'z Arts while in Paris. His notes, however, give a much more detailed description of this event. Because of the uniqueness of this party and Webb's humorous account of it, it was decided to include it in this chapter as well.

When Webb was asked if he wanted to go to the Bal des Quat'z Arts, he said, "I would love to, but I am terrified, because I have heard what they do to you if you are not one of the student body. One of the heads of the committee came to see me and said he would assure me that it would be all right. He would be at the door at the entrance at one o'clock and take me right there. But he said, 'Don't speak English. You know you have to come in a Babylonian costume.' So we went to get our costumes. Mine consisted of just a toga. He said, 'Don't wear a jock strap because if someone gets a little familiar and finds you have a jock strap on, out you go.'

"So we all went for our costumes, and then I saw Conde Nast. He had the most elaborate costume—a great osprey and all that. I said, 'Conde, are you sure you're doing the right thing? This is a Babylonian ball.' [Conde Nast was an American who owned several magazines, including *Vogue, Vanity Fair, House and Garden,* and *Glamour.* He published French editions of several of his magazines.] At any rate we danced early that night, and we went to our dressing rooms and got dressed. We had to get out of the car about half a block away and we all linked arms. Nobody could speak very good French, and so we ooh-lah-lah-ooh-lah'd the whole way. The whole conversation was ooh-lah-lah. When we arrived, we were led across the floor and we were taken to the opposite side and put in a box with a group of students. We had to walk up to our box on a ladder. So we got up there, and there were a couple of students who were friends of the director, and their costume consisted of nothing but blue paint—that is all—nothing but blue paint and a tin cup hitched to a particular part of their body.

"It was all very, very Babylonian, and we looked down and just below us was a girl with nothing on but a bunch of cherries. Now Frenchmen are not particularly good looking with nothing on but beards, and these men were dancing around, trying to grab the cherries with their mouths. Back of the boxes there was a garden. I peeked, and was so confused that I quickly drew the curtains. I was terrified to go down and dance in the snake pit. Suddenly we heard a great yell—whoooo—and a group of these man creatures were rushing to the exit and here was Conde Nast being put out bodily. You couldn't get back in again because they put a great big black cross on your back.

"This man, the director, had his mistress there, and it got quite late, and I got a little more courage up and I asked her to dance, so we danced. That was all right. Dwight Wiman went downstairs and someone put their hands under his skirts, and he was almost put out . . . everybody left . . . by that time I had courage—a real Babylonian. I would not want to do it again, but I did not want and would not have wanted to miss any of it. Finally we all left, and by that time everybody loved everybody else. Down the Champs Elysees we went—jumped into the fountain, and were still ooh-lah-lahing."

Reflecting on his "wild years," Webb said, "If you form a certain psychology for yourself or a certain pattern, you are able to go anywhere and observe, take what is amusing at the moment but never let it become a part of you. God knows these years were mad and wonderful years, but I never became a part of it. I always looked upon it in an objective way. I was always an observer."

CHAPTER 8

Great Plays, Then the Great War

In the late 1920s, Clifton Webb had a chance to meet some of his relatives. He also had a meeting with his father, seeing him for the first time since he left Indianapolis as a child.

"When I was in Chicago a cousin of mine that was living there came to see me. I had not seen her since I was a kid in Indiana, but she told me my father was there and asked if I'd like to see him. So a meeting was arranged, and he, and my mother, who was there with me, all went out to dinner. It was a very amusing meeting inasmuch as we hadn't seen him in so many years. They carried on like a couple of school kids. It was really rather pleasant to see. After that, through the years, we corresponded.

"He'd remarried and was living in St. Louis. I found him most affable, still tall, dark, and handsome, with a great sense of humor and an infectious laugh. Whenever he came to New York, he and Mabelle and I would dine together. When I was playing in St. Louis in 1934 with *As Thousands Cheer*, we lunched together. He told me that he hoped I bore him no malice about the way he treated my mother when I was a child. He was very anxious for me to like him. I told him that I couldn't look on him really as a father because I hardly knew him, and after all, what happened in their youth happens to a lot of young people who get married too young.

"In 1937, I received a telegram of his death. Following that I received a letter from his lawyers, that he left me some timberland in Louisiana, and, according to Louisiana law, any offspring was to receive one-third of the estate. This came as a great surprise, it being the first time that I had ever been left anything by anybody. Later on, when I was playing

The Man Who Came to Dinner in St. Louis, I met his wife, who came to the hotel where I was staying. We lunched together, and all during luncheon I was very conscious that my mother, who was there at the time, was peeking from behind a panel, trying to see what her successor looked like."

With the success of *The Little Show* and *Three's a Crowd*, Webb and Mabelle were able to rent a stylish apartment at 410 Park Avenue in Manhattan to complement their "weekend" house in Greenwich, Connecticut, that he had named High Acres. He also hired a maid and chauffeur: "So we could live like human beings."

In 1932 following *Three's a Crowd*, Webb appeared in what some have called "the fourth generation" of a series of revues that began with *The Little Show*. This revue sired two other hits: *Three's a Crowd* and *The Band Wagon*. Max Gordon produced and made sure that Arthur Schwartz and Howard Dietz were not above composing music for a fourth revue that followed a similar musical pattern found in their other recent hits. The "new" show was called *Flying Colors*. It opened on September 15, 1932, and ran until June 25, 1933.

Brooks Atkinson, commenting on this repetition, said, "Now that the freshness of style has worn off in the fourth generation, the aristocracy of musical entertainment needs new blood." But other critics didn't care. They loved all the Max Gordon shows regardless of their similarity.

Gordon was not alone in following a successful show with several similar efforts. *The Earl Carroll Vanities* gave birth to ten shows, all much the same other than a few trimmings like the visually delightful sets of nineteen-year-old Vincente Minnelli.

In *Flying Colors*, Webb was again teamed with Tamara Geva. Patsy Kelly was cast in what might have been a Libby Holman role, and comedian Charles Butterworth was the monologist instead of Fred Allen. This show featured two pairs of dancers. In addition to Webb and Geva, the eccentric dance team of Buddy and Vilma Ebsen danced to the harmonica melodies of Larry Adler. Vocalist Jean Sargent sang "Alone Together" while Webb and Geva performed an elegant, sinuous dance that was described as "the best choreography of the evening." They danced on a specially designed stage that slowly receded into darkness. Norman Bel Geddes was the designer of the crisp, modernistic sets. One of the funniest sketches was called *The American Plan*, in which Webb and Kelly ran a hotel for the suicidally inclined Depression victims. Charles Butterworth finds that the higher the floor, the more expensive the room. Webb and Kelly carefully check off the jumpers as they fall.

THE IMPERIAL THEATRE

TAMARA GEVA, CLIFTON WEBB, PATSY KELLY AND CHARLES BUTTERWORTH

FLYING COLORS

8.1. Program for *Flying Colors*. *Left to right:* Tamara Geva, Clifton Webb, Patsy Kelly, and Charles Butterworth. The David L. Smith Collection.

Flying Colors originally played to top ticket prices, but after three and a half months the prices were drastically reduced. The show ran for 188 performances and even with the reduced prices managed to turn a small profit.

By now it was obvious that Clifton Webb's stock had begun to rise in theatrical circles. He proved that he was a capable and serious actor, ready for the next big step. This came in the form of a new revue with music and lyrics written by Irving Berlin and a book by Moss Hart. It was an amusing and original gimmick. Newspaper stories were turned into revue numbers. Headlines were illustrated with songs and sketches. It was called *As Thousands Cheer*.

Marilyn Miller was asked to join Clifton Webb in this revue. Critic John Mason Brown called Miller "a Degas figure turned American . . . a Titania of the jazz age"; she was "Ziegfeld's most dazzling star." Like Webb, she was a Hoosier, born to a vaudeville family in Evansville, Indiana. Webb tried to get her to join him in *Flying Colors*, but she wasn't interested. Fellow Hoosier Cole Porter tried to get her for *The Gay Divorce*. Earl Carroll wanted her for the next edition of his *Vanities*.

8.2. Marilyn Miller portrait, signed, "To my girlfriend (Mabelle) and Cliffy. Loads of love, Marilyn."
The David L. Smith Collection.

At this time she had made three films. The first two were film versions of her stage hits, *Sally* and *Sunny*. The last was an original screenplay written just for her, *Her Majesty, Love*. Released in December 1931, it was a disaster. Her contract was abruptly terminated. The magic she had on stage did not translate to film. She would soon turn thirty-five, and Broadway was in bad shape, offering tickets to many shows at cut-rate prices.

Webb had known Marilyn Miller since he had been cast in her musical success, *Sunny*, in 1925. They became bosom pals. Miller loved to go out partying with Webb after the show, even though it always meant including Mabelle in their plans. Miller didn't mind because she found Mabelle to be a delight. She was full of fun with a zany belief in spiritualism and the occult.

Miller had been a singing and dancing star since she was a child in vaudeville. Moss Hart and Irving Berlin had been considering her for their show, but finally ruled her out. In *The Life and Times of Moss Hart*, author Steven Bach quotes Hart: "We wanted someone refreshing, vibrant, youthful." However, when Hart was seated next to her at a dinner party he said, "All the thrill of the days when I saw this lovely dream girl on stage came back to me. I think I had been very much in love with her, and very much in awe, too. She was so gay that night. She seemed the most alive person in the place. She talked about many things. Her eyes danced and I fell in love with her all over again. I thought maybe I should wire Irving Berlin, who was in Bermuda at the time. Perhaps we were making a mistake in not considering her."

Berlin agreed with Hart, but when he approached Miller, she thought she was not right for the show. This was not a typical Marilyn Miller show. A witty satire on current events and famous people called for her to do much more than just sing and dance. Clifton Webb, who already had a number of hit revues to his credit, promised to help her get ready. He knew Miller well enough to know that she was a wonderful clown and mimic. He kept telling her that she was underestimating her talent. With Webb's persistent assurance, she agreed to be in the show. She got top billing but only a flat twenty-five hundred dollars a week. Without Webb's influence, she probably would not have done it.

When *As Thousands Cheer* opened September 30, 1933, at the Music Box, the audience gave Miller a standing ovation. There were several show stopping numbers. One was Miller and Webb's rendition of the exquisitely staged rotogravure production of *Easter Parade* designed by Hassard Short.

The weather headline brought forth "Heat Wave," hotly sung by Ethel Waters. The comic section was turned into a skit with Miller dressed as a long-haired tot cavorting with cartoon characters Popeye, Mickey Mouse, and folks from the "Toonerville Trolley" strip. Society and headlines were taken care of with songs like "Supper Time" and "Not for All the Rice in China."

Waters almost stole the show from Miller and Webb. She produced a blazing rendition of a young woman causing a "Heat Wave by letting her seat wave." Then, under the headline "Josephine Baker Still the Rage of Paris," she did a bluesy rendition of "Harlem on My Mind." However, it was the second number in act 2 that stopped the show. Waters appeared underneath a headline that read, "Unknown Negro Lynched by Frenzied Mob." Behind her was a silhouette of a man with a rope around his neck hanging from a tree. She sang that it was "Supper Time" and that she should set the table but couldn't

> 'Cause that man o' mine
> Ain't comin' home no more.

8.3. Program cover for *As Thousands Cheer* (1933). The David L. Smith Collection.

Irving Berlin had never written a song like this. It had an incisive and critical thrust. Many were surprised that Berlin could and would write this kind of song. During out-of-town tryouts, people begged him to cut the number. He refused. To complicate matters further, Webb, Miller, and Broderick are supposed to have refused to take curtain calls with Waters. Berlin is said to have replied, "Fine, there will be no curtain calls then."

In her autobiography, *His Eye Is on the Sparrow*, Waters makes no mention of this supposed incident. There is no mention of it in the two biographies of Irving Berlin or the biography of Marilyn Miller. Waters says this, "'Supper Time' was in the second act. Marilyn Miller and Clifton Webb had to follow it with a flippant bedroom dance. They didn't like the idea of trying to be cute and amusing right after the people had heard that grim, overwhelming song."

The only source for this incident is Mary Ellin (Berlin) Barrett's memoir of her father. She said that after the Philadelphia tryout, the white stars refused to take a bow with Ethel Waters. "He would respect their feelings, of course, my father had said, only in that case there need be no bows at all." It is difficult to believe that, as liberal as most actors are, Webb, Miller, and Broderick would have conspired to deny Waters her share of the spotlight.

On the contrary, Miller and Webb got into a friendly duel with Waters over who could stop the show the longest. Waters had the edge since Berlin had given her "Heat Wave," "Supper Time," and "Harlem on My Mind." They were all hits and all were potential showstoppers. But the big winner was almost always "Easter Parade," which closed the first act. The scene opened with strollers frozen behind a scrim. Everything was in browns and tans, depicting the Easter Parade of 1883. When Miller and Webb stepped out of the sepia-tone background and the parade came to life, it was the magic moment of the show.

Noel Coward was happy for Webb's success but became a little irritated when he heard that Webb said a tableau used in Coward's *Conversation Piece* might have got its inspiration from the "Easter Parade" sequence in *As Thousands Cheer*. Coward wrote the following letter to Webb, dated March 27, 1934,

> Clifton, my little dear,
>
> I hear weecked, disquieting rumors that you think I cribbed the tableau idea of Easter Parade for my dainty *Conversation Piece* and oh dear, oh dear, I honestly and truly never even thought of it and was absolutely delighted with the originality of my plan. Now I realize that it must have been sitting in my subconscious mind. Anyhow you will be delighted to hear it is as effective as ever and, may I say, you wicked old drab, that if I had thought of it I will tell you honestly and deeply and from my heart I *would* have stolen it without a qualm and even, if possible, have pretended that you got the idea from me first . . . so there. In *Conversation Piece* it is actually slightly better than in *As Thousands Cheer*, because I used the silences in order to allow dialogue to be heard . . . also, instead of doing it once, I do it over and over and over again until the audiences go mad with irritation.
>
> Any more nonsense from you and I shall not only kill myself but Rockefeller, Ghandi [Gandhi], and all the Mdvani brothers and then where will your show be? In the meanwhile perhaps you

would write me a letter saying you love me very much and telling
me about your life from A to Z.

Goody Goody,
Noel
P.S. Love from the King and Queen

Webb was at his best in this revue. He had a chance to showcase the
diversity of his talent. He played Mahatma Gandhi, John D. Rockefeller,
Douglas Fairbanks Jr., and a room-service waiter in Noel Coward's suite.
Webb had little time to change costume and makeup for each character, but he managed to pull it off magnificently. He must have enjoyed
mimicking his friend Noel Coward. The headline was "Noel Coward, Celebrated Playwright, Returns to England." The working-class cabin staff
is turned into cosmopolitan wits simply by cleaning the master's room.
Helen Broderick, Marilyn Miller, Ethel Waters, Leslie Adams, and Webb
played the cabin staff.

The scene takes place aboard the *Normandie*. Coward has just left the
ship. Webb is a room-service waiter who mimics many of Coward's mannerisms, Miller is a chambermaid, and Waters is a scrubwoman. Having
spent five days catering to every whim of Coward, they are all so dazzled
by his residue in the room that they carry on like players out of *Design
for Living*. Miller as the chambermaid floats about the room a la Lynn
Fontanne with a feather duster. As the housekeeper, Broderick enters
the room, surveys the scene, and flatly says, "Well, I'll be goddamned!"

"Gandhi Goes on Hunger Strike" featured Webb as Gandhi and Helen
Broderick as evangelist Aimee Semple MacPherson. Moss Hart came up
with the idea of having these two meet. Because they both are experts
at grabbing headlines, MacPherson suggests they form a team to sell religion. Gandhi likes the idea and they bound off the stage doing a soft-
shoe dance.

"Joan Crawford to Divorce Douglas Fairbanks, Jr." was the headline
for Miller (Crawford) and Webb (Fairbanks) having an argument over
who would get top billing for "a divorce the industry can be proud of!"
Crawford and Fairbanks managed to stay married until 1935.

"World's Wealthiest Man Celebrates 94th Birthday" featured Webb
as the ancient Rockefeller. Webb layered on the makeup then took a
toothpick to put heavy lines on his face. John D. is presented with a huge
birthday cake shaped in the form of Rockefeller Center. His son tells his
father his present is something called "Radio City." Webb then goes after

8.4. Clifton Webb as Mahatma Gandhi in *As Thousands Cheer* (1933). Billy Rose Theatre Division, The New York Public Library for the Performing Arts, Astor, Lenox and Tilden Foundations.

them with a carving knife, croaking, "This isn't a birthday present . . . it's a dirty joke. You sell it right back to the feller who sold it to you."

Webb was given the final number in the show. It was not the standard reprise, but an entirely new song, "Not for All the Rice in China." Webb, who could be both debonair and daffy, gave it the perfect delivery. The song had a list of all the commodities a lover would not exchange for his sweetheart: "all the rice in China," "all the grapes in France," "all the kilts in Scotland," "all the onions in Bermuda," and "all the beans in Boston."

Helen Broderick played Mrs. Herbert Hoover, who was preparing to vacate the White House as Franklin D. Roosevelt was about to move in. She went about stripping the White House bare, including portraits of George Washington and any light bulbs she could unscrew.

The critics were enthusiastic to say the least. Heywood Broun said, "The best revue I've ever seen." Brooks Atkinson wrote that "no doubt some one will be able to suggest how *As Thousands Cheer* could be improved," but made it clear that he could find no room for improvement. John Mason Brown said, "Mr. Webb continues to grow in versatility from

8.5. Clifton Webb as John D. Rockefeller Sr. in *As Thousands Cheer* (1933). Billy Rose Theatre Division, The New York Public Library for the Performing Arts, Astor, Lenox and Tilden Foundations.

one season to another. In addition to his dancing and his sure instinct for comedy, he has now become a master of make-up; his Mahatma Gandhi, his Douglas Fairbanks, Jr., his elder Rockefeller and his waiter who has modeled himself on Noel Coward are astonishing achievements in grease paint and mimicry."

Unfortunately, it wasn't long before Miller began to have sinusitis problems and migraine headaches. She missed several performances. Each time she returned she would suffer a relapse, and by spring she was wondering how long she could continue. She managed to keep performing until the following July, when her contract expired. She decided not to renew it.

This would be Marilyn Miller's last show before her death at age thirty-six from an infection caused by a botched operation on her sinuses. She surprised a lot of people by showing she had an untapped flair for sophisticated comedy. *As Thousands Cheer* became one of Broadway's all-time greats. It was the best show Irving Berlin had written and had more hit songs in it than any other Berlin show until *Annie Get Your Gun*. It finished a forty-nine-week run in 1934 with a total gross of $1,200,000, at $4.40 the top ticket price. Its big box office was especially notable because it achieved such great success while the country was still in the depths of the Great Depression.

This success prompted MGM to approach Webb with a film contract for three thousand dollars a week. MGM wanted someone to compete with Fred Astaire, who was with RKO. They were of the opinion that Webb was more handsome than Astaire and he was just as good a dancer and actor. Webb said, "MGM had been making overtures to me for sometime. On November 27, 1934, I signed my contract at three o'clock in the morning with Metro-Goldwyn-Mayer."

Unfortunately, Webb's entrance into the film capital gave the moguls at MGM second thoughts. He arrived white-gloved and top-hatted, with Mabelle on his arm and a French poodle named Ernest (named for Oscar Wilde's *The Importance of Being Earnest*) trailing along on a leash. He was to star in a musical with Joan Crawford in a film entitled *Elegance*. It was based on the life of the famous ballroom dancer Maurice Mouvet. Webb knew Mouvet. He had even danced with Mouvet's ex-partner, Leonora Hughes, in Paris.

Eddie Knopf and George Oppenheimer wrote the script with Webb in mind. Mouvet was known simply as "Maurice" when he was the idol of two continents from 1910 through the 1920s. He was noted for creating many dances and dance steps. He was the innovator of the "American" tango as it is danced today and the infamous Apache dance that became one of his most successful ballroom-exhibition acts. He even performed it before the King (Edward VII) and Queen of England. His life was a colorful one; he was born in a tenement district of New York City and rose to become one of the most famous and successful dancers in the world. He had many dance partners, but the most well known was Florence Walton, whom he married in 1911 shortly after meeting her while performing in the Ziegfeld Follies. He died of tuberculosis in 1927 at the age of thirty-eight. Clifton Webb was to play Maurice and Joan Crawford was to be Florence Walton. By this time, Webb had extensive experience performing most of the dances attributed to Maurice, including the tango, the Apache dance, the Maxixe, the Maurice fox-trot, and others.

Crawford, who had already danced with Astaire in *Dancing Lady* (1933), felt pretty confident about her dancing ability. However, as preliminary rehearsals began, Crawford reputedly was embarrassed by her inability to keep up with Webb and was not too happy with the myriad of dance steps she was required to learn. She also found that it was a man's picture, and probably wanted to avoid additional embarrassment

8.6. Clifton Webb in 1934, ". . . more handsome than Fred Astaire and just as good a dancer."
Hurrellphotos.com/Hurrelleditions.com.

by appearing on screen with the effete Webb, who was then an unknown. The other big problem was that it was next to impossible to find
any female Hollywood "star" who was a good enough dancer to perform
with Webb.

In August 1935, Louella Parsons reported this version of Crawford's
departure from the picture: "The gossip that Joan Crawford will not be
starred in *Elegance* is true. The story is so much a man's part that Crawford voted against it. Seems all the fat lines went to Clifton Webb and the
woman's part was not what Crawford expected, so she bowed out of the
picture."

In August 1944, Webb was interviewed by Hollywood columnist Rob-
bin Coons, who asked him about the Crawford picture. Coons reported
that the picture didn't get made because Crawford's dancing couldn't
match Webb's. Webb said this report disturbed him and proceeded to
give his version of what happened.

"I came to Metro to do the film *Elegance*. Joan was to co-star, and I
was the guest of Joan and her husband, Douglas Fairbanks, Jr., when I
arrived. But the script was all mine . . . the girl's part was secondary, and I
told the studio and told Joan that it wouldn't be fair to her, an established

picture star, to play second fiddle to a newcomer from the stage. That's all there was to it. They worked over the script, but it never developed satisfactorily. I left without making a picture and *Elegance* hasn't been made to this day."

Obviously, there were many reasons why this film was never made. Crawford justifiably did not like the plot of the film and the fact it was a "man's picture." She may have, indeed, been reluctant to dance with Webb for several reasons. However, the fact that Webb and Crawford remained friends seems to indicate there was no animosity between them. Webb decided he was not welcome in Hollywood at this time, and Crawford might have understood his predicament and sympathized with him.

Further evidence of Crawford and Webb's friendship can be found in an undated letter she wrote to Webb. It appears she was reluctantly saying good-bye. Thus, it could be the letter was written as Webb left Hollywood to go back to New York.

> My dearest, precious, adorable, sweet, personal, private poopsie:
>
> My heart ached when we said good-bye. There were so many many things I wanted to say but my throat was too full and tears were so near I dared not speak, even now I cannot put into words how we miss you. It's a blessing I didn't go to the station for I would have created a scene.

Everyone was aware that Webb was acerbically witty, a brilliant performer, and the hit of several Broadway shows. In spite of this, the studio didn't quite know what to do with him. Webb cooled his heels for eighteen months and collected his salary. He swam, attended many parties, and met a lot of important people. In short order, he and Mabelle became regulars in the Hollywood social scene.

One of the big party givers was the American countess Dorothy Di Frasso. She was born into wealth, inheriting twelve million dollars from her father, Bertrand Taylor. She became a countess in 1923 when she married Count Carlo di Frasso. Her parties in her Beverly Hills home were memorable. One particular party in the summer of 1935 came to be known as "The Tape Recording Party." Present at this party along with Webb were Cary Grant, Claudette Colbert, Marlene Dietrich, Betty Furness, George Cukor, Olive McClure, and William Haines.

The countess, known for her malicious sense of humor, had photographer Jerome Zerbe hide recording devices underneath all of her garden benches. A few weeks after that party, the countess invited the same group to another party. She then played back the conversations. The prank was not as funny as she thought it might be. After receiving urgent requests from several of the guests, including Webb, not to play the recordings ever again, she agreed to do just that. Whether the recordings were destroyed is not known.

Webb became fast friends with Di Frasso and was with her at the last party she attended before her sudden death. In 1954, Webb attended a party with her at the El Rancho Hotel in Las Vegas. It was known that she had a heart condition, and friends said she had been eating nitroglycerin pills "like popcorn." She told Webb, "Too bad that I am going to die so soon. I have been having such a good time." She and Webb boarded the Union Pacific's Los Angeles Limited to return to Los Angeles, where she could see her doctor. The next morning Webb went to check on her in her roomette and found her lying fully clothed, wearing a diamond necklace worth $175,000. She was covered with a full-length mink, and her baggage contained another $100,000 in jewelry. She was dead at the age of sixty-eight.

When it became apparent there was no progress on any film project, Webb finally asked to be released from his five-year contract. Back in New York he gave an interview at the Lombardy Hotel. He said, "There are two very important factors in an artist's life—one is his talent, the other time, and both of these have been wasted." He referred to Hollywood as "a land of endowed vacations."

In 1945, after he had made his breakout film, *Laura*, Webb provided additional details on his previous sojourn in Hollywood.

"I swam and played tennis on weekdays when honest people were digging ditches or mending shoes. I didn't lift a finger to earn my keep. Not my fault. However, I was screaming for work, but nobody listened. An actor must act, and while I had a wonderful time, I wasn't working, so I wasn't happy."

On October 12, 1936, Webb returned to the stage. He opened in the Theatre Guild's production of *And Stars Remain*, written by the Epstein brothers. Helen Gahagan was the star. It was a drama about a family of Manhattan aristocrats converted to humanity by a rude, young political idealist. It ran for seventy-eight performances. This was a major switch for Webb. He played straight drama, no singing or dancing. Some critics thought it a remarkable change. One critic said that Webb, "showed wonderfully how an actor-dancer with a full technical equipment for comedy can build a believable character out of a handful of vacuous lines."

Webb refused to see anything remarkable in it. He pointed out, "John Barrymore began as a musical comedy juvenile, Ina Claire had been a "Follies" star, David Warfield was once a Jewish dialect comedian with Weber and Fields, and George M. Cohan had gone from revues to Eugene O'Neill." However, Webb's drama days were short. He returned to musicals with his next stage appearance.

Webb's good friend Cole Porter informed him he was writing a musical for him. Porter and Webb had been friends since the ill-fated production of *See America First* in 1916. When Porter and Moss Hart opened their show *Jubilee* in 1935, it was filled with inside jokes, one of which featured a reference to Webb and Mabelle. The song was "Picture You Without Me."

> Picture Ogden Nash without a rhyme,
> Picture Bulova without the time,
> Picture Staten Island without a ferry,
> Picture little George Washington without a cherry,
> Picture brother Cain without his Abel,
> Picture Clifton Webb minus mother Mabel,
> Mix them all together and what have you got?
> Just a picture of me without you.

In 1943 Porter's *Let's Face It* opened on Broadway. One of the songs was entitled "Farming." It also included a reference to Webb and Mabelle, but the lyric was rejected before production.

In September of 1937, Cole Porter had just returned from Paris and was spending a relaxed weekend at the Countess Edith di Zoppola's country house in Mill Neck, near Oyster Bay, Long Island. He had been an avid equestrian since his childhood days in Indiana. He organized a riding party and selected a horse that struck his fancy. He was warned that the horse was known to be skittish. He ignored the warning and set out on the bridle path. A clump of bushes frightened the horse and it shied and reared. Porter failed to kick his stirrups free and the horse fell back and rolled, crushing one of Porter's legs. It then tried to regain its feet, but staggered and went down again, falling on the opposite side. This time it pulverized Porter's other leg.

Doctors told Porter's wife, Linda, that the legs should be amputated. Linda would not permit this, thinking it could destroy his spirit and he would never be the same; Porter's mother, Kate, agreed. Porter had already started to write a musical for Clifton Webb. He even referred to it as "The Clifton Webb Show." At this point Porter had finished three songs: "You Never Know," "At Long Last Love," and "From Alpha to Omega." Webb visited Porter and tried to cheer him up. Porter replied, "Don't worry. The show *will* be finished."

Legend has it that when Porter was lying on the ground waiting for help with his legs crushed, he took out a notebook and worked on the song "At Long Last Love." The song had already been copyrighted but did not have a verse. At any rate, Porter at some time finished the song and it became an enduring favorite. Webb was privileged to introduce it on stage.

Before *You Never Know* was finished, Clifton Webb almost appeared in a rather unusual musical. George S. Kaufman and Moss Hart were working on a musical set to open in the spring of 1938. However, it was scrapped by April 1937. The show was to be called "Curtain Going Up," about the writing of a musical in which Kaufman, Hart, and Gershwin would appear onstage as themselves (with the more reserved Ira speaking offstage). Webb was to co-star with Ina Claire. The show could never have been produced since George Gershwin died July 11, 1937.

In New Haven, on March 5, 1938, *You Never Know* opened to a sold-out audience. Webb was teamed with his old friend Libby Holman and Lupe Velez, who was known as "the Mexican Spitfire." Also in this show was the dance team that appeared with Webb in *Flying Colors* in 1932: Buddy and Vilma Ebsen. It was soon apparent that Webb and Holman were working with mediocre material. Just as bad was the fact that Lupe Velez was stealing the show from them. After New Haven, the show moved to Boston, then to Washington, D.C. All the while changes were being made in the book and the score. To top it off, Velez began to hate Libby Holman. She even threatened to kill her. Webb gave her a straight talking-to. "Lupe, you must not say such things. One day you'll turn them all against yourself." These were prophetic words since Velez did eventually commit suicide.

When the show reached Philadelphia, Webb thought it might be salvageable but still needed some doctoring. Webb persuaded J. J. Shubert to call in George Abbott to try to fix the problems. The show went to Pittsburgh, Detroit, and then Chicago. The notices were mixed. The final date of the road show was in Porter's and Webb's home state. *You Never Know* opened on May 23, 1938, for a three-day engagement at the English Theater in Indianapolis.

The show finally got to the Winter Garden in New York. The critical reviews were mild. Fourteen weeks after the opening, the show closed.

8.7. *The Importance of Being Earnest* with Derek Williams, Helen Trenholme, and Clifton Webb.
The John and Betsy Neylon Collection.

The night before it closed, J. J. Shubert came to Webb's dressing room. "Clifton, if we put things back the way they were, don't you think we could get a run out of it?" "Not with me," Webb replied.

You Never Know was a genuine bomb even though Porter had written a fine selection of songs for it. Despite its poor reputation, it has been revived frequently in summer stock and even had an Off-Broadway revival (eight performances) in 1973. Webb and Porter enjoyed each other's company and remained close friends.

Having had his fill of musicals for a while, Webb decided he would take on something that had proven its durability, a new production of Oscar Wilde's *The Importance of Being Earnest*. Less then two months after *You Never Know* closed, Webb opened with *Earnest* at the Vanderbilt Theater on January 12, 1939. It was not as durable as Webb had hoped. It closed after sixty-one performances.

In the summer of 1939, Webb decided to appear in a stock revival of *Burlesque*. Webb and Libby Holman played the roles originated by Hal

8.8. Clifton Webb as "Skid" in *Burlesque* (1939). The David L. Smith Collection.

Skelly and Barbara Stanwyck on Broadway. The play was used primarily as a vehicle for their amusement. Holman's second husband, actor Ralph Holmes, and Topper, her son, tagged along. They drove leisurely from town to town in Webb's blue-and-white Rolls Royce.

Painting was always an intriguing avocation for Webb. He not only painted and collected paintings, but was the subject of at least one portrait by a noted artist. On April 20, 1939, a showing of paintings by Augustus John was held at the Seligmann Galleries in New York. It was entitled "Noteworthy Subjects of the Theatre." Webb's portrait was featured along with portraits of Tallulah Bankhead, Katharine Cornell, Katharine Hepburn, and Otis Skinner. One critic spoke of Webb's portrait: "A most remarkable sitting of Clifton Webb in a white tie and top hat completely collapsed in a chair. This is one you should see."

Webb continued to paint. His training in art school, as outlined in an earlier chapter, helped him create some very good paintings. At age eighteen, he had a one-man show of his portraits and still lifes in New York. The author saw several of Webb's paintings in the John and Betsy Neylon collection, and, as a non-expert, I would classify them as high-quality, excellent renditions in realism.

8.9. Undated self-portrait painted by Clifton Webb. The David L. Smith Collection.

Webb was also a collector of paintings. Among his notes is a statement (dated May 7, 1941) from the Wildenstein Galleries in New York confirming his purchase of two paintings, *La Capeline Rouge*, portrait de Madame Monet by Claude Monet, and *Viaduc a l' Estaque*, by Cezanne. In December 1949, Webb asked Noel Coward to buy three paintings for him in Europe. Apparently, Webb neglected to place a limit on the price. Reports state he was shocked when he received the bill. Webb continued to paint, with frequent help from artist Luigi Lucioni.

Presumably in the early 1940s (since Webb seldom mentions dates in his notes, it is difficult to pin down many events), Webb talked of more painting and more celebrities. "I received an invitation to go to Sagamore, the Vanderbilt camp in the Adirondacks, which was left by Alfred Vanderbilt to his son, Alfred Junior. His mother, Margaret Emerson, is a great friend of mine. I painted every day, bowled, played games.

"I spent a weekend with the Wiman's in Greenwich, Connecticut. I decided I would like to buy some property there. I went out with the real estate agent on a dark, rainy day, took one look and said, 'That's it.' I telephoned my mother, and she came up complete with galoshes, and also said she thought that was a good idea. I got in touch with William

Ballard, the architect who built Libby Holman's house at Stanford. I told him approximately the type of house I wanted and went ahead and made plans.

"We reopened *The Man Who Came to Dinner* in Detroit and had a long, successful run. After that I started off on a cross-country tour. I remember my mother writing me from New York. She bought herself a shovel and broke the first ground. She also sent me some dirt that spilled out of the envelope. It was the first thing that I have ever owned remotely relating to the soil. I had lived in hotels and apartments before that time."

In 1940, while touring as Sheridan Whiteside in *The Man Who Came to Dinner*, Webb discovered that Laurence Olivier and Vivien Leigh were coming to the United States in their own production of *Romeo and Juliet*. Webb had seen Leigh as Scarlett O'Hara in *Gone with the Wind* and was captivated by her. He desperately wanted to meet her.

"I wrote Larry, whom I had known through the years, that when they came to Chicago they should arrange to give a special matinee for people in the theatre who wouldn't get a chance to see them otherwise. In my letter I wrote, 'What about that dream girl? I can't wait to meet her.'

"I'd only seen her in *Gone with the Wind* and fell madly in love with her. After their opening night in Chicago, a party was arranged for them at the Ambassador Hotel, where we were all staying. I arrived before they did. When they finally arrived, Larry and I embraced one another, and then he suddenly thrust into my arms a vision and said, 'Well, here she is.'

"She broke into a southern accent and said, 'I'm delighted to meet you, honey child.' I thought she was one of the most beautiful creatures I had ever seen, with a wonderful sense of humor and great intelligence. The notices for their production were scathing, and they were deeply hurt. I told them not to pay any attention to what Chicago said. I was sure they would come off with flying colors in New York."

Unfortunately, Webb's prediction was wrong. Critics savaged the production. The press publicized the adulterous affair that started their relationship and questioned whether or not Olivier was giving his all to the war effort. The couple had put most of their own savings into the production, and the failure of this venture left them in severe financial straits. Webb enjoyed their companionship while they were in Chicago.

"All during their stay in Chicago we were together constantly. When they opened in New York, the critics were just as unkind, and again they were deeply hurt. I remember spending a weekend with them at Katharine Cornell's house, at Sneden's Landing in New York. Larry was

CHICAGO STAGEBILL

8.10. Clifton Webb as Sheridan Whiteside in *The Man Who Came to Dinner*. The David L. Smith Collection.

very anxious to get back to England to do his bit. They finally sailed with heavy hearts."

Webb closed *The Man Who Came to Dinner* in Cleveland, Ohio, on March 15, 1941. After he visited with Louis Bromfield and his wife, Mary, in Mansfield, Ohio, the production moved on to Pittsburgh. After closing in Pittsburgh, he returned to Greenwich, anxious to see his house. He had Luigi Lucioni help him mix colors for the outside of the house and for various rooms inside. He said, "We worked all day on that."

On May 16, 1941, Webb drove to New Haven, Connecticut, to see *The Man Who Came to Dinner*, with Alexander Woolcott starring in the play based on him by Moss Hart and George S. Kaufman. Webb recalls, "I sat in the front row, and a more nervous actor I'd hardly ever seen. It was obvious that acting was not his forte."

Webb and Mabelle moved into their new home in Greenwich on May 31, 1941. "For about two weeks we slept on mattresses on the floor until our furniture arrived." While there, they learned of the death of Sam Harris, which Webb said "shocked the theatrical world."

8.11. *Left to right:* Laurence Olivier, Mrs. Darryl Zanuck, Clifton Webb, and Vivien Leigh at the opening of the Sadler Wells Ballet, October 20, 1950. The David L. Smith Collection.

On July 15 of that year, Webb attended Grace Moore's "annual anniversary party." "She was taking off the next day for her concert tour around the world, which she did by plane. I asked her husband, Val, if he'd like to lunch the following Sunday, because I'd asked Geraldine Farrar for lunch on that day.

"Sunday I was working in the garden, not realizing it was practically lunch time, when suddenly a car drove up, and out hopped Geraldine, who was having her first driving lesson. She asked me if it were going to be a formal lunch, because if that were the case she had brought her jewels in a bag. I was in dirty dungarees. I told her I hardly thought so. So, she proceeded to park her jewels in Mother's bedroom. As always, she was most fascinating at lunch and spoke so beautifully about Grace Moore. Val was fascinated by her, and I remember her telling him about certain passages in *Tosca*, which Grace was scheduled to do the following season . . . how she could save herself. Unlike so many prima donnas, she was very helpful to the younger singers."

Cheryl Crawford, a Broadway producer and one of the founders of the Actor's Studio, and John Wildberg, a copyright attorney turned producer, were running a theatre in Maplewood, New Jersey. They called Webb and asked him if he would like to do a week of *The Man Who Came to Dinner*. He said, "I told them I would, provided I could have a charming actress, Doris Nolan, whom I had seen in the play with Woolcott, and Claudia Morgan, whom I'd seen with Monty Wooley. They were procured. When we opened on August 4, 1941, in Maplewood, the two girls were astonished that they were getting laughs they never got before. The week was highly successful, and we had to play an extra matinee."

Shortly after this latter production of *The Man Who Came to Dinner*, Webb received a call from John C. Wilson. Wilson was an American and the general manager for the original production of Noel Coward's *Private Lives* in 1931. He made his directorial debut with Coward's *Blithe Spirit* in 1941.

Coward wrote a letter of advice to Wilson about the casting of the American version of his play.

> As far as the New York company of *Blithe Spirit* goes I think Leonora [Corbett] will be fine. Gladys Cooper I am frightened of, because she is frightfully bad at learning words and it is a very long part needing the utmost precision. Clifton [Webb] I feel sure will be the best bet. He is a beautiful comedian and the slight hint of precious-ness won't matter and I think he will give it distinction. I have a feeling Edna May Oliver will be superb as long as she does not overplay. I am sure that Edna Best would be good as Ruth but a little lacking in attack and I think on the whole, if you could bear it, Peggy [Wood] would be the best. We know what a good actress she is and she really has got drive. If I can't get over, you shall have complete detailed script with every move marked and extra bits of business and cuts. I would rather you directed it than anybody else. I have implicit faith in your taste and discretion.

Obviously, others noted that "slight hint of preciousness" to which Cow-ard refers, but it seldom seemed to present a major stumbling block for Webb. It may have narrowed his options as an actor, but, except for his brief sojourn to Hollywood in the 1930s, it did not prevent advancement in his chosen profession. He simply was too good to be ignored, whether he performed as a singer, dancer, or actor.

Coward first met Webb in the 1920s. They swiftly became fast friends, although in later life Coward became increasingly irritated with him. Graham Payn, who was the star of many of Coward's shows and was his confidant and friend for thirty years, says this of Coward's relationship with Clifton Webb in his book, *My Life with Noel Coward:* "Clifton's man-ner was an attempt at an American 'Noel Coward,' which may explain Noel's ambivalent feelings. He saw his mirror image, and there were days when he wasn't in the mood to face it! Certainly, Noel and his ambience fascinated Clifton and he was extremely hospitable to all of us."

Wilson sent the script for *Blithe Spirit* to Webb and asked him to read it, and if he liked it, he would put Webb in it. Webb said, "I read it and I

8.12. Clifton Webb with Noel Coward. The Graham Payn Collection.

was enchanted with it. I called him up and said, 'When do we start?' He told me he'd like for me to come down to New York and discuss the cast. The first time I read it, I read it as a whole. The second time I read it, I realized that I had a tough assignment, as the part was not easy to play.

"In reading it, I could see only one person in the part of the medium, Madame Arcati, and that was the brilliant actress Mildred Natwick. I lunched with Wilson and we discussed the cast, and he told me that Noel had cabled him that he would like Peggy Wood in the part of my second wife. A beautiful English actress who was in this country, he thought, would be good for my first wife. I had never seen her, or met her, but she had been rehearsing two plays of Coward's, *This Happy Breed* and *Present Laughter*, when war was declared. She had then come to this country. Her name was Leonora Corbett. He then asked me whom I considered would be good for the part of Madame Arcati, and when I mentioned Mildred Natwick, he thought I was mad. He had only seen her as Prossy in Katherine Cornell's production of *Candida*. I then asked him if he had ever seen her in a musical with Jimmy Durante and Ethel Merman called *Stars in Your Eyes*. I had, and she was very funny, and held her own on a stage with fast company. He still thought I was crazy, so I ordered him another cocktail. By the time he drank that I could tell that I was winning my point, for he went to the telephone, called his office, and asked them to try and find out where Miss Natwick was playing. I knew she was in an engagement in summer stock somewhere in New Jersey.

"The result was he sent her a script, and after reading the first act she called him up in a complete dither and said, 'If the second act and third acts are as good as the first, I can't wait to start.' She was engaged to play the part.

"The Wilsons, Jack and Natasha, asked me to dine at their charming home in Wilton, Connecticut, and then go to the opening at Westport of *Liliom*, which Jack had directed and in which Tyrone Power and his wife, Annabella, were appearing. They also had asked Miss Corbett. They thought it would be a very good idea if I met her. I was delighted with her: tall, thin, and extremely beautiful, and with a stinging wit. I also realized that she might be quite difficult. After the play the Wilsons had a charming party at their home for Tyrone and Annabella. I found Power quite changed from the starry-eyed young man I'd met in Chicago in 1934.

"Meanwhile, I was very busy planting, and I realized that I was meeting a new type of gyp artist, a nursery man. On Thursday, September 18, 1941, we started rehearsals of *Blithe Spirit*, and when Peggy Wood and Leonora Corbett met I realized that there was going to be trouble ahead, for those two personalities should never have come within a hundred miles of one another, let alone on the same stage, in the same play.

"Miss Corbett, a brilliant actress when she wants to be, started pulling a few old-fashioned tricks on me. I saw what she was trying to do and said nothing, until one day she tried to upstage me once too often. I asked Mr. Wilson who was directing this play, he or Miss Corbett. The result was we settled everything then and there, and I gave her to understand that she couldn't pull any of those old-fashioned tricks on me. Poor Peggy Wood was completely baffled by her.

"We opened on October 9, 1941, in New Haven. The next day Jack and I cut twelve minutes out of the running time, as we found that Coward had repeated himself, especially in the last act; and as I said to Wilson, 'Don't forget this is America, we don't have to explain the jokes twice.'

"From New Haven we went to Boston and opened October 13 at the Wilbur Theatre. The play was a great success. I remember George Cukor coming to Boston with Victor Saville to see the play. Cukor was one of Metro's top directors, and Metro had sent him up to see it with the idea of buying it for pictures. I'd known George for a great many years, and I had great respect for his knowledge and ability. He came back to the Hotel with Jack and me and proceeded to say what he thought. He gave me some very helpful hints about the playing of the part, for which I was deeply grateful.

"From Boston we went to Washington, where we packed the National Theatre to the doors. On Tuesday, November 4, 1941, we gave a benefit for the British War Relief, and on November 5, we opened at the Morosco Theatre.

"The play received brilliant notices from all the critics, and I was delighted especially for Jack Wilson, who stepped out on his own for the first time as a director/producer. Miss Corbett made a tremendous hit, not only with the public but with Mr. John Royal. When we arrived at the Morosco Theatre, we were all highly amused at the way her dressing room had been decorated by Royal—all in gray and very expensive. I suppose that was done to match her makeup on the stage." (Corbett, playing the ghost Elvira, had gray makeup with gray clothing.) John Royal was an NBC vice president who was in charge of the network's international broadcasting. He was twelve years older than Ms. Corbett. They were married September 7, 1942.

Webb reported that there was a great discussion about which production of *Blithe Spirit* was best. The British and the American productions were playing simultaneously. The London production was directed by Coward and featured Kay Hammond as Elvira, Margaret Rutherford as Madame Arcati, Cecil Parker as Charles, and Fay Compton as Ruth. Webb was highly pleased when word came back from people who had seen both productions that they thought the American production had the edge.

Wolcott Gibbs wrote in the *New Yorker* that Webb "has just the correct wispy elegance and achieves, I should say, one of the best performances of his career." Another critic remarked that Webb could "turn a line with as much neat dexterity as Coward could write it."

Shortly after the opening at the Morosco Theater, Webb began to fill ill. "I couldn't understand what was the matter, so I thought I'd better go to my doctor and find out. He started to take my blood pressure. After pumping the thing up the third time he said, 'This bloody machine must be broken.' Such was not the case, so he said, 'What have you been do-ing?' I said, 'Nothing, just working hard.' I was working extra hard with war work activities. My blood pressure was 75, my blood count was 76, so I had to have a transfusion. This was my very first experience in that sort of thing, and I remember going to the hospital. The day I went to the hospital to have my blood matched, the attendant asked if I was the donor. I said, 'Hell no, I'm in here to get, not to give.' I went to the hospital Saturday night after the performance and Sunday morning they started in on me. I happened to look at the name on the bottle and found it decidedly Teutonic, so I said to the nurse, 'I hope this isn't Nazi blood I'm getting in me.' She gave me a scowl. So, I had to watch myself for some time to come, and the doctor put me on a hamburger three times a day."

CHAPTER 9

The War Starts, *Blithe Spirit* Leads to *Laura*

In late November 1942, Clifton Webb and Mabelle were living in Greenwich on weekends and in New York during the week at the Gotham Hotel. As was the case for most Americans who remember the start of World War II, Webb never forgot where he was when he heard the news. He said, "Like millions of others on December 7, 1941, we were sitting in my studio listening to the symphony when the news was flashed of Pearl Harbor. Naturally, we were all quite stunned. The following Friday a committee met in the American Theatre Wing. In the basement of the 44th Street Theatre, which some years before had been known as Justine Johnstone's Little Club, the Stage Door Canteen was born. We all contributed our services, washed dishes, served the GI's, and made ourselves generally useful. Alfred Lunt and Lynn Fontanne, Katherine Cornell, Gertrude Lawrence, and everyone in the theatre pitched in and made it a great success."

It should be noted that the American Theatre Wing had been operating as a branch of the British War Relief. With America's entrance into the war, it became the American Theatre Wing War Service, an American agency. Among those active in the Wing were Helen Hayes, Burgess Meredith, Clare Boothe, Ilka Chase, Ray Bolger, Gertrude Lawrence, Cornelia Otis Skinner, and Clifton Webb. *Variety* said, "America is in war, and show business, ever alert to interpret the American spirit, is pledged to play its inimitable role. Let it be said that Americans will be proud of its performance." Clifton Webb worked conscientiously in this regard and was often a leader in efforts to bring entertainment to the troops.

At the urging of the government, millions of Americans started Victory Gardens. Webb recalled his Victory Garden experience.

"The spring of 1942 we moved to the country. Everybody was starting Victory Gardens. I planted three cornfields, two tomato patches, and all of the various vegetables. I had much more corn than I could possibly eat, so I thought I would sell it. Nobody would buy it, so I thought I'd give it away. So, I'd bring in great bags of corn to various members of the cast, which was very inconvenient for them because if they were going out to supper after the show, they'd have to leave it somewhere. I don't imagine they ate very much of it.

"Everybody in Greenwich was very war conscious. The Theatre Wing was giving instructions in first aid. Every night one would look out front and see, in the most expensive seats way down front, men in shirt sleeves, no coats, no ties."

Webb found that New York and especially Broadway were greatly changed because of the war. He remembered, "In crossing town from the Grand Central Station to the theatre, it was a very odd feeling to find oneself blacked out. To see Broadway without all its glittering lights gave one a very eerie feeling. Katharine Cornell was doing some special performances of *Candida* for the Army and Navy Relief Fund. When Cornell decided to reopen *Candida*, she cabled George Bernard Shaw, asking him to waive the royalties. Several days after rehearsals began, her husband answered the telephone. It was a telephone operator at his office with an answer from Shaw. She read, 'All that your genius has earned for me has been eaten up in war taxation. Not another cent can I afford.' Here the operator, who should have been an actress, paused, and Mr. [Guthrie] McClintic started some frantic mental arithmetic based on the 16 percent royalty that would be due the author. Then, the voice continued sweetly reading, 'But, as a birthday present to you personally, I give my royalties on the five performances you desire.' The cable came on April 18, which was neither Miss Cornell's, nor her husband's birthday. But it was gratefully received, nevertheless."

Webb was very active in providing entertainment for the troops. He said, "On May 3, 1942, we gave a special performance to the cadets at West Point, which was quite a thrilling experience and a wonderful audience. On the program at West Point, it was mentioned that the idea of bringing Broadway plays to West Point for the cadets came from Lt. Alexander H. Mininger Jr., of the Philippine Scouts, who, to quote a note in the program of the performance, 'went to a heroic death, and posthumous award of the Congressional Medal of Honor, in a gallant and single-handed attack against the Japanese forces near Abucay on the Bataan Peninsula, January 12, 1942. Lt. Mininger was cited in the official dispatches. It was young Mininger's idea last year when he was chairman of the Cadet Lecture Committee to get Broadway productions for his fellow cadets. Boris Karloff and other members of the cast responded generously to the idea and as a result *Arsenic and Old Lace* was given. In writing his thanks afterward for what help he had been able to give in arranging the performance, young Mininger expressed the hope that 'this will not be the last time that Broadway and West Point get together.'

"'To make that hope a reality,' said the program note, 'and to further perpetuate his name, Lt. Mininger's comrades offer this production of *Blithe Spirit* with its star-studded cast.'"

March 24 was Mabelle's birthday. She was seventy-two. Webb gave a birthday party for her at the theatre where he was playing. He said, "Among those present were Gloria Swanson, Elsa Maxwell, Katharine Cornell, Tallulah Bankhead, Valentina and George Schlee, Danny Kaye, Moss Hart, Guthrie McClintic, and others."

Webb listed several productions that were given for the benefit of the armed forces. One of these was rather unusual, but was certainly a big hit with those who were privileged to see it. Webb described the event: "On March 10, 1942, there was an enormous show at Madison Square Garden for the Navy Relief. A group of us did the "Floradora Sextet." Ed Wynn, Vincent Price, Danny Kaye, Boris Karloff, Eddie Cantor, and myself dressed in the Floradora costumes of the period, played the girls. Leonora Corbett, Eve Arden, Sophie Tucker, Tallulah Bankhead, Peggy Wood, and Gertrude Lawrence played the boys. The place was jammed to the rafters. We rehearsed very seriously. I remember following Boris Karloff on, who was trembling with nerves, but when we made our entrance to the Floradora music, a howl went up which shook Madison Square Garden to the rafters. They never stopped laughing all through the sextet, and at the end the applause came like a cloudburst.

"During this season, Irving Berlin's soldier show, *This Is the Army*, was packing them in. Also, all sorts of offers came for *Blithe Spirit* from Hollywood, but Noel Coward turned a deaf ear to all of them. There were benefits right and left, and the people of the theatre always came through in every way possible. I worked day and night for war relief, entertaining.

"In April, Beatrice Lillie was opening in Manchester, England, in a new review. Just before she went on she received a telegram that her son, Robert, had disappeared when his ship went down in Asiatic waters. Like all good troupers, 'Beattie' knew that the show must go on and had the stage manager put a notice on the bulletin board backstage asking the company not to mention the news to her. It was a great tragedy to her, and heartbreaking to all of us who had known Bobbie through the years, and I don't think to this day she has quite gotten over it. Fortunately, she was working and proceeded to throw herself into more and more work. When the show closed she went out and entertained the troops. When she came back to America, all of us who knew her well and loved her did not know quite what to say. She seemed disinclined to talk about it. It wasn't until three years later that she brought the subject up and was able to talk about it quite calmly and objectively. One felt that there was a hurt in her heart that she could never repair. He was a wonderful boy, just like his mother, and with a sense of humor like his mother's."

Webb discovered that a certain branch of the service was not getting much attention. He decided to do something about it.

"On January 23, I was having supper after our play with Lynn and Alfred Lunt. I was telling them of a story that I had been told by a young member of the Coast Guard who was stationed in a remote part of Florida. They had no means of entertainment at all. They were completely isolated and the only game they had was a deck of dirty cards. The chap told me how, on one New Year's Eve, he took a ride along the beach on his horse, and when twelve o'clock came the only person he could say 'Happy New Year' to was his horse, whom he kissed. From what he related, the members of the Coast Guard were the forgotten men. So, I decided something ought to be done about it. I went to various members of the casts of various shows playing and asked them if they wouldn't contribute books, games, radios, and so forth. They were all highly responsive.

"I bought a ping pong table for the boys in this particular camp. My apartment at the Park Lane Hotel was stacked full of books. I sent them all down and got a most grateful letter from the various boys. I was relating this story to Lynn and Alfred [Lunt], and I had just said that I thought it would be a good idea if I told Alex Woolcott the story about these conditions that prevailed that he might use it in one of his broadcasts. Just then Alfred was called to the telephone. After about five minutes he returned to the table looking a little white. Margalo Gilmore had rung up to tell him that Alex had just died. He was stricken during his broadcast. We were naturally very upset, as we knew it would be a great loss to those who loved him and to whom he had been a friend.

"The fabulous Tallulah Bankhead was playing *The Skin of Our Teeth*. I took Mother to see it and we enjoyed it enormously. We went backstage to see Tallulah, who let it be known in no uncertain terms that she and

Mr. Fredric March were not seeing eye to eye in numerous ways. Poor Freddie was in rather the same spot as I was in *Blithe Spirit.*

"In April, we played another benefit at Madison Square Garden for the Red Cross and repeated the Floradora Sextet. On the thirtieth of April we moved back to Greenwich. Mabelle had not been feeling well, so I took her for an examination. The doctor found that her heart was affected and put her to bed for twelve weeks. Naturally, this was very worrying for me.

"On Sunday, May 23, I went to dinner with Mrs. Wiman at their home in Greenwich. After dinner, Libby Holman came in. She and Mrs. Wiman and I were sitting talking. Suddenly Holman started a tirade against Mabelle. At first I couldn't believe my ears. I thought she must be joking, but when she repeated the same remarks for the third time, I realized that she must be serious. If she had any cause for talking the way she did, I could have understood it, but all through the years of our friendship, or what I thought was our friendship, Mabelle had always been the first to come to her defense.

"She started the tirade by saying, 'I'm ruthless. I hate my mother.' That, in itself, was enough for me. Then she proceeded to say, 'I would have married you, but Mabelle stopped it.' I felt like saying, 'I might have had something to say about that.' But, I was too stunned and thought it better to say nothing.

"When she finished I quietly left the house, quite shaken. I couldn't believe it possible that anyone who claimed to be a friend could turn so. But that night I buried Libby Holman under a great many feet of sod. The next day, I could think of nothing else, and then I knew that if I told Mabelle, she would not be able to understand why Libby had said the things that she did. The following night I went to Elsa Maxwell's birthday party at Neysa McMein's. The thing preyed on my mind, so I told Neysa and Grace Moore, and they agreed that I should never speak to Miss Holman again."

In *Dreams That Money Can Buy: The Tragic Life of Libby Holman*, author Jon Bradshaw gives a different version of this event. Bradshaw says, "Only once was Libby forced to sample someone else's dismissive scorn. That summer, she drove over to Tantallon, Steve Wiman's Greenwich home, for cocktails with Steve and Clifton Webb, her oldest friend. By ten that evening, the three friends were exceedingly drunk, and Webb began to blubber about his tyrannic mother, Mabelle . . . how she abused him, how she schemed and pried and meddled. Libby, who had listened to Webb's maternal lamentations for fifteen years, became exasperated.

'Cliftuary, Mabelle's ruined your life,' she said. 'Why don't you chloroform the old cunt?'

"Webb glared at Libby, his eyes glistening with surprise and pain. Putting down his glass, he rose to his feet and in a clipped, reedy voice said quietly, 'Libby Holman died tonight.' He tossed his head and strode briskly from the room. Libby and Webb would never see one another again. Webb went so far as to forbid the mention of Libby's name in his presence; and if some unsuspecting stranger referred to her, Webb always stiffened, explaining that Libby Holman, whom he had once known long before, was 'a black angel of death.'"

Webb's label for Holman had a ring of truth to it. Libby was a bisexual and became involved with Louisa d' Andelot Carpenter, who was a DuPont heiress. Carpenter dressed as a man most of the time. Eventually, they began living together. Zachary "Smith" Reynolds of the Reynolds Tobacco family happened to see Libby on stage in *Three's a Crowd*. Smith was there every night, always in the same seat in the front row on the aisle. He became enamored of Libby and pursued her relentlessly. Louisa recommended she marry him in that she would then be endowed with wealth the rest of her life. Libby did marry Reynolds in 1931 and had one child with him, Christopher, whom she referred to as "Topper."

The marriage was soon in trouble. Smith wanted Libby to give up the stage. She refused. Smith became preoccupied with kidnappers and began carrying a gun wherever he went. He insisted that Libby have a gun and gave her one. In 1932 Smith died from what was said to be a self-inflicted gunshot wound. Libby was pregnant at the time with Christopher. Investigators felt that it was not a suicide, and Libby and Ab Walker (a close friend of Smith) were accused of murder. The trial caused a sensation but the Reynolds family intervened before it was concluded and all charges were dropped. Libby inherited seven million dollars from Smith's estate.

When Christopher was born, Webb was named his godfather. When Louisa Carpenter adopted a daughter she called "Sunny," Webb was named her godfather. On January 9, 1939, Libby gave an extravagant party in her Manhattan duplex to celebrate Topper's sixth birthday. Topper had developed an appreciation for jazz, and Libby hired Benny Goodman, Teddy Wilson, Gene Krupa, Lionel Hampton, Helen Ward, and Billie Holiday to perform. Topper dressed in a sailor suit and said he was going to stay up till midnight. At one point in the party, Webb took Topper as his dancing partner and together they performed an Apache dance, leaping and twisting onto the sofas, the tables, and chairs. Libby,

Helen Ward, and Billie Holiday sang an upbeat version of "Happy Birthday." Then as the lights were dimmed and a huge cake was brought in, Libby sang "You Are My Sunshine" to Topper, who finally fell asleep and was put to bed.

Every January Topper received a silver goblet from his godfather. But one January the goblet did not arrive. Libby and Webb were no longer speaking. When Topper asked why there was no goblet, Libby said, "I don't even know if the old faggot is still alive." Topper was shocked.

Libby Holman was married three times. After Smith she married actor Ralph Holmes and then Louis Schanker. In 1942, she decided to back a play called *Mexican Mural*. She and Montgomery Clift were the stars. Clift was just twenty-one years old. The play ran on Broadway for only three weeks. Libby and Clift were immediately attracted to each other and spent much time together during the run of the play and for some time after it closed. Ralph Holmes committed suicide in 1945. In 1950, eighteen-year-old Topper died in a mountain-climbing accident on Mount Whitney. Libby Holman committed suicide in 1971. Webb's name for Libby, "the black angel of death," was prophetic indeed.

Blithe Spirit closed in New York on June 5, 1943. It would re-open in New York on September 6, 1943, but would run for only thirty-two performances before going on tour. The tour stop in Los Angeles proved to be a defining moment in Clifton Webb's career.

After the show closed in June, Webb said he was in great need of a rest. On July 16 he helped celebrate Grace Moore and Valentin Parera's twelfth wedding anniversary. On July 30, he went to visit Katharine Cornell and Guthrie McClintic at their summer home in Chip Chop on the water. For thirty years, Cornell summered on this eighteen-acre peninsula in Martha's Vineyard. It was named Chip Chop to conform to East Chop and West Chop, two other points on the island. The property consisted of a shingled main house, two adjoining guest cottages, a pool, and a cabana. It took eight years to build. Construction was held up during the war, and as a result, the house was not finished until 1945. Therefore, at the time of Webb's visit, the house was still not finished.

Stories of what went on at this house are numerous. Vivien Leigh visited when she was in deep despair. Cornell persuaded her to do the mad scene from *Hamlet*. The acting was said to be extraordinary. Someone taped it, but no one ever found the tape. The house was preserved by the new owners, and the bathroom walls are still decorated with signatures of the Lunts, Helen Keller, Rex Harrison, Noel Coward, Laurence Olivier, and others. Cornell designed her kitchen with no windows, only a large skylight. She wanted her guests to enjoy skinny-dipping without having to worry that her servants were Peeping Toms.

Webb said it was peaceful and charming. There were no telephones. He recalled the scene: "Kit and I would drive to the village to do the marketing. I'd watch her milk the cows. During this visit I first met Gregory Peck, who was playing a summer stock engagement on the mainland. He came over to read for Guthrie for a play that he was going to do with Gladys Cooper. Guthrie took him into the studio, and Kit and I sat nervously, hoping everything would turn out all right for him. When they returned, we knew that Guthrie was pleased. We all drank a toast to his success. When the play opened later on in the season, although it wasn't a great success, he made a personal hit, which led him to fame in Hollywood."

Preparations began to take *Blithe Spirit* on tour. Webb said, "In the beginning of August I had to listen to several people try out for Leonora Corbett's part, who didn't feel that she wished to go on tour. After listening to several readings, we selected Haila Stoddard, a most charming girl." At this time Webb seemed to get caught up in the patriotic fervor of those war years as he began to think about doing something for his country.

"On August 30, we began rehearsal of *Blithe Spirit*. Some of the members of the local committee in Greenwich had been calling me up, asking me if I would do something for the bond rally they were to have. I told them that if I could arrange it I would try to give a performance of *Blithe Spirit*. They thought that was an excellent idea. It was all arranged. So, on September 3, in the local theatre, we gave a performance. One could only be admitted by buying a bond. We were able to make about five hundred thousand dollars for my community.

"On Sunday, September 5, we gave an invitational dress rehearsal for soldiers just before opening the following night. We were a little apprehensive as to how it would go with that type of audience. They began to laugh at the rise of the curtain. They never missed a point throughout the show.

"On September 10, Peggy Wood and I attended a USO luncheon at the Hotel Astor. Various people on the committee spoke as to how important it was that we should continue to devote as much time as we could to entertaining the soldiers at various camps. When they finished, I realized that nothing had been said about entertaining any of the wounded in the various hospitals throughout the country. I then proceeded to tell them that I thought that was very necessary as there were a great many already, and would be a great many more. They thought it was a very good idea.

"We were fortunate in having in our company people who could do numbers as well as straight sketches. Peggy Wood had been in musical comedy and operetta; Mildred Natwick had played in a musical; Haila Stoddard hadn't, but was very anxious to try; a little girl who was the general understudy had done various things in local camps with great success.

"We started to plan our show and called ourselves 'The Blithe Spirits.' We had an opening chorus written for us. Peggy did several straight singing numbers, Millie did a sketch that Beatrice Lillie had made famous, and I decided to do a takeoff on Sinatra, whom I had never seen, but naturally had heard a great deal about. I also did a number with Haila Stoddard that I had done in the *First Little Show*."

Webb said the group rehearsed very seriously. Little by little the show began to take shape. Shortly thereafter, Webb discovered that Frank Sinatra was opening at the Wedgewood Room at the Waldorf Astoria. He said, "I thought, considering I was doing an imitation of him, I'd better see him. So, I engaged a table and asked Jack Wilson and his wife, Neysa McMein, Guthrie McClintic, and Cole Porter and Mabelle."

None of Webb's group had ever seen Sinatra. They were certainly aware of him by virtue of his publicity. Webb said he could hear the screaming of young females from his dressing room at the Booth Theater, which was close to the stage door of the Paramount Theater, where Sinatra was playing.

Webb's initial impression of Sinatra was positive: "When he entered the room at the Waldorf we were all surprised at his charm and modesty, which was quite contrary to what we had expected. When he began to sing, we all realized that the stir he had caused had some reason. When he finished, he came over to the table, very simple, unaffected, and completely charming. I told him I was doing an imitation of him. He said, 'Gee, that's great!' Mabelle said, 'I am one of your bobby-soxers.' It seemed to please him very much."

On October 2, 1943, *Blithe Spirit* closed in New York. The following day, the cast and crew headed for Philadelphia. They continued to do double duty; while doing the play they also continued to rehearse their *Blithe Spirits* little show. The cast sold bonds in Gimbel's window and appeared on local radio stations. The show closed in Philadelphia on October 16. The following Monday they headed for Baltimore. It was there they gave their first little show for the Coast Guard. Webb was ill and was unable to join the rest of the cast.

When the touring group arrived in Boston, Webb found that the USO showed virtually no interest in his little show.

"I took it upon my own shoulders to see the various heads about giving our performances. I interviewed Major Winthrop about appearing at Fort Devens. On November 4, we appeared at the Fort Devens hospital for the wounded. We all took it very seriously, and the girls wore their best frocks, which thrilled the boys. It was a very depressing sight to see all of the boys out front, some wheeled in, some on stretchers, most of them had just arrived the day before from Africa. After the main show, which ran an hour and twenty minutes, we went into the wards and talked to them. We automatically found ourselves using a new language, as we were told that the worst thing to do was to show pity. One had to kid them and act as if nothing had happened, which was not an easy assignment."

Webb and his *Blithe Spirits* group played for hospitals in Butler, Pennsylvania; Cleveland, Ohio; Detroit, Michigan; and one memorable show for amputees at Mare Island. It was there that he asked for four boys to walk across the stage at a given time. Webb said, "I was standing in the wings with them and explaining when I wanted them, they were to just walk across the stage in a perfectly ordinary manner, and that a girl would follow them. When I used the expression 'in an ordinary manner,' I heard one of the boys whisper to another one, saying, 'He doesn't know.' In other words, they thought that I didn't know that they had wooden legs."

Webb said the boys were given an opportunity to dance with the girls on stage. He said, "In this particular hospital it was rather a sad sight to see them dancing around. Some of them hadn't learned to control their wooden limbs as yet." Another memorable point Webb remembers: "A charming little girl joined us for this particular appearance and came on and did a splendid dance. When she finished she picked up her skirts to show the boys that both of her legs were wooden."

Looking back on these experiences, Webb said, "They were a wonderful audience, didn't miss a point. Doing these revues affected me emotionally. I'd go on stage and I wouldn't know which act I was in. It was the effect of seeing all those wounded boys."

"I will never forget those audiences . . . the faces of lonely and sick men, lighting up to laughter and appreciation of our revue. No other Christmas ever meant as much to me."

When *Blithe Spirit* played in San Francisco, it was quite a treat for Webb. He had never visited that city. He said, "I lived at the Mark Hopkins Hotel. I was thrilled by what is called 'The Top of the Mark,' which has an extraordinary view of the entire city. Also, Fisherman's Wharf was very amusing. Of course, the hills terrified me driving. We took a ride on the cable car, and we went all through China Town. I thought it was extraordinary. Wonderful food at the Palace Hotel and a place called Jacques. I remember we took a boat from Oakland and saw for the first time the Golden Gate Bridge and the harbor and the Oakland Bay Bridge. We broke all records of the house, and they were very annoyed that we couldn't stay longer. San Francisco is a great theatre town."

The next stop for the tour group was Los Angeles. Upon arrival, Webb had a car and chauffeur waiting for him to take him to George Cukor's home. He stayed with Cukor in Beverly Hills during the engagement. Cukor gave him a big party on his first night there.

One night after a performance, Webb said a newspaper friend brought a young couple backstage. He said, "I was a little stunned when he said, 'You know, Mr. Webb, this is the first time I have ever seen a *round* actor.' I couldn't find an answer to that remark, and my face must have shown it, so he repeated it. I then found myself looking down at my waistline, wondering if I had put on weight unnoticed. After a slight pause, he explained that heretofore he had seen only 'flat' actors, meaning those on the screen, but never a 'round' actor, which he termed people who acted on the stage." Little did Webb know at this time that he would soon be joining the 'flat' actors in Hollywood.

While in Los Angeles, Webb visited Danny Kaye at his house. Moss Hart happened to be there. He was directing his stage play *Winged Victory* for Twentieth Century Fox. Webb recalled, "We sat around the pool and Moss happened to say, 'I bet after you open in the play tonight, you'll have plenty of movie offers.'" Webb replied, "'I wouldn't work in this blankety-blank place if they gave me a million dollars a week.' With that, I got my car and went to rehearsal. The opening night was a huge success with many of the local celebrities out front."

After the performance that evening, a party was given for Webb at Lady Mendl's house. There he renewed an acquaintance with Felix Ferry, also known as "Fefe." Webb had met him in Paris. Fefe ran Fefe's Monte

Carlo Beach in Monte Carlo and had opened another club, Fefe's Monte Carlo, in New York. He had recently gone into the agency business with Leland Hayward. He asked Webb if he would be interested in doing a picture. Webb replied, "I don't think so, I prefer the theatre." The next morning Fefe telephoned Webb at Cukor's and asked if he'd meet him and go to Twentieth Century Fox to see Otto Preminger. Webb said, "I'd be delighted to see Otto again, because I'd met him in New York through Tallulah Bankhead."

Felix Ferry was a close friend of Preminger. Preminger was a regular at Fefe's Monte Carlo. Ferry was a Rumanian, and his club had all the ingredients that appealed to Preminger. Preminger felt it was important to frequent the right places and be seen in luxurious surroundings. Besides, he enjoyed relaxing in the company of lesser mortals like Felix and other chums from the Europe of his youth. Little has been mentioned about Felix Ferry's importance in starting the movie career of Clifton Webb. But it was Ferry who put things in motion that led to Webb being cast in *Laura*.

Preminger said, "Felix Fefe, who knew everyone, knew Clifton Webb, who at that time was playing in Noel Coward's play *Blithe Spirit* downtown in Los Angeles. Felix invited me to come there with some other people, and I was fascinated by Clifton Webb. I had never seen him, or knew who he was, and we met and I felt he must play this part. I told him so."

The summoning of Webb started on a morning in 1943 when Otto Preminger arrived at his office at Twentieth Century Fox. He found two scripts on his desk. A brief glance at one of them, entitled *Army Wives*, didn't appeal to him. Although he thought little of the script, Preminger wound up directing it because he was given the opportunity to both produce and direct. The film was a minor one and was released under the title *In the Meantime, Darling*. Once this small film was out of the way, Preminger began work on the other script, *Laura*. He felt certain it would provide more promise. He found the story to be compelling, generating curiosity and suspense.

The story was based on a novel by Vera Caspary. Fox paid Caspary a very frugal thirty thousand dollars for the rights to a novel, a play, and a serialized magazine story. Caspary first wrote her story as a play, *Ring Twice for Lora*, in 1939. She then adapted it into a novel entitled *Laura*. The novel was serialized in *Collier's* magazine in 1942 under the title *Ring Twice for Laura*. The principal characters were all fascinating. There was beautiful Laura Hunt, who is thought to have been murdered, a neurotic and frustrated snob named Waldo Lydecker, and a very masculine detective named Mark McPherson. Preminger threw himself into revising the script. He and Caspary clashed frequently over the script, but Preminger was firm in his belief that he knew far more than Caspary about what was needed to turn the material into a successful film.

Preminger managed to get the completed script to Darryl Zanuck. At this point, Preminger was primarily a producer who was itching to be a director. He secretly hoped Zanuck would allow him to direct the script he discovered. Zanuck liked the script and gave it a green light. Lewis Milestone was asked to direct but turned it down. This gave Preminger hope that he would now be chosen to direct. Instead, Rouben Mamoulian was selected. Disappointed, Preminger began to cast the film.

Webb's version of the events that led to his being cast in *Laura* in 1944 differs from Otto Preminger's version. Preminger is quoted as saying he had not seen Webb before viewing him on stage in *Blithe Spirit*, yet Webb says he met him previously in New York. It is possible he met Webb earlier but had not seen him perform.

Preminger wanted to make a test with Webb to show to Zanuck. Rufus LeMaire, the casting director, informed him that Webb had made a test at Metro. However, when Preminger met Webb at a party and told him he was waiting to see that test, Webb replied, "My dear boy, I was at Metro for eighteen months and never faced a camera. Never made a test!" The next day at an executive luncheon Preminger accused LeMaire of lying. He said, "I talked to Webb last night and he never faced a camera." Then Preminger turned to Zanuck and said, "Now, don't you think it would be fair to let him make a test?" Zanuck gave Preminger permission to shoot a test.

Webb provides this version of his first meeting with Preminger at his office. He said Preminger asked if he would be interested in doing a picture. Webb said, "I thought it would be stupid to stamp my foot and say no, so I said, 'It depends entirely on the picture and the part.' He [Preminger] said, 'Well, if you did a part, what kind of a part would you like to do?' And I said, 'A charming son of a bitch.' So, he lifted a script from his desk and handed it to me. It was called *Laura*. So, I read it and obviously realized it was a wonderful part and right up my street."

Webb asked his friend George Cukor if he would read the script and tell him what he thought. Cukor said that if Webb was thinking of starting in pictures this would be a great part for him.

"Preminger called up and asked me what I thought, and I told him I liked it immensely but that I had a contract with Wilson for the run of the play, which meant I couldn't close until the first of June. They were very anxious to begin the picture as soon as possible. I then gave the script to Jack Wilson to read and he said, 'To Hell with the play, we'll close. You must do that part.'"

Preminger wanted to film Webb doing two scenes from the *Laura* script. There are reports that Webb, acting like a prima donna, refused to do the scenes from *Laura*. However, in his notes Webb logically explained why he refused to do the *Laura* test.

"I told him this would be quite impossible because I had a night performance and a matinee the next day, and I felt I could not learn the lines in such a short space of time, and I couldn't give any characterization to it if I were rushed into it. I told him that if he wanted to see what came off as far as I was concerned, I would do two scenes from *Blithe Spirit*, a comedy scene from the first act and the narration at the very close of the play where I bid my wives, my spirit wives, goodbye. So, we left it like that. He telephoned me the next day and told me they'd agreed to let me do it. I then asked Valerie Cossart, who was playing a part in the show, as well as being Peggy Wood's understudy, if she would make the test with me. She said she'd be delighted."

Preminger went back to Zanuck and told him Webb would not do scenes from *Laura* but instead wanted to film scenes from *Blithe Spirit*. Zanuck said, "I'm not filming the damn play. I am not interested in the play. I want him to do this from the script." Preminger knew Webb would not do scenes from the script. He said, "I took a terrific gamble. I got a very good cameraman and photographed Webb without permission from Zanuck. I knew it was great, and I took the test to Zanuck. He didn't say anything and we screened it. Zanuck looked at me, and being a professional, he liked it. He said, 'You son-of-a-bitch, I told you I don't want to see the play, but O.K.'" Preminger said, "Later on Zanuck and Webb became the greatest of friends, he practically lived in Zanuck's house in Palm Springs."

There is no question that Webb made a test using scenes from *Blithe Spirit*. There is a question as to whether or not he made another test with Jennifer Jones. Louella Parsons, in her column dated March 25, 1944, stated, "Clifton, who made a test for *Laura* opposite Jennifer Jones, will make his first appearance on the Fox lot." Parsons's column on April 3, 1944, has a headline, "Jennifer Jones to Do *Laura*." In that column she talks as though Jones was all set to do the film. "Jennifer Jones is expected to report at 20th Century Fox May 1 to start on *Laura*. Under terms of the contract Darryl Zanuck cannot announce any other actor for the picture, because he loses Jennifer if a substitute is named before he receives an official answer."

According to Preminger, Jones was the first choice. Jones had just won an Oscar for *The Song of Bernadette* and was in the process of divorcing Robert Walker as she and David O. Selznick became a twosome. Selznick did not think *Laura* was right for Jones and successfully discouraged her from accepting. After Jones refused the role, Fox filed a suit against Jones for $613,600, an amount they said represented the loss of the services of Jones, "an Academy Award winner." The suit was later settled, and Jones went back to Fox to make *Cluny Brown* in 1946.

Preminger suggested Gene Tierney as a replacement. When Tierney was offered the part, she replied, "If Jennifer Jones doesn't want it, why should I?" Zanuck said, "The role is right for you. You'll be good in it. And, you'll see, this one will help your career." Tierney had reservations, but she had a hunch Zanuck might be right.

The night before his *Blithe Spirit* test, Webb called Cukor and asked him if he'd help him prepare for it. He said, "Cukor was waiting up for me and he sat with me until the wee small hours and gave me some very helpful advice and went over the two scenes that I was going to do." Since Webb was a stage actor, Cukor coached him on becoming much more intimate and conversational for the screen test. The next morning the first scene was shot with Webb and Valerie Cossart with Preminger directing. Cukor and Webb both knew what Zanuck's objection to him might be and did their best to avoid—"that hint of preciousness." Webb said, "I talked very softly as if I were talking to someone in a room." Webb said, Preminger was "very patient, and considerate." After lunch, Webb did the other scene alone. Preminger was pleased with the tests. He said Webb was very good. "He didn't fly."

The following day, Fefe called Webb and said, "Just seen the test, and it was sensational." Webb commented, "That was a word I found out later that they use out here for everything from aspirin to zanite." Fefe wanted Webb to come right over and see it.

"This was about five in the afternoon. I told him that would be impossible, as I had to dine at six in order to make the show by quarter of eight. So, I made an appointment to see it the following day, Saturday, before the matinee. George and I went together and went into the projection room, and I sat between him and Otto Preminger, feeling very scared at what I might see on the screen, because I had made it very clear that unless I liked myself and felt that I had a quality, nothing would induce me to accept this proposition. The first time they ran it, Cukor and Preminger were so busy talking across me I really didn't get a chance to look at it very clearly. At the end, Preminger said, 'Well what do you think?' I said, 'Run it again, and for God's sake be quiet.' This they did. When it was all over I said that I felt quite pleased with myself."

That night *Blithe Spirit* closed in Los Angeles, and Cukor gave a farewell party for the cast. The next stop on the tour was in Oakland for just one night. Webb said he got a wire there saying, "Decision cannot be made about your playing the part until tomorrow." Rouben Mamoulian wanted Laird Cregar to play Waldo Lydecker. Webb wired Jack Wilson, "Oh what a beautiful morning, oh, what a beautiful day. Baby's right back where he started. Mamoulian wants Cregar they say. Love and kisses."

Darryl Zanuck was also somewhat set on Laird Cregar playing Waldo Lydecker. Zanuck wrote a note to Preminger: "If we decide to use Laird Cregar (who was a Fox contract player), you should again look at those scenes in *Blood and Sand* in which he was so magnificent as the sardonic super-critic."

Preminger did not want Cregar. He said, "Zanuck and Mamoulian wanted a man called Laird Cregar, who at that time played all the heavies. I, who had worked very hard on the script, felt that the only possibility to make this a success was if people did not know from the beginning that this amusing and very urbane and civil character was the villain."

Blithe Spirit's next stop was Portland, Oregon. While there, Webb received a wire from Fefe that said, "Mamoulian, after seeing other tests, entirely in your favor. Decision now rests with Darryl Zanuck." Webb said, "Meantime, Mabelle was going mad in New York, wondering what was happening. From there we went to Seattle, Washington. It was then decided that I was to do it."

Webb promptly went into action.

"When it was decided, I was on the long distance telephone from Seattle about the housing situation in Beverly Hills. I found I could get Constance Bennett's house at Holmby Hills, which pleased me very much, as I knew the house, having been there when she first built it in 1935. The next thing was to get some servants . . . more telegrams, more wires. I had the script with me and I was figuring out my clothes plot.

When it was settled what I was going to wear, I telephoned my tailors in New York with instructions what I wanted them to make me up. I also instructed Mabelle to go to Mainbocher and shoot the works."

Webb sensed that he might be leaving the stage forever. "I played my last performance in Minneapolis and at the end of the show when I had to say farewell to my wives, I found the words wouldn't come out. I was saddened at leaving the company after three years. The company all stood in the wings, crying. We took our calls, and the orchestra played *Auld Lang Syne*. I arrived in New York Monday, the seventeenth of April, and spent five hectic days putting the house in Greenwich in cold storage, running to tailors, shirt makers, trying to see a few of the plays. The following Friday we entrained for California with suits in boxes and shirts in boxes, Mabelle's Mainbocher in boxes, and my French poodle at the end of a brand new leash and collar—all set for Hollywood."

Webb was exhausted but found time to relax and study the script while on the train. When they arrived at Pasadena, Fefe met them at the station.

"He was now my agent and I was his first client. From there I was rushed to the studio to discuss my wardrobe. The next morning at eight o'clock I found my body being made up; at nine o'clock I found myself sitting in a bathtub. While I was sitting, waiting to be called, a young man came up to me and made himself known. He was Dana Andrews. He was very friendly and warm and put me at my ease. I was naturally nervous, but trying to appear completely detached. I sat in that bloody tub for two days in hot water, until at the end of the day I had shriveled like a prune. All the stagehands were most courteous and the property men couldn't do enough for me to make things easier and comfortable. They brought me coffee and Coca Cola."

Webb recalled the first time he saw the rushes. "When I saw myself sitting in the bathtub looking very much like Mahatma Gandhi, I felt I might vomit. After it was over Dana saved my life with a big swig of bourbon. The first shock of seeing myself had a strange effect on me, psychologically, as it made me realize for the first time that I was no longer a dashing young juvenile, which I must have fancied myself being through the years in the theatre."

Webb said the first week of shooting was brutal. He recalled, "I arrived home whipped, nervous, and discouraged; had my dinner on a tray and would go to bed." He began to regain his stamina about the second week, when he decided he'd give a party. "I invited about eighty people. I had known most of them from New York. It seemed to me at the time that

9.1. At poolside in California, *left to right:* Hedda Hopper, unidentified person, Bea Lillie, and Clifton Webb. The John and Betsy Neylon Collection.

everybody seemed to be here. I had the audacity to invite Hedda Hopper and Louella Parsons to the same party. I was told by several of my guests that only I would have the courage to do such a thing. These two ladies of the columns were apparently bitter enemies and could never be invited to the same party at the same time. I paid no attention to this fiddle-dee-dee because I entirely disapprove of such adolescent behavior."

As the evening wore on, Webb discovered something remarkable. "I was standing with my back to the door, talking to Milestone [Lewis], the director. Suddenly his face went blank and I thought he'd been struck dumb. When I asked him what was wrong, he said, 'Just look back of you and see if you see what I see.' I did this and found Louella and Hedda standing at the bar with their arms around one another. This bit of news traveled like wildfire naturally."

During the course of the party, Webb discovered Dana Andrews standing around alone. "I asked him what was the matter. He startled me when he said, 'I didn't realize that one doesn't get asked to a party like this unless they make a thousand dollars a week or over.' This rather stunned me because I didn't realize that one's social position was rated by their weekly paycheck."

Webb started *Laura* with Rouben Mamoulian as the director. He doesn't elaborate on the melodrama involving Mamoulian and Preminger and how Preminger was finally appointed the director by Zanuck. He simply says, "After two weeks of shooting under Mamoulian's direction, he retired from the picture and Otto Preminger took over the reins. Up to this time his position on the lot had been that of producer. I found him a most sympathetic director, having had his own theatre in Vienna and having been an actor himself, he knew what a stage person could go through." Webb must have been pleased with Preminger's promotion to director. He was fully aware that Mamoulian wanted Laird Cregar for the role of Lydecker.

Preminger's machinations to get promoted from an underling in a B-picture unit to the director/producer of *Laura* are well known. Preminger had a seven-year contract with Twentieth Century Fox to act and direct. However, Zanuck had not hired him. When Zanuck met him he was not impressed. Zanuck informed him, "You will produce, but you will never direct." Shortly after the shooting of *Laura* began, the rushes were reviewed and they were terrible. Preminger said, "Webb was not good. Dana Andrews had no sex appeal." Zanuck asked Preminger, "What is wrong with this picture?" Preminger said, "Being an actor, I acted it out." Zanuck said, "Why don't you explain that to Rouben?" Preminger retorted, "Rouben doesn't listen." After three days, the rushes were no better.

One day in the executive dining room with all the directors and producers present, Zanuck announced, "I think I'll take Mamoulian off the picture." After lunch, walking down the hallway, Zanuck waved to Preminger with his polo stick and said, "You're on." It was the beginning of a long and profitable relationship between Zanuck and Preminger.

The casting of *Laura* is legendary. When Rufus LeMaire heard that Preminger was considering Webb for the part of Waldo Lydecker, he said, "You can't have Clifton Webb play this part. He flies!" Preminger said, "What do you mean? I didn't even understand what he meant. I already knew that Clifton Webb was a little effeminate, but that didn't bother me at all."

In the finished script, Lydecker was supposed to be a jealous heterosexual, but Preminger wanted to restore some of the gayness that was apparent in the original concept of the role. He was convinced Webb would be perfect for the conniving, clever, yet misogynous murderer. It is possible Preminger even purposely cast other known gays in supporting roles. Critic James Naremore observed, "Any movie that puts Clifton

Webb, Judith Anderson and Vincent Price in the same drawing room is inviting a mood of fey theatricality."

Price and Webb were old friends from their New York days in the mid-1930s. Price said, "I first met him in New York when I was in *Victoria* [*Regina*]. He and Mabelle one day took me out to dinner. He said, 'You're the top young actor in New York today, and you need to be included in all of the things here.' Clifton would always put me in any kind of benefit that he had a chance to." It must have been pleasing for Webb to see Price cast in *Laura.* He may even have spoken to Preminger on Price's behalf. At any rate, Price was forever grateful to Webb. He said, "Clifton was the kindest man I ever knew in my life." Price's daughter Victoria said, "I'm not sure they socialized much, but I do know that my father was very proud of being in that movie and thought that Clifton was superb."

Zanuck had provided a prophetic guide for the casting, saying, "All of the people, Mark included, should seem as if they stepped out of *The Maltese Falcon. . . .* [E]veryone has a distinct, different personality. This is what made *The Maltese Falcon.* It wasn't the plot. It was the amazing characters. The only chance this picture has of becoming a big-time success is if these characters emerge as real outstanding personalities. Otherwise it will become nothing more than a blown-up Whodunit."

Everything seemed to fall in place nicely after Preminger took over the film. There was the matter of the score and theme music. Alfred Newman, head of music at Fox, decided he didn't want to waste his time writing music for this troubled film. He assigned a young composer named David Raksin to work with Preminger. Preminger wanted to use Duke Ellington's "Sophisticated Lady" as the theme. Raksin suggested a Gershwin tune, "Summertime," might be used. But the rights were not available. Raksin was experimenting with a tune of his own. One day Raksin entered Preminger's office and asked if he could play his own tune for him. Preminger had a little piano in his office and Raksin began to play. When Preminger heard it, he was impressed. He said, "I don't know much about music, but I like this. Let's put it in." Raksin's music was perfect. If you believed that Dana Andrews really was in love with Laura, then you can thank David Raksin's music. Raksin's music set the stage for the film. It is the first thing you hear before the opening credits. The music, along with the portrait of Tierney, created a memorable opening for the film.

It wasn't until after the film was released and requests by the thousands came in asking for a recording of the song that the publishers realized the value of the music. The problem was there were no lyrics for it. Johnny Mercer was promptly hired to write the lyrics, and "Laura" became a standard. It was a big break for Raksin. He went on to write the entire score for *Laura*. His work promoted him to the Hollywood A-list, where he was given the opportunity to work on a number of big-budget films.

Hedy Lamarr, who was considered for the role of Laura, was asked why she turned the role down. She is supposed to have said, "They sent me the script, not the score."

Vincent Price recalled, "When we all went to see *Laura* on opening night we had never heard the score! So we sat there and thought, 'Isn't that marvelous?'" Raksin's *Laura* theme became one of the most famous movie themes ever written.

The portrait of Laura was to be a painting by Rouben Mamoulian's wife, Azadia. She was at that time a popular Hollywood artist. Preminger felt it lacked the mystic quality he wanted. He sent Tierney to pose for Frank Powolny, the studio photographer who had photographed Tierney many times. Preminger took the photograph, enlarged it, and had it lightly brushed with paint to create the effect he wanted.

Gene Tierney had never seen Webb on stage. She marveled at his professionalism and polish. "It was pleasant to observe at close range the professional respect between Clifton and Preminger. The role of the acid-tongued Waldo Lydecker was the most demanding of all, with long stretches of dialogue. There was a wonderfully brittle edge to Clifton, his manner, his speech, the way he moved."

Richard Barrios in his book *Screened Out* says of Webb's voice and manner of speaking, "The voice alone would have carried the performance: the tone a courtly buzz saw, the razor diction dining on consonants as if they were truffled squab." Indeed, it is a rare thing to see an actor and a role so perfectly matched as was Webb and Waldo Lydecker. Critic Molly Haskell said this of the pairing of Tierney and Webb, "They make a dazzling team . . . Tierney's career woman and the epicene, knife-blade-lean New York intellectual who launched her." Other reviewers commented on the effeminate overtones evoked by Webb as Waldo. Bosley Crowther called Webb "a *sybaritic* villain." The *New Republic* stated that his "perfumed literary style of talking expresses a lot of auntyish effeminacy."

Obviously, Webb was aware that this was a big step in his career. He was under a great deal of pressure. He knew the part was made for him, and he knew he could deliver. Tierney said that she felt Webb was rather "tightly strung." Her feelings proved to be correct; she said, "After we

9.2. Gene Tierney and Clifton Webb show off their sartorial splendor in *Laura* (1944). Twentieth Century Fox photo. Courtesy of The Academy of Motion Picture Arts and Sciences.

finished filming, he suffered a nervous breakdown and checked himself into the famous Silver Hills Sanitarium in Connecticut. He came out rested and restored."

Webb recounts his ordeal during the making of the picture: "*Laura* took ten weeks to make and I was becoming more exhausted with every approaching day. Benzedrine in the daytime to keep me going and sleeping pills at night was not a very happy combination."

Webb recalled his first impression of Tierney. "I didn't meet Gene Tierney until we were well along in the picture, and I must confess I had never seen her on the screen. Her beauty and gayety enchanted me, even though she did baffle me in the beginning by turning on her heel and telling her secretary she wanted corn beef and cabbage for dinner, in the midst of a tense dramatic scene."

Seldom has a movie featured two people who were so elegantly and tastefully clothed. Louella Parsons said, "Gene Tierney wears clothes out of this world." Costume design was by Bonnie Cashin, but Tierney was married at the time to Oleg Cassini, and one may wonder how much he had to do with her striking wardrobe. Similarly, Clifton Webb must have had a lot to say about his outfits because he made a point of saying he carefully looked over the script to see what he would need and ordered all his clothes from his favorite tailor in New York City. Webb's principal indulgence had always been his wardrobe. He justified such expenditures by insisting that clothes were essential to his career. He claimed that they were his tools, just as a plumber's wrenches were his.

Finally, the film began to wind down and Webb was happy to be shooting the last scene. "My last shot in the picture was to be taken at night. It showed me walking back and forth in front of Laura's house, with the snow pouring down. Dana had finished shooting before I did but said he wouldn't let the picture finish without his being there, so he came over to the studio. We sat and watched them icing the streets. Great hunks of ice were crushed up and blown through a sprayer."

By this time, Dana Andrews had observed Webb's sartorial elegance and began to wonder about his own taste in clothes. Webb says, "Dana Andrews became very clothes conscious after he had seen the clothes I had worn in *Laura*. He asked me, 'What is the matter with my suits?' And, I told him they weren't the clothes of a gentleman, much too exaggerated, which I found was the trouble with tailors in California. They looked more like zoot suits. And, the odd thing is that the moment a person would come from the West to the East you could spot them immediately by the cut of their clothes."

For many years, Webb had a valet to help him maintain his "best dressed" reputation. He called the valet "Romano" because he looked somewhat like Ramon Navarro. Webb claimed to have introduced the white mess jacket to America and the dark red carnation worn with white tie and tails.

On the wearing of a handkerchief in one's coat pocket, he gave this advice, "Never pointed, never square. It should always be, of course, pear-shaped!" For many years during his heyday in Hollywood, Webb frequently made the "best-dressed men" lists. In the late 1940s he said, "I was nominated again as one of the ten best-dressed men, for the tenth time, along with the Duke of Windsor, Anthony Biddle, Fred Astaire, Edward Stettinius, Anthony Eden, and the Duke of Spoleto."

Webb was now ready to shoot the last scene of *Laura*.

"I emerged from my trailer in winter overcoat, muffler, and galoshes and took my position. It was a shot in which I was talking with the camera in front of me. Suddenly they turned on huge fans behind me, which sent me sprawling on my face. That was remedied, so I started to walk and walked first for a long shot and then for a medium shot and then for a close-up, and when I finished that I was taken to my trailer, given a complete change, rubbed down with alcohol, and started all over again.

"The next shot was under Laura's window. I had to keep looking up at her window and wait for a man to emerge from the front door. The extra that they engaged to do this shot was not very good, and when he came out the door he acted as if he was getting a breath of spring air. The result was we had to do it over and over again. Meantime, my eyes were getting filled with corn flakes, which is what they use to represent snow. So, every time the fellow would come out in a jaunty spring fashion and they'd stop the camera, I had to rush to a nurse they had on the set and have her swab out my eyes. After about two hours of this it was getting me down. We finally wound up at 4:30 in the morning."

After the film was finished and Zanuck saw it, he told Preminger, "You made a chorus girl out of Gene Tierney and we must re-do the last third of the picture." Zanuck added new narration as seen from Tierney's point of view. He brought in a writer and dictated a new script. Zanuck's new ending would disclose that the whole search for the killer is revealed to be a dream. Preminger was there, listening with a sour face. Zanuck stopped and said, "You don't like it?" Preminger confirmed that he didn't. Zanuck told him if he didn't like it, he could get somebody else to direct. Preminger reluctantly directed Zanuck's new material. The rough cut of the new version was finished and was ready to be viewed.

Preminger said, "This is why you have to believe in fate, or something. The guest [at the screening] was Walter Winchell. In the last row of this four or five row projection room was Walter Winchell with a girl." The room darkened and the film began. Preminger was very pleased to hear Clifton Webb's well-modulated voice crisply and elegantly intoning the opening narration: "I shall never forget this weekend—the weekend Laura died . . . a silver sun burned through the sky like a huge magnifying glass. . . . It was the hottest Sunday in my recollection. A heavy silence lay on the town. I felt as if I were the only human being left in New York. And in a sense it was true. For with Laura's horrible death I was alone—with only my crowding, poignant memories of her."

As the picture went on, particularly the repartee between Clifton Webb and Dana Andrews, there were laughs from Walter Winchell and giggles from the girl." After the film ended, Winchell got up and said, "Darryl, that was big time—big time. . . . Great, great! But you are going to change the ending? What's happening at the end? I don't understand."

Preminger said that Zanuck was, in reality, a very flexible man. Instead of being mad, he looked at Preminger and said, "Do you want to have your old ending back?" Preminger replied in the affirmative. He threw out all of the re-takes and put the old ending back.

After the shooting was finished, Webb and Mabelle took off for New York. Webb said, "Kate Hepburn gave us a farewell dinner. When I got back to New York there were a great many interviews to be done with people of the press department of Twentieth Century Fox. It was while I was there that I began to get what is commonly referred to as 'nerves.' I didn't know what it was, but I'd suddenly call up, or have someone call up for me, and get me out of a dinner party. Then it got worse. So, I consulted my doctor, and on the fourth of October I went to the Doctor's Hospital. I told Otto Preminger that I wanted him to write me after they had their first sneak preview of *Laura* and let me know how the audience took me. I wasn't quite sure whether the audience would get my type of humor in pictures. So, while I was at the Doctor's Hospital he sent me a two-page telegram saying that they had a sneak preview and the audience was with me from the very beginning, and I had nothing to worry about. I thought it was a very charming thing for him to do.

"Before I entered the hospital I had arranged with the studio to have a private showing of *Laura* at the Fox Little Theatre on West Fifty-sixth Street. I told them that I wanted to see it first before anybody else saw it. So, one afternoon they ran it for me and I left the hospital and went down to see it. They were all very enthusiastic and turned to me and said, 'What do you think?' And I said I thought it was pretty good. But, my nerves were in such a state I really didn't care one way or the other. On the tenth of October I left the hospital and we had this social preview. My mother sent a list of our friends she wanted invited to the publicity department. They were all very thrilled but were afraid they wouldn't have enough seats for everybody who wished to come. I went to see it and sat in the back row, very nervous. At the end they were highly enthusiastic.

"On the fourteenth of October, we moved to Greenwich. My nerves were still very bad. They kept getting worse and worse, so I called our doctor in Greenwich and asked him to come over and see me, after a terrible day. He and Mother took me to New Canaan to the Silver Hills Foundation. I had a nurse, as I was frightened to be alone. She was a wonderful woman, Mrs. Willy, who had great experience in this sort of thing. Every morning I talked to the psychiatrist. I returned to Greenwich on the nineteenth of November."

Webb still wasn't able to shake off his nervous condition. He decided to go to another psychiatrist. "On Saturday, the thirtieth of December,

I was taken to Dr. Lawrence Kubie, one of our great analysts. I started with him and went to him every day, seven days a week. Meantime, he told me to go around and try and busy myself with as many things as possible. So, I did radio and went to the opera and to the theatre."

Webb did a lot of radio work after he went to Hollywood. However, a *Lux Radio Theatre* version of *Laura* on February 5, 1945, featured Gene Tierney, Dana Andrews, and Vincent Price, but Otto Kruger played the Waldo Lydecker part. There were two more radio recreations of *Laura* in which Webb appeared with Tierney and Andrews. The *Screen Guild Theater* aired *Laura* on August 20, 1945, and *Hollywood Star Time* aired their version of *Laura* on January 13, 1946. There were eight radio adaptations of *Laura* from 1945 to 1954 on various network programs. Webb acted in radio adaptations of several of his other starring roles on *Lux Radio Theater*, including *Sitting Pretty*, *Mr. Belvedere Goes to College*, *The Man Who Came to Dinner*, and *Cheaper by the Dozen*. He even appeared on the mystery shows *Inner Sanctum* and *Suspense*.

Laura paid off for everyone involved in the film. Webb received an Oscar nomination for best supporting actor. Preminger received an Oscar nomination for best director. *Laura* was nominated for best screenplay. The film was also nominated for art direction–interior decoration. The cameraman, Joseph La Shelle, who had never worked with a first unit before, won an Oscar for best photography. Curiously, the haunting musical score by David Raksin was not even nominated. The only Oscar garnered by the film was for best cinematography. Webb lost the supporting actor Oscar to Barry Fitzgerald, who was nominated for both best actor and best supporting actor for the same film—*Going My Way* (something no longer possible).

Reflecting on his loss of the Oscar, Webb said, "I was nominated after *Laura* for the Oscar. Barry Fitzgerald got the award, but I was very pleased because I got the Critic's Award for my performance."

Shortly thereafter, thanks to the immense success of *Laura*, Dana Andrews was able to raise his social position. Webb said, "Before they released *Laura* I don't think they knew they had the success in it that it turned out to be. When it opened in New York, it opened with very little advance publicity, and ever since then it has been referred to at the Twentieth Century lot as the *Laura luck* because out of that picture Otto Preminger became a producer-director, Dana Andrews went from $500 a week to $150,000 a picture, and they tore up Gene Tierney's old contract and gave her a new one." *Laura* was shot for a little over $1 million. The film grossed twice that amount.

Laura is now one of the most beloved and enduring films of the 1940s. It is considered a landmark film in the emerging genre of film noir. The noir world was a dark place, psychologically and morally as well as in its cinematography.

Clifton Webb was overwhelmed at the power of motion pictures. He said, "After *Laura*, the fan mail poured in from the most extraordinary places all over the world. My great public seemed to be England, Ireland, Scotland, and even Helsinki." When *Laura* first played in London, it was very well received. Webb reported this reaction from critic James Agate, who Webb said normally "loathes Americans": "Waldo . . . or may I call you Mr. Webb? I like you, I admire you, and I hope to see you soon again. Let us occupy ourselves with Waldo for a moment. The actor's name is Clifton Webb, and he is a find of the first water. He is long and lean . . . in the 30s, perhaps. . . . [H]e has an elegant, drawling, very English voice. . . [H]e delivers his lines with a perfection of timing seldom heard on either stage or screen in these degenerate days. In a word, he has the art of speaking his part as if every remark were a pearl of wit, which in this case it certainly isn't. When he says to the intruding detective: 'Why do you not avail yourself of that triumph of modern science, the door bell?' It sounds like some purple patch out of Congreve."

Laura had such impact that it inspired others to try adaptations of it. In 1945, it was announced that Otto Kruger would play Clifton Webb's part in the stage play of *Laura*. In the late 1960s, Truman Capote decided he would turn Lee Bouvier Radziwill, Jacqueline Kennedy's sister, into an actress—perhaps a movie star. Even after a disastrous turn in a dinner theatre production of *The Philadelphia Story*, Capote persisted. He convinced ABC to carry his adaptation of *The Voice of the Turtle*, starring Radziwill. On second thought, he decided an adaptation of *Laura* would be better. Radziwill would take Gene Tierney's part, and George Sanders would take Clifton Webb's part. The show was telecast in January 1968. *Time* magazine said that Radziwill was "only slightly less animated than the portrait of herself that hung over the mantel." Radziwill's acting career was brought to a dismal end. She was no Gene Tierney and Sanders was no Clifton Webb.

CHAPTER 10

More Movies, More Parties, and Garbo

Apparently, Webb had an option with Twentieth Century Fox that depended on the outcome of *Laura*. Obviously, they liked what they saw. However, Webb's initial contract with Fox was for only one picture, *Laura*, at $4,000 a week. Webb said, "The studio had taken up my option and I was to come out to do *The Razor's Edge*." The studio had not yet bought the rights to Somerset Maugham's novel, but it didn't take a genius to see that Webb was the perfect choice for the role of Elliott Templeton. Maugham was an old friend of Webb's, and both Webb and Maugham began to exhort Fox to buy the novel. Webb said, "While I was doing *Laura*, having read *The Razor's Edge*, I was very anxious that they do it because I was dying to do Elliott Templeton. So, they bought it."

Zanuck's friend, agent-producer Charlie Feldman, had the rights to Maugham's book. Zanuck paid Feldman $53,000 to relinquish his rights. Maugham was a shrewd businessman as well as a successful author. He received $250,000 against a 20 percent share of the film's net profits.

It was going to be awhile before work could begin on *The Razor's Edge*, so Webb and Mabelle began to look for a house in California.

"On Friday, May 25 [1946], we closed the house in Greenwich. On May 29, we left for California. Meantime, I'd written the real estate agent here to get me a house and told him I wanted something with a view and a swimming pool. The second time I came back to Hollywood, when I did *Laura*, having not been here for ten years, I found the attitude completely changed towards people in the theatre. I felt when I was out here before they were rather resentful, but now, all the barriers had been let down, and they seemed to welcome them."

While looking for a house, Webb and Mabelle stayed at the Beverly Hills Hotel. They went to dinner parties, and Webb joined a group that regularly met to do calisthenics. Eventually, a house in Bel Air was rented. Webb referred to Bel Air as "the Forest Lawn of the Living."

At a dinner party one night in 1946 at director Lewis Milestone's house, Webb sat next to Ingrid Bergman. "I had never met her before," he said. "After dinner, she, Milestone, and myself stayed at the table talking." Their talk was interrupted when they heard a commotion coming from another room.

"One could hear the strains of jitterbug music coming from the living room. Upon going in, I found Bergman's husband (her first), Dr. Lindstrom, jitterbugging in a most strenuous way. Up to this moment I hadn't realized that he had a mad passion for dancing this type of thing. But, I learned that whenever he goes to a party, he takes three complete changes with him, which he carries in a brief case, and upon entering the first thing he does is inquire where the men's room is. He parks his brief case and when things get a little too warm for him, or he gets too warm himself, or possibly his partner, he goes out and makes a complete change. This night at Milestone's he brought three changes, but at two in the morning he ran out and had to borrow the necessary articles of clothing from Milestone."

One day Webb decided to drop in on his friend Elsie Mendl. Little did he know this little, unplanned visit would introduce him to one of the cinema's iconic legends. It was around cocktail time when Webb entered Mendl's house.

"She was sitting in the little library off the main drawing room. There was also another person there whose face I couldn't see, as it was practically covered by a large drooping hat. When I walked in, Elsie took me by the arm and led me over to the person under the hat, then Elsie said, 'Greta, I want you to meet one of my oldest and dearest friends.'"

Startled, Webb recalled: "I found myself gazing into the most beautiful face I've ever seen in my life, the great Garbo. I sat down. We talked. I said, 'What are you drinking?' She said, 'Vodka.' I said, "I think I'll have some too.' She said, 'Come, we'll have some together,' and proceeded to lead me to the bar. We sat there quite some time, chattering gaily. I also found that this person of wondrous beauty had the most delicious wit and the greatest sense of humor.

"A few days later a mutual friend of hers and mine, Minna Wallis, invited us to dine. We were put next to one another on a sofa, and I became more and more amazed at her quick wit and subtle observation. Valentina and George Schlee came out to stay with us, and my tennis

10.1. Clifton Webb and Greta Garbo at one of the Russian Easter parties given by Valentina, a leading dress designer and close friend of Garbo and Webb. Jerome Zerbe photo.

court was the scene of great activity. Kate Hepburn, a magnificent player, George Schlee, Garbo, and myself had many gay matches."

Webb became so serious about tennis that he hired tennis legend Bill Tilden to give him lessons. Tilden was also giving lessons to other stars, including Katharine Hepburn. Webb did not think his tennis game was improving much as a result of the lessons. He said, "It was too late for me to start." But he was still in good shape, his body athletically trained from all those years of dancing. He enjoyed the game and continued to play "Kate Hepburn and Garbo would come and play with us, and then every Sunday I'd have tennis exhibitions."

In 1946 the Ballet Theatre was playing in the Hollywood Bowl. One afternoon Webb and Mabelle were entertaining a group of dancers from the ballet when the butler announced that a Miss Garbo had arrived. Webb said, "I went out to see her, and she said she'd come over for a swim; did I mind? I told her I was delighted. She had her swim, and I went out to the pool and asked her if she wouldn't like to come in and join us. At first she demurred, but after I told her they were all charming little people from the ballet, she decided she would. Suddenly she appeared in the door, and everyone emitted a great gasp, as, naturally, they were thrilled to the marrow at meeting her. She proceeded to entertain them with one story after the other, at which she is expert. She had them all charmed, and they couldn't believe that they were in the presence of the 'Great One,' who, after all, was a very amusing, warm, human being, like the rest of us."

Webb and Mabelle already knew a lot of people in Hollywood. He said, "By this time Ethel Barrymore had decided to give up the theatre for pictures and was living out here." Webb learned that Ethel Barrymore entertained infrequently. Her invitations, therefore, were not taken lightly in Hollywood. Her guests at these infrequent dinners included such literary lights as Somerset Maugham, Aldous Huxley, and Christopher Isherwood. The Cole Porters, the Irving Berlins, Artur Rubinstein, and Vladimir Horowitz represented Broadway and music. George Cukor, Charles Brackett and his wife, and producer Edwin Knopf and his wife were regular guests as were Webb's old friends Elsie de Wolfe and her husband, Sir Charles Mendl.

Webb was effusive about the Barrymore dinners: "The most civilized meals ever served in Hollywood were devoured by dazzling galaxies of diners." Webb and Mabelle were one of the privileged couples that were regular attendees.

At that time, Webb recalled, "Joan Crawford was then married to Philip Terry and was in the throes of wedded bliss, apparently. Somerset Maugham was staying with George Cukor and working on the screenplay for *The Razor's Edge*. He also joined our exercises, which consisted of Cukor, Constance Collier, Miss Garbo, Somerset Maugham, and myself. Two or three mornings a week we'd meet at Cukor's very early and have this gentleman put us through our paces to various tunes played on the gramophone. Sometimes it was rather difficult for Somerset Maugham and Constance Collier to keep time; they were always just a little behind the beat, which was quite understandable as things were being done at a very rapid tempo."

These were the days of many parties in Hollywood, and no one was more delighted to be a part of these festivities than Clifton and Mabelle. Webb recalled, "At a dinner party one night, that I gave, at which Irving and Ellin Berlin, Kate Hepburn, Spencer Tracy, 'Willy' Maugham, George Cukor, Garbo, and Madeline and Bob Sherwood were present, the latter entertained us until the wee small hours going through his repertoire of popular songs, of which he knows every word, starting with 'When the Red, Red Robin Comes Bob-Bob-Bobbin' Along.' Bob loves to go into his routine at the drop of a scotch.

"Paulette Goddard and her husband, Burgess Meredith, entertained beautifully in their home in Santa Monica. Cole Porter had very amusing Sunday luncheons, and Cobina Wright and Elsa Maxwell were vying with one another as to who was going to give the most amusing party."

Webb and Marlene Dietrich had been pals for some time. He had this recollection of a party that featured both Dietrich and Garbo as guests: "When Marlene Dietrich arrived after her wonderful work that she had done during the war, she was given a party by Joe Schenck. The gardens were lighted and the buffet and cocktail bar reached a full city block in length. On the twelfth of August, I gave a tea party, a real tea party, on my terrace. Ethel Barrymore, Kate Hepburn, George Cukor, Sir Charles, and Lady Mendl attended. I asked Garbo and Dietrich, as I was anxious to see how the two glamour girls would take to one another. Miss Garbo arrived first. She is always very prompt and jolly. Miss Dietrich arrived last and made a wonderful entrance. When I introduced them, I suddenly felt as if we'd entered the regions of the unknown. Dietrich was marvelous. We were all anxious to hear about Marlene's war experiences, and she told of the time when she was the first person to enter German territory. The person in command of the entertainment was very worried and surrounded her with MPs for fear the Germans might try to molest her. When she came out into the street after her performance, they made a rush for her, and all they said was '*Die Blau Angel*,' which they remembered her having done in Germany years ago. She mentioned how far-reaching the screen was."

In Maria Riva's biography she quotes her mother: "It didn't matter that Clifton Webb knew he was amusing, because he actually was. My mother often read his letters aloud, pointing out where she thought him especially clever or outrageous."

Webb met Dietrich through the Countess di Frasso in the early 1930s. In 1936, Dietrich was in London shooting a film at Denham Studios. Maria Riva's biography of her mother includes one of the amusing letters he wrote to Dietrich. Webb had just returned to New York after his ill-fated adventure in Hollywood, where he did nothing for eighteen months. He knew that Dietrich hated her role in *The Garden of Allah* (which had just been released), and so he addressed her by her name in that film. Similarly, he called Jeanne Eagels "Mrs. Dubinsky" which enraged her.

10.2. Clifton Webb and Marlene Dietrich in the 1930s. The John and Betsy Neylon Collection.

Dear sweet Miss Enfilden:

I was more than happy to get your postcard if for no other reason than to know that in all of the dizzy whirl you still remembered
little me. . . . I arrived, en suite, last week, and the shrieks of "Le
(or perhaps I should say "La") Webb" could have been heard in
Laurel Canyon, the ex-abode of that vibrating raper Brian Aherne,
or maybe I shouldn't have brought that up. On the train coming
back was Granny Boyer, which practically made the trip perfect
and filled with excitement as you can well imagine. . . .

Madame Dracula de Acosta came over to the house to go to dinner with us on the day of your departure. She was thrilled to the
bone because you had sent her "eight dozen lilies" which she said
was "The Old Sign," whatever that means. Well dear, I happened
to be in the florist you had sent your flowers from and in a very
nonchalant manner inquired if you had sent eight dozen lilies to

anyone. When the florist fainted dead away, I knew then and there that Mme. Dracula de A. had been lying just a teeny weeny bit. . . .

. . . N.Y. is grand, and I must say it is a relief to get back to people who do talk of something else but "my public, my long shots, my close-ups." . . . All one has to do is get away from that self-etherized group to realize how little they mean outside of that glorious sunlit terrain.

I shall probably be crying for it this winter when I am up to my "whatsis" in snow and slush. . . . My days of "whoopie poo" are at an end. I go into rehearsal next week. Am doing a play with the Theatre Guild, about the grandest part one could wish for. I almost did "On Your Toes" in London. I had visions of being crowned along with dear David at the Coronation. [Webb always referred to the Duke of Windsor as "David."]

I also had visions of all the crowned heads of Europe at my feet . . . and spots North . . . and I must say I was greatly excited for a very short time at the outlook. . . . If you see Noel, just casually ask him what went on in Garbo's flat in Stockholm. My dear girl . . . I SAY NOTHING!

By now you are probably palpitating over some illegitimate son of a frowsy old Earl. On the other hand, perhaps not. If I remember rightly, the English haven't got enough of that "zum, zip and zowie" for you my puss.

Do, if you have a chance, and even if you have not a chance, drop me a line and let me know a little bit what goes on. . . . I love you so very much, and even though you are the toy of London, being whoopsed off your feet (in more ways than one I HOPE!), shall be delighted to get any news. As you know, I am MAHD for you.

Love to Maria and Rudi if he is with you. Bless you.

Your little mother

CLIFTON

(Public gentleman number 1)

In the letter Webb refers to actor Brian Aherne, with whom Dietrich had one of her many affairs. The "Madame Dracula de Acosta" to which he refers is Mercedes de Acosta, poet, playwright, costume designer, and lesbian lover of several Hollywood personalities.

Riva reported how her mother felt about Webb: "I like Clifton. You know, he never goes anywhere without his mother, Mabelle. That's why he has never married. Dear Clifton . . . does liven up a party. Wonderful sense of humor! He's one of the intelligent ones, like Noel Coward!"

Garbo had an affinity for Webb in the same manner as Dietrich. She loved to be in his company. Webb constantly urged Garbo to be more social. He felt more people should be able to enjoy her personality. Louella Parsons reported in her column in June 1944, "Greta Garbo, who is becoming more and more social, so much so she can no longer be called a recluse, was at Minna Wallis' house for dinner the other eve with Clifton Webb, Fefe Ferry and Norma Shearer." Webb delighted in telling how she surprised everyone in August 1945. "Greta Garbo broke all tradition by having six people for cocktails. She was excited and perfectly charming, like a child with a new toy. She said she'd never done such a thing before."

Webb had Garbo as a guest at his house many times. She played tennis there, as witnessed by this statement from Tallulah Bankhead in her autobiography, "I've had tea with Lloyd George, tiffin with Ramsey MacDonald, and I've aced Greta Garbo on Clifton Webb's court." Webb said, "Tallulah Bankhead would come every day at one o'clock and take a lesson. She was determined to learn. She'd stand for an hour in the blazing sun while we were all dropping under the trees from the heat."

It seems a tennis court was a premiere attraction for Garbo. She was a rather frequent guest of Ernst Lubitsch and Cedric Gibbons, both of whom had tennis courts. Garbo is supposed to have attended séances at Webb's home in the 1950s. These séances were certainly arranged by Mabelle, who had a keen interest in the occult and supernatural.

Another amusing Garbo story from Webb happened in 1945 at a thirteenth wedding anniversary party for Mr. and Mrs. James Pendleton. Pendleton was a highly successful New York decorator. Webb remembers, "scores of friends dropped in for a buffet supper and dance. Greta Garbo and I were causing screams of laughter from a gallery of people watching us jitterbug in the garden in the moonlight. Among those present were Lillian Gish, Mary Pickford, Allie and Ed Harbach, Norma Shearer, and Charles Farrell. In connection with that same party, there appeared in Hedda Hopper's column the following: 'Clifton Webb dancing . . . not on the floor, but on the lawn, with Garbo, and at Jim Pendleton's party. He caught cold and couldn't do his *Suspense* show [radio], which was taken over by Joseph Cotten.'"

After acquiring the rights to *The Razor's Edge*, Darryl Zanuck made arrangements to borrow George Cukor from his home studio, MGM, to direct. Cukor had read the manuscript and liked it. Lamar Trotti had written the adaptation, and Zanuck did not like it. Cukor told Zanuck he could get Maugham to write the screen adaptation. Zanuck feared that Maugham would ask for too much money. However, when Cukor phoned his old friend with the proposal, Maugham said he'd write it for nothing.

Maugham came to California and stayed with Cukor while writing the screenplay. When it was finished, Zanuck said he liked it but that he had heard from Tyrone Power, who begged Zanuck to wait until he was discharged from the service since he wanted to play the leading man. According to Webb, "George Cukor began testing young men to play the part of Larry in *The Razor's Edge*. Meantime, it was discovered that Tyrone Power was about to be released from his duties with Uncle Sam."

After hearing from Zanuck, Cukor called off the testing. By the time Power was discharged from the Marines in late 1945, Cukor was committed to another project for MGM (*Desire Me*). Zanuck decided to sign Edmund Goulding as the director. The Maugham screenplay was dumped, and Zanuck went back to the Trotti script. According to Mel Gussow in his biography of Zanuck, Zanuck felt bad about the work Maugham did on the screenplay for which he received no remuneration. He asked Cukor what he could do for Maugham to repay him for his effort on the screenplay. Cukor told Zanuck that Maugham would be delighted to be given a painting. Zanuck then told Maugham he could go and select any painting he liked from any dealer he liked. He could spend up to fifteen thousand dollars. Pleased, Maugham wrote to Cukor, "I have bought at the expense of 20th Century-Fox a very fine Monet."

Webb knew that, as Elliott Templeton, he would have the juiciest part in *The Razor's Edge*. Templeton seemed to be fashioned from the prejudices of both Maugham's own personality and Clifton Webb's personality. He was a snobbish Midwesterner who much preferred the salons of Paris. The Templeton character was based on an American who had lived most of his life in England. Sir Henry "Chips" Channon eventually took British citizenship. Thus Webb had the benefit of playing a part based on a real person.

In order to follow up on Webb's success in *Laura*, Fox decided to put him in another film while waiting for *The Razor's Edge* to work out its problems. Webb said, "Meantime, I signed to do a picture to fill in the time, called *The Dark Corner*, with Mark Stevens and Lucille Ball. When they sent me *The Dark Corner* to read, I liked it very much. It was a screen treatment that had been done by the author, very cleverly written, a psychological drama. So, I agreed to do it. When I received the script, they had changed it into a 'whodunit,' and after we finished it and it was shown, I wondered, 'WHY they'd done it.' They tried to fashion my part in it on the lines of Waldo Lydecker, the part I played in *Laura*, which didn't fit this character at all."

Webb was right. Fox was anxious to capitalize on the Webb image as seen in *Laura*. Thus, the script for *The Dark Corner* was re-written to do just that. Webb was asked to come up with an acerbic smile as the sort of uncle who yearned secretly to knife a nephew.

The Dark Corner has been categorized as belonging to the "film noir" genre. Some have classified *Laura* as belonging to this genre. Thus Clifton Webb's first two films of note were of similar type, with Webb the villain in each. Fortunately, this trend did not continue since Webb's next film (*The Razor's Edge*) had him playing a character that retained the essential ingredients of the Waldo Lydecker character but without the murderous intent.

Webb was pleased to have Henry Hathaway as the director for *The Dark Corner:* "I enjoyed working with Henry Hathaway, who is responsible for directing documentary films that Mr. Zanuck had made, such as *The House on 92nd Street* and *13 Rue Madeleine*. However, I found it rather difficult working with the young lady who played my wife [Cathy Downs]. I'm sure I wasn't the only one. I don't think Henry Hathaway found it any too easy directing her. But, her beauty was extraordinary, and when it was all out and seen on the screen, she came off admirably, another example of what can be done by a director, a cameraman, and a cutter."

Critic reviews said, ". . . tough-fibered, exciting entertainment" and "superior performances." Lucille Ball, who was loaned to Fox from MGM for the picture, said, "Most of my scenes were with Mark Stevens and I never did know what the rest of the people were doing. I guess I'll have to go see it." Ball was having marital problems with Desi Arnaz and said, "I can't say my performance was superior. I had a staring, numb, fogbank look." She was genuinely surprised when the movie did so well. Webb finished *The Dark Corner* on January 28, 1946.

Darryl Zanuck took an almost immediate liking to Clifton Webb. Perhaps he could see that Webb might be developed into a moneymaker for his studio. Zanuck didn't have enough money to buy stars—he had to make them. Webb was very grateful to Zanuck for giving him his big break. He felt a certain loyalty was due him. Eventually, however, as they began to know each other better, it was obvious they sincerely enjoyed each other's company. Richard Zanuck said of Webb, "He was

10.3. Darryl Zanuck and Mabelle Webb kicking up their heels. The John and Betsy Neylon Collection.

easy to confide in. You could trust him. Besides, my father always liked odd people. He seldom became friendly with the stars. Instead he loved to be with people like Gregory Ratoff and Mike Romanoff." Zanuck even became friendly with Mabelle and loved to joke and cavort with her.

In November 1945, a column in the *New York Times* stated, "Mabel Webb, the mother of Clifton Webb, has been signed by Jesse L. Lasky for a part in *Thanks God, I'll Take It from Here*." Webb said, "Mervyn LeRoy had persuaded Mabelle to act in this picture. LeRoy had it all set, but I put my foot down. I said one actor in the family is enough." Mabelle did not appear in the picture. It was released under the title *Without Reservations* (1946) and starred John Wayne and Claudette Colbert.

Webb said, "Whenever possible, I'd spend the weekend with Darryl and Virginia Zanuck in their charming home at Palm Springs. During the two years that I had been out here off and on I had grown deeply fond of them." Webb became friends of the Zanuck family. One time he gave Zanuck's daughter Darrylin some money to have an outing in the desert with her college friends. It turned into a disaster because the girls met a

10.4. Clifton Webb at a preview with Susan Zanuck and Steve Cochran. The John and Betsy
Neylon Collection.

group of Harvard boys and things began to get out of hand. The police
were called and Zanuck had to go bail out several who were arrested.
Zanuck was not very pleased with Webb's largesse.

In 1953, Webb escorted Zanuck's daughter Susan to President Eisen-
hower's inaugural ball in Washington, D.C. Susan, dressed in a brand-
new gown, entered and stood at the head of the grand stairway on
Webb's arm. As she began to go down the stairs, she tripped, broke the
heel of her shoe, and tumbled unceremoniously down the stairs. She
picked herself up and shouted at Webb, "You nasty man. You pushed
me!" Webb's reaction was not recorded.

When Susan's coming-out party was being planned, Zanuck was told
he would be expected to dance the first dance with his daughter. It was
a waltz and he didn't know how to waltz. Clifton Webb immediately
volunteered to be Zanuck's instructor. Behind closed doors, with Jule
Styne playing the piano, Zanuck and Webb danced cheek to cheek, Zanuck puffing his cigar all through the lesson. This was made even more

hilarious in that Webb was much taller than Zanuck. Thus Webb was doubled-over in order to be more of a match for his boss's height.

Zanuck seldom dealt directly with actors. Only a few could be considered his "friends." Among those who managed to get reasonably close to this "loner" were Tyrone Power, Reginald Gardiner, and Clifton Webb. Webb might have been his best friend. No one called Zanuck by a nickname other than Clifton Webb. For no known reason, Webb always called him "Bud," his only recorded nickname.

Zanuck's sport of choice was polo. He owned twenty polo ponies, and he played regularly with his cronies. One day a ball came flying at his face. It struck his hand and smashed his mallet against his face. He was a mass of bruises and had a broken nose. After this, he gave up polo and donated all his horses to West Point. He then started looking for something that was less of a blood sport. Clifton Webb was instrumental in coming up with a sport that became Zanuck's next big passion.

"One morning I happened to drop by the Zanuck's and found them trying to play croquet with a children's set. I asked them what they thought they were doing. The only way one could possibly play croquet was with an English set, such as we had used during my croquet days in Port Washington, Long Island. Darryl immediately inquired where he could get one. I told him the only way I knew was through Abercrombie and Fitch in New York, but I doubted if they had any because I don't think they had imported any during the war. He lost no time, however, getting in touch with Abercrombie and Fitch, only to be told that they didn't have any.

"He finally found a set that they had at the Western Costume Company, a place where they rent all sorts of things, props, costumes, to the various studios. The next weekend I arrived at their house to find them setting it up. I gave him a few basic rules that I learned in the East, and we started to play and he became an avid devotee of the game. So, naturally, everybody had to learn to play croquet."

Zanuck found that it could be a bitterly competitive, highly emotional, very vocal, and exacting game. The front lawn at Zanuck's house in Palm Springs became, in the late 1940s, the croquet capital of California. Zanuck was its ruler, as well as the chief umpire and premiere player. Moss Hart said, "Though a neophyte at the game, Zanuck has true croquet spirit. He trusts no one but himself, never concedes . . . no matter how far behind he may be . . . and hates his opponents with an all-enduring hate." In his autobiography, Director Jean Negulesco quotes a letter from Moss Hart to trade-paper columnist Edith Wilkerson:

Croquet is a noble game; its basic element is skill, but its first requisite is a right code of ethics. Played correctly, it is a game of savagery, passion and deep, almost mystic, fulfillment. To find it sullied by such tomfoolery as "peaked caps," a gaping throng of goons, and such players as Fefe Ferry, Clifton Webb, Tyrone Power, et all. is more than I can take. I came up in croquet the hard way and for long summers was only allowed to watch. After this I was placed on a scrub team in the late afternoons when the big games were over. And even then I would have spit on Clifton Webb as a partner.

Webb said he introduced the game of croquet to Zanuck, Tyrone Power, and others because he saw that even though it could be a grueling contest, it allowed him to remain nattily dressed through the most devastating match although Zanuck and others often stripped to the waist.

Richard Zanuck, who witnessed many of the matches but never played, said that Louis Jourdan was the best player, with Howard Hawks and Jean Negulesco coming in second. Webb had other somewhat unusual interests in addition to croquet. In an interview with Webb, the *Indianapolis Star* provided this insight: "His hobbies are writing for his own amusement, dogs, hockey and prize fights."

It wasn't long before Zanuck's house wasn't the only place to play croquet. Tyrone Power put in a court of his own. Webb played there as well: "A group of us, every Sunday, would have a standing date to go to Tyrone Power's and play croquet, stay for dinner, and after dinner we'd play 'The Game' or various different pastimes."

Croquet became such a passion, especially with Zanuck, that he had floodlights installed so he could play at night. One time Olivia de Havilland came storming out of her room at three in the morning and demanded that her husband stop playing and come to bed. After a moment of stunned silence, the game continued.

On May 18, 1946, Tyrone Power had his usual croquet gathering. Clifton Webb did not attend, since he had accepted an invitation to a party at Joan Crawford's house. Webb told this story of that night at Power's house as he learned it from others.

"Among others attending that evening were Mr. and Mrs. David Niven. She was known as 'Primmy.' It was at this party, after dinner, they were playing a game in which all the lights were turned off, that she opened a door, thinking she was stepping into a cupboard, and fell down a flight of stairs into the cellar

"The next day on the set, I heard about the accident. I called David up that evening and asked him how she was. He said she was unconscious, but the doctors thought she'd be all right. The next morning when we were shooting, I was talking about her to the script girl and she happened to say, 'Isn't that awful about Primmy Niven?' And I said, 'I just talked to David last night, and he said she was better.' And she said, 'She died last night.' It caused all of us a terrible shock. David had a beautiful memorial service for her."

Primula Niven was just twenty-eight years old. She and David had two sons at that time. David Niven Jr. was four years old and Jamie Niven was just five months old. She had recently arrived from England, and this was her first Hollywood party. Fred Guiles in his biography of Tyrone Power provides the details of the accident. "When she fell down the stairs, Cesar Romero knew instantly what had happened and, knowing the house, he found the light switch and the cellar door. Lying at the foot was 'Primmy.' Annabella and Lillie Palmer began to attend her. Lillie put her head in her lap and Annabella applied cold compresses. An ambulance arrived, and Primmy was put inside with David following. Everyone waited in shock for David to phone from the hospital. Instead he came back to the party. He said she was going to have to stay absolutely quiet and in the dark for a few days but, 'She'll be fine.'"

The next day David visited her at the hospital and she recognized him. He was urged to go home and get some sleep. About 11:00 p.m., he received a call saying a blood clot had developed and they were going to have to operate. She died during the operation.

After finishing *The Dark Corner* and before starting *The Razor's Edge*, Webb went to Palm Springs, where he had cocktails and dinner with Bill and Mousie Powell. After dinner, they went to a restaurant called the Stables. Webb described the scene: "After dinner, the pint-sized Mousie inveigled us into going into the bar, where she began pouring coins into the juke box. When Cole Porter's 'Begin the Beguine' began to play, I found myself for no reason taking to the floor, and also for no reason, I found myself doing an exhibition dance. When I sat down, completely winded, I realized I had done the wrong thing, insofar as I'd really tipped my hand that there were a few good steps still left in the old legs. I'm sure it was then and there that Darryl decided in his most determined way that I was going to do a dancing picture, or else."

But Webb had determined long ago that he was through dancing. He became very upset while touring with *The Man Who Came to Dinner* when a critic referred to him as a "Hoofer." Webb said, "I'll show them!" He had planned for the day he could hang up his dancing shoes in favor of straight comedy. He stuck to his guns, never dancing in a movie other than an occasional twirl with Maureen O'Hara in *Sitting Pretty* or Betty Lynn in *Cheaper by the Dozen*.

On March 29, 1946, the filming of *The Razor's Edge* began with Edmund Goulding directing. Webb didn't care for the finished script.

"A great many changes had been made from the original script of Mr. Somerset Maugham, and I'm sorry to relate I don't think they improved it. We all worked very hard and very arduously because we all loved the story of *The Razor's Edge* and we were anxious to do everything we could. I found it a little trying, personally, because it's very difficult to do comedy without an audience if you have such long rehearsals."

Obviously, Webb was still getting acclimated to the vagaries of movie making. He recalled, "I remember in the scene in Sulka's in Paris; it was a long, tiring scene, all done in one shot. We started to rehearse at nine o'clock in the morning and, due to certain camera difficulties, we didn't get our first shot until ten minutes before six. By that time, the sparkle had left. It's different if you are playing tragedy; you can sit all day and emote for hours, but you can't be funny and spontaneous. I always felt that I could have done the Sulka scene better if I hadn't been so physically tired by the time we really shot it."

One of the supporting actors in the film was the veteran Lucille Watson. Watson wrote a parody of Edmund Goulding's style of directing. Apparently, Webb wasn't the only one who didn't care for Goulding's directing style. "As we all know, he [Goulding] loved to act every part, which, for me personally, was very confusing as I had my character well defined, having known in Paris the four different men that Somerset Maugham had woven the character around." Webb said that he thought Watson's parody was highly amusing and "explain[ed] exactly what happened on the set. He had everybody entranced but me, and I'm afraid I remained cold to this type of thing to the very end."

RAZOR'S EDGE: FIRST IMPRESSION
May I be you? Thanks, chum!
Look, I'm Gene. See, here I come . . .
The music plays . . . Tum-tum, tum-tum;
I'm very beautiful . . . Look, here I go . . .
(This is not acting, it is just to show.)

The music plays, "Spring Flowers"
Tra-la! This is Ty Powers'
Entrance. Here we "Pam"
May I be you? See, here I am,
And here is Maugham . . .
Bartlet, may I be you?

Clifton, my pet, it's warm,
You're in a stew.
Where's the old woman?
Oh, I beg your pardon!
See, I'm Lucille, here in the garden.

The music plays, the breezes flutter.
No, no . . . no! This is not Utter
McKinley! We're at a dance!
This is Chicago, we are not in France.
(The bloody fool! I hate
The Common Man! I'm more alive
Than he at twenty-two, I'm fifty-five.)
But don't mind me . . . I have a "limey" voice;
I was a butcher-boy, but not from choice!
Ah, well! May I be you? Thanks, here I go . . .
(This is not acting, it is just to show.)

In late May of 1946, Webb was working on *The Razor's Edge* when he became ill. "I was taken with a chill, but I continued to work. On the thirtieth I came down with pneumonia and was taken to the Cedars of Lebanon Hospital. While I was in the hospital, I kept getting word from the studio. I told them I thought it was much better for me to do the death scene there. They could shoot it right there in my hospital room very easily, because that was the last scene in the picture.

"On June 24, I shot the death scene, which we only did once. When I had finished doing it, all the stage hands and electricians, property boys, and the entire company there, applauded, which pleased me greatly."

The beauty of Webb's performance as the esthete bachelor Elliott Templeton is that, although he played a detestable character, he never became detestable. It was a role that fit him well, much as the Lydecker character in *Laura*. The difference was that Templeton is an obviously gay man who is markedly effeminate and who entertains using his sister as a substitute for a spouse.

It was probably the deathbed scene that nailed down Webb's second Oscar nomination. It is the highlight of the film. He created a beautiful characterization of the dying egocentric Elliott Templeton. He is shown in his bed wearing silk pajamas, lying on an embroidered pillow with the letters "E. T." prominently displayed. He discovers that he has just received an unexpected invitation to a party from Princess Novemali (played by Cobina Wright Jr.), his old nemesis. He dictates a reply: "Mr. Elliott Templeton regrets he can not accept Princess Novemali's kind invitation owing to a previous engagement with his blessed Lord." There is a slight pause and then he says, "The old witch!"

It was in this scene, more than any other, that Webb managed to make Templeton's insufferable snobbery curiously poignant. Apart from Webb's brilliant performance as Elliott Templeton, the movie was not generally well received. Pauline Kael called it "almost as irresistibly funny and terrible as *The Fountainhead.*" However, she was kind to Webb. She said, "Clifton Webb does a memorable high camp number as an expatriate snob." Despite mixed reviews, *The Razor's Edge* was one of the highest grossing movies of the year. It garnered four Oscar nominations. Webb was nominated for Best Supporting Actor; Anne Baxter was nominated for Best Supporting Actress. The film also received nominations for Best Art Direction and Best Picture. Only Baxter won. However, both Webb and Baxter won Golden Globes. Thus, after making just three pictures since his return to Hollywood, Webb received two Oscar nominations, a Golden Globe, and a Critic's Award.

After the release of *The Razor's Edge*, Noel Coward's representative, Jack Wilson, approached Webb to appear in Coward's *Present Laughter*. Wilson told Webb that if he would do it, Coward would release the play for America.

Webb said, "I decided I thought it would be a very wise thing to do to get back to the stage. So, I had him send it to me. I read it and thought it very amusing. Noel had been playing it in London with great success. Noel wrote it for himself, about himself, which he sometimes denied. Nevertheless it's true. After a great deal of communication, I decided I'd do it. On July 5, I left for Arrowhead Springs, to study my script. Sunday afternoons were charming, playing croquet at the Zanucks in the afternoon, staying on for dinner and seeing a picture afterwards.

"On July 25, I gave a farewell dinner at Romanoff's for the Zanucks and Frances and Samuel Goldwyn. On July 27, I left for New York. I'd called Grace Moore, asking if I could have her apartment at the Savoy Plaza. That was arranged. I was besieged with the press department of Twentieth Century Fox for interviews. They started publicity on *The Razor's Edge*. Every minute of the day was taken up with it.".

Webb was startled at what had happened to New York in the short time he'd been gone. "When we arrived in New York after fourteen months in California, I realized that a tremendous change had taken place. People were hurrying to get nowhere. Traffic was impossible. If one would try to walk on the streets, you would be bumped into. I thought then, 'Time has made a change.' I realized it was no longer the New York that I had known for so many years. A certain hysteria prevailed. Broadway looked like Coney Island. I said to myself, 'I don't think I could ever live here again.'"

Webb helped in the casting of *Present Laughter*. He said, "I sat one day in the Empire Theatre listening to sixty young men read for the part of the mad poet. I was startled at how little talent there was. On September 3 [1946], we started rehearsals. On September 24, we went to Wilmington to open. We opened September 26 at the Dupont Theatre."

Shortly after the play opened, Webb began to get signals that all was not right with this production.

"Tallulah Bankhead, who was staying with Mrs. Carpenter in Wilmington, came to see the play. They had been to the races all day, and I fancy had one or two Southern Comforts. She laughed so loud in the oddest places that the audience paid almost more attention to her than they did to us on the stage. After the play we went to Mrs. Carpenter's for supper. Jack Wilson and two or three members of the cast went with us. When we walked in, Tallulah greeted me with a charming remark, 'Well, how does it feel to stink up the stage?'

"I didn't quite know how to take this, but I thought it best to laugh it off. She then proceeded to announce to all of us how much she disliked the play, and how bad the direction was. I felt this was a very stupid thing for her to do before minor members of the cast. If she had anything to say, she should have said it to Jack Wilson and me, privately. When we left, I don't think the other members of the cast had been swept off their feet by Miss Bankhead."

Critics did not praise the play but were kind to Webb. In fact, he said, "I came off with flying colors. It was a very difficult play to play. It should have been played by people with great facility. Such, I'm afraid, was not the case." Apparently, the problem was the cast, particularly the minor players, who caricatured their roles too sharply. This prevented Webb from properly highlighting the piece. As far as the play itself, one critic said, "It is an excellent illustration of the miracles that can be performed with a soap bubble. The play is not even good theatre, yet it is entertaining theatre, and offers one of the most delightful experiences of the season."

Present Laughter moved to Boston, and it was there that Webb became ill with the flu. He missed five performances. Since he had no understudy, the theatre went dark. His doctor told him he didn't want to take any chance since there was a New York opening staring him in the face. Webb managed to play a Saturday matinee and a Saturday night in "a very weakened condition."

While in Boston, Webb and Jack Wilson began to work on how to allot seats for the New York opening. Webb said, "As usual, telegrams and telephone messages had been coming in right and left from various people wanting us to be sure to put them down on the first night list, and also, as always, everybody wanted to be in the front row." After much soul-searching, Webb and Wilson managed to come up with a plan to allot the seats for opening night.

The gala opening came and, as is the custom, everybody was supposed to be in their seats by 8:40 pm. But Webb said, "At 8:40 all our delightful friends, over whom we had taken a great deal of trouble, I'm sure were still sitting in the Colony telling one another how too, too divine everything was. We held the curtain twenty minutes. The critics were there, beginning to chew their fingernails. We rang up five minutes past nine, and when I came on stage about five minutes after the opening, all of our delicious little pals, the pretties swathed in rich furs and warm jewels, came streaming down the aisles, chattering at the top of their voices, waving to one another, making dates to meet one another later at '21,' stepping over people, and completely disregarding what was going on on the stage."

Webb said he and the other cast members could hardly hear the dialogue being spoken. "All in all, it was the most disgraceful behavior I have ever seen in the theatre." The next day Webb was delighted to find that this unbelievable behavior did not go unnoticed by the critics. Brooks Atkinson devoted an entire paragraph to their shameful behavior, as did critic John Chapman.

Webb wrote to Noel Coward, giving him the gruesome details of the Broadway opening. Coward replied in a letter dated November 13, 1946.

Dearest Mr. W.

I adored your letter, Oh dear what a rousing 8th dimensional fuck-pig that first night must have been. My heart has been bleeding for you so much that I have had to have transfusions. I am so sorry to tell you that there isn't a working script. I just went flipping about in my insouciant butterfly way doing whatever came into my feathery little head, but I never chased Roland Maule [a talentless playwright in *Present Laughter*] round the stage so Dwight [Wiman] must be out of his mind (at least I don't think I did). I may have chased him down stage a little. Obviously the thing to go after in the rest of the cast, above everything else, is speed and attack but you know that as well as I do. I so long to see you play it and who knows there may be a slight chance of me coming over in the New Year but this is in no way certain.

I am now in the middle of rehearsals and so far everything is going beautifully. Mary [Mary Martin] is perfectly enchanting and I think will knock them cold. Everything is under control and I am looking if possible prettier than ever. I am doing my hair in a new way. People complain that it makes me look a bit too chocolate boxy but that is of course personal jealousy.

Give my dearest love to wicked Gold Tooth [Mabelle] and a great deal to yourself.

The crosses following this sentence denote mad, moist, tempestuous kisses.

X X X X X X X

N.C.

In the letter Coward is referring to his musical *Pacific 1860*, which opened in December 1946 and starred, in her British debut, Mary Martin with Graham Payn. The play was one of Coward's few flops.

Coward did make it to America in the new year. He arrived on February 3, 1947, and promptly came to see the performance. Webb said, "The entire cast was very nervous, as well as myself. After the show I waited for him at the door leading from the orchestra under the stage. I introduced him to the cast and went to my dressing room. He had come with Neysa McMein and Hope Williams. He suddenly bounded into my dressing room, white around the gills, and in a raging temper he said, 'How dare Jack do that to me?' He said he'd never seen such a cast in all his life, and how I managed to play with them was beyond his imagination.

He said he understood why the critics had laced into the play, the way it was being played. I told him it hadn't been an easy job for me. Also, I told him what Guthrie McClintic had said when he'd seen the show, which was, 'He wouldn't have acted with them. He would have shot them!'

"Afterwards we went to supper at Margaret Case's, of *Vogue* magazine, and Noel then took Jack Wilson in one of the bedrooms and proceeded to lace into him. Jack came out looking rather warm and said he'd better go home. After this upset, he hied himself off to Palm Beach."

In his diary, Noel Coward spoke of his displeasure with the American production of *Present Laughter*. He said, "Went to *Present Laughter*. A gruesome evening. Clifton was excellent, lacking in fire and virility but compensating by comedy technique. The production of the play was lamentable. The cast was tatty and fifth rate."

Although Coward was outwardly complimentary on Webb's performance, his secretary Cole Lesley, in his book *Remembered Laughter*, had a different take. Lesley said it was in America "where Clifton Webb first played Garry Essendine in *Present Laughter* as waspish and bitchy. Garry is a larger than life portrait of Noel, written by himself, which does give a good if exaggerated idea of what he was like to live with, and his relations with 'those around him.' Garry is quite funny enough as he is, without adding venom that is not there, and Noel disliked Clifton's portrayal very much indeed."

In their *About Town* column, New York critics Babette and Judith Brimberg said, "In portraying a typically Coward character, Clifton Webb is so supremely competent that one is tempted to consider *Present Laughter* the new Webb play. There are perhaps a dozen actors and actresses who possess that rare quality of stage presence, and Mr. Webb is one of these. His unspoken appearance in a scene is enough to lift it off its feet; his gestures and mannerisms, his delivery of dialogue could not be more perfect."

Nevertheless, Webb was devastated by this experience and said, "It was during these days that I made up my mind that I was no longer stage struck, and that the theatre I had been in all my life and had loved so dearly had no more allure for me." He never again appeared in a stage production.

The Razor's Edge was now close to opening in New York. Webb said, "Great publicity had been started via the newspapers and radio and enormous billboards were all over town, about the opening of *The Razor's Edge*. It was to open at the Roxy on November 19, which happened to be my birthday. [This was Webb's fifty-seventh birthday.]

"My plan, as I wanted to be at this gala event, was to close *Present Laughter* on that night. The opening of the film was to be a strictly invitational affair. Valentina [Schlee] designed a new frock for Mabelle to wear at the opening. Three telephones never stopped all day long with people calling up asking if I couldn't use my influence to try and get them an invitation. I was told that I had to be ready about 7:30 p.m., as I was to be picked up by a large car, with a guard. I had planned to give a small dinner beforehand at the Colony, but found that impossible. So, I arranged for Jack and Natasha Wilson to dine with Mabelle and me approximately at 6:45 pm. I ordered a large and expensive dinner. Mabelle arrived on time and waited and waited. I tried to calm my nerves with a couple of vodkas. Natasha suddenly arrived alone with the news that Jack had fallen asleep at his osteopath's."

This was Webb's first big film premiere. Neither *Laura* nor *The Dark Corner* had an opening that approached the extravaganza that was about to unfold before Webb's astonished eyes.

"Everybody one ran into seemed to be going to the opening. In fact, that was all anybody was talking about. Jack eventually arrived at a quarter past seven. The expensive Chateaubriand was brought on. The champagne was about to be poured, when suddenly I saw myself being summoned by my escort, in the person of a guard, furnished by Twentieth Century Fox. So, Mabelle, dripping with orchids and ermine, and I rushed out. We got into the car provided by Fox with the chauffeur, a guard, and escort. And we were whisked over to the offices on West Fifty-sixth Street, where they were to wait for the signal telling us what time we were supposed to start in this vast parade to the Roxy Theatre.

"It had been arranged that all traffic from Forty-ninth Street to Fifty-second Street on Seventh Avenue was to be rerouted. The block above and the block below the Roxy Theatre had great planks put up to keep the gaping public back. Searchlights were flashing in the sky from every direction. When we got to the Roxy and started to turn left so that I could be seen by television and movie cameras, making a grand entrance, something went wrong with the traffic scheme. We were told to continue to Sixth Avenue. This upset the little man driving us considerably, who kept repeating he knew he'd lose his job as I was supposed to be on the air at eight o'clock. I, having had no dinner, decided to relax and let come what may. So, down forty-ninth we drove, back to Broadway, up Broadway, crowds screaming and yelling, kids jumping on the running board of the car, people being pushed aside by the mounted police. We finally arrived in front of the Roxy Theatre and were hustled

10.5. Clifton Webb and his mother, Mabelle, at a premiere, with Mabelle "looking like Clifton in drag." The David L. Smith Collection.

through the crowds. Newsreel cameras were grinding and loud speakers were announcing the arrival of the various personalities. I was rushed to a microphone, where I told thousands of eager listeners how glamorous the whole thing was; how delighted I was to be there, when personally I'd much rather have been sitting in a bar with a hamburger and a glass of beer. Mabelle was every inch the delighted mother and took on a rapturous expression which refused to come off."

Webb and Mabelle were rushed up to some private offices in the theatre building. Webb said, "Tyrone was there, and Gene Tierney. I was offered a drink, but settled for a Hershey bar. We all talked on the telephone to Darryl Zanuck, who was at Palm Springs eagerly awaiting the returns as they came in. We were then taken to our respective seats by our guard, and the picture began to unfold. I must say I was delighted at the response of the audience when I first appeared on the screen, and my death scene brought forth a round of applause. Just before the final fade-out, I was tapped on the shoulder. Mabelle and I were hustled out by our guard through a side entrance and into a waiting car. As we were walking up the aisle, the lights suddenly went up and the people began to pour out. There was a certain silence pervading the air, the type of silence, when one is theatre-wise, has a certain ominous significance. I felt instinctively that the great and near-great had not liked it very much, which disappointed me heartily, as I felt that Darryl Zanuck had done a courageous thing in putting Maugham's story on the screen."

Webb's instinct after he heard the audience reaction to the film proved to be correct. Howard Barnes of the *New York Herald Tribune* wrote, "At its best, this 20th Century Fox production has a dramatic depth which is rarely explored in Hollywood." On the other hand, Bosley Crowther said, "Tyrone Power, who returns in this picture after a long war service career, tries exceedingly hard to play a 'good' man on little more than frequent statements that he is. His face glows like Mr. Sunshine's and he affects a sublime serenity. . . . Goodness is back and Mr. Power has got it. At least that's what it says."

Despite critical reviews, the picture did very well at the box office. The fact that it featured a star-studded cast and was a sumptuous production certainly had something to do with its monetary success. One can only wonder, if George Cukor had directed and Somerset Maugham's screenplay had been used, how much better would the film have been?

After the premiere, Webb and Mabelle went to the Plaza Hotel, where he had arranged a birthday party for himself. "I had four tables reserved for my particular guests. There were about three hundred people. Emil Coleman's orchestra was there. Among my guests were Vincent Astor and his lovely wife, Minnie. He presented me with a charming old English snuffbox. Mr. and Mrs. Cornelius Dresselhuys had a large birthday cake waiting for me. Everybody was most complimentary about my performance in the picture. Champagne flowed like water. Emil Coleman struck up a Cole Porter tune, and Gene Tierney and I opened the dancing. But, I'm afraid I could think of nothing but that I had no dinner. Also, I realized that I had a matinee to play the next day.

"At the given moment the lights were turned out, and Emile Coleman struck up 'Happy Birthday' and an enormous birthday cake was wheeled in, fortunately, with only one candle. The entire group sang 'Happy Birthday' and I managed to blush modestly. As Mabelle and I made our way to our hotel, the thought flashed through my mind that I was well over twenty-one and still hadn't seen the day, fortunately, when I was having to sell cigarettes."

In February 1947, Clifton Webb learned he had been nominated for Best Performance by a Supporting Actor for *The Razor's Edge*. He said, "I was very thrilled at this, but I didn't particularly like the phrase, which I have never approved of, at least the word 'supporting,' because I don't consider the part of Elliott Templeton a supporting part. I contended then, which I have continued to cry from the hilltops, they should change their phraseology to 'the best character performance' as against 'the best supporting role.'"

On March 13, 1947, the Academy of Motion Pictures Arts and Sciences presented their Oscars. Webb was not able to attend because he was still on the road with *Present Laughter*. He said, "I listened to it over the radio. The next day I received the following wires from Virginia and Darryl Zanuck:

Dear Clifton:

Although it did not bring you an award, you would have been thrilled by the applause that greeted your name at the Academy affair. It's unfortunate that you were up against a popular military figure (Harold Russell for *The Best Years of Our Lives*), and while I do not want to take anything away from him, it goes without saying that the finest performance of the year was given by Eddie Goulding's protege, Clifton.
Darryl

Then from Mrs. Zanuck:

Dear Clifton:

I am sure my disappointment in last night's award was far greater than yours, and everyone here feels the same as I do. When the cut was run on the screen of you doing your last scene, the applause was terrific. It was unfortunate you were up against a veteran whose sympathy became a personal thing with many who voted for him. I definitely think he should have a special award. Well, anyway, honey, you were not in *The Best Years*, but you gave the best performance of the year. All my love and hope you can visit us in Palm Springs before the season closes. The weather is divine, and we miss you.
Love to Mabelle.
Devotedly, Virginia.

Webb lost to non-actor Harold Russell, who in *The Best Years of Our Lives* played a part patterned after his own experience, a war veteran who lost both arms below the elbow.

Webb did receive another award from the Hollywood Foreign Correspondents Association. He said, "I was given the Golden Globe Award, symbolizing the press of the world, mounted on a polished granite column with the name and achievement of each winner engraved on a gold panel, encircling the base of the stately trophy." Douglas Fairbanks Jr. was the master of ceremonies and presented the award. Webb was unable to accept the award personally since he was still appearing on Broadway.

CHAPTER 11

A Top Box-Office Draw

Clifton Webb knew that someday Darryl Zanuck would bring a script to him that would require him to put his dancing shoes back on. He had made the mistake of exhibiting his dancing ability at a few parties. These impromptu exhibitions seemed to prove that "there was still life in the old legs." In November 1946 Webb received a letter from Zanuck with a script for a musical he wanted Webb to do.

"It was called *Dancing in the Dark*. Zanuck had purchased the music by Arthur Schwartz from the revue *The Bandwagon*, in which Fred Astaire and his sister, Adele, starred in 1931. He asked if I'd consider doing it. He thought it a magnificent part. He'd be very grateful if I would consider it as he was short of product."

Zanuck asked Webb to read the script, stating that he thought it could be a "sensational starring role" for him. However, Zanuck said that due to a Technicolor commitment, he did not think they could hold the starting date beyond January. He asked if Webb could return to Hollywood, or if he had to stay with the play through the winter season.

"He didn't realize that I had a run of the play contract that had to run until the first of June, so I wired back that I had to stay. I wasn't very anxious to do a dancing picture anyway. However, he sent me the script, which I thought was fairly good. So, I wired him that I would do it, but I couldn't give him any idea when the play was going to close, as we were doing an enormous business at that time."

It was eventually arranged that Webb would do *Dancing in the Dark*. He was told to report in California on May 26. He was rather pleased to get word that he would be back in Hollywood.

"I was getting tired and bored with the play, and suddenly during the matinee the thought flashed through my mind, 'What am I doing all this hard work for? California and pictures is the best place for me.'"

Present Laughter closed March 15, 1947. As much as he enjoyed the stage, he had come to the realization that a play was much harder work than making a movie. He decided he needed a rest before reporting to the studio.

"I was tired and weary from carrying the weight of the play on my shoulders. So, I decided to take a little holiday before going to California. I arranged through a great friend of mine, Mimi Brand, to take a couple of apartments in Del Rey Beach, which is just far enough away from Palm Beach to be safe. Terence Rattigan, the playwright [*Oh Mistress Mine*], along with Lynn and Alfred Lunt, Beatrice Lillie, Dorothy Dickson, and myself, all left for a holiday. For two weeks we had a madly amusing time."

Webb said he did not get much rest on this "vacation" but did have a "great deal of fun." Before returning to New York, Webb and Mabelle went to Greenwich, where they started packing furniture to be put in storage.

"I realized that my Greenwich life was over. The people that were instrumental in my building there were of the past, the Wimans were divorced, and Libby Holman was nothing but a memory. I decided there was no point in my holding on to the place any longer. I felt very sad when I saw everything being put in boxes and crates, as I had given a great deal of care and thought to the creating of my home. On May 6, 1947, when the last bag had been put in the station wagon, Mabelle and I drove off, and I never turned back."

Shortly after returning to Hollywood, Webb found that the picture industry had "gone into a great slump and all the studios became panicky. The story for *Dancing in the Dark* had been completely changed." He found the title of the film was now *Julie*. On June 10, the movie was cancelled. Webb said, "I can't say that I was too bitterly disappointed." He then experienced a period of inactivity for which he was still getting paid. He said, "Although I was collecting a handsome salary every week, I would have preferred to have been working."

The story of *Dancing in the Dark* and *The Bandwagon* are intertwined. Although *Dancing in the Dark* (which was a song in *The Bandwagon*) was not filmed at this point, it did become a Fox musical in 1949. The story line concerned the efforts of a studio's production head to film a revue called *The Bandwagon*. The production head was named Crossman, which was Darryl Zanuck's pseudonym (Melville Crossman). Crossman, played by Adolphe Menjou, sends a conceited has-been actor to New York to sign up a potential young star for the big film. Presumably, Clifton Webb would have played the conceited actor, but instead the role was given to William Powell.

Webb was correct in saying he wasn't "too bitterly disappointed" in not playing the Powell role. The plot was rather silly and *Dancing in the Dark* is now considered a minor entry in the history of Fox musicals. In 1953, MGM made a film of *The Bandwagon* that originally appeared on Broadway in 1931. The Broadway production was notable to say the least. Arthur Schwartz and Howard Dietz composed the music. Hassard Short again proved his mastery by creating a series of spectacular moods and effects. George S. Kaufman provided the skits and Fred and Adele Astaire lit up the stage with their dance routines. The result was a smash revue.

Thus it was not a stretch for MGM to decide to make this wonderful revue into a film musical. Clifton Webb was originally scheduled to play the part of Jeffrey Cordova, a Broadway director. Fred Astaire and Cyd Charisse were the other leads. In his autobiography, Vincente Minnelli, who directed *The Bandwagon*, said, "Clifton Webb was originally offered the part. He opted instead for the role of John Philip Sousa in *Stars and Stripes Forever*. Clifton suggested Jack [Buchanan], a great English music hall star, for the part. We took him up on the suggestion, for we sensed Jack could supply the impulsive, scatter-brained explosiveness we were looking for."

Webb was anxious to play John Philip Sousa in *Stars and Stripes Forever* (1952), and immediately following that came *Titanic* (1953). Both of these pictures were major productions. If Webb had accepted the role in *The Bandwagon*, it would have been necessary to "loan" him to MGM since he was a Fox property. But perhaps one of the primary drawbacks for Webb was the fact he had not danced professionally for several years. Undoubtedly, he was not too keen about dusting off his dancing shoes to compete with Fred Astaire. Buchanan was good but one can only imagine what it would have been like to see Astaire and Webb together doing such numbers as "I Guess I'll Have to Change My Plan," a song Webb introduced in *The Little Show* in 1929.

In early September of 1947, Webb received a call from a friend who was in "the literary world." "He telephoned me from New York telling me that he had just read the galley proof of a book called *Mr. Belvedere*. He told me the story roughly. It was about an author/writer who hires himself out as a babysitter. He told me that I should go to Zanuck and have them buy it for me. I followed through on this the next day. I told him what I had heard, and he began to laugh. I asked him why the hysteria, and he said he'd bought it five weeks ago for Monty Wooley. There was a pregnant pause, and I asked him if he had a gun handy, and he laughed a little more and said, 'You silly so and so, we bought it for you.' That was indeed good news. He had an advance copy of it and gave it to me to read, which I promptly did. I realized it would make a swell picture."

It would not only make a "swell picture," but usher in a whole new image for Webb. After playing consecutive "nasties" in *Laura*, *The Dark Corner*, and *The Razor's Edge*, here was a chance to play a somewhat nasty but loveable babysitter. Although the budget was not very big, Fox put some good people to work on it.

"F. Hugh Herbert, considered the top-flight comedy writer in these parts, was put to work on the script; and Walter Lang, one of Twentieth Century's ace directors, was going to direct it. I was sent the first rough draft, and I realized it was a great opportunity for me. As time went on, I had long sessions with Walter Lang about how it should be played. I also took the liberty of changing a few of the lines. Walter was in complete agreement with everything I suggested. I then thought it would be a very good idea to get a crew cut, as I didn't want to look like the usual writer, with long, flowing hair. In other words, I wanted to play him against what people usually expect a writer to look like. When I suggested this to Darryl Zanuck, he was not a little amazed, but after I explained why I thought it was a good idea, he saw the point and was highly enthusiastic."

Zanuck was sold on the Belvedere character. He could smell the money. He said, "We have a sensational character in Belvedere . . . original, fresh, wonderful. This is a perfect setup." What made it perfect was that they could have Belvedere do almost anything and still be believable. Zanuck said, "The wonderful thing about Mr. Belvedere is his superior attitude, his sureness, and it is amazing that an audience will completely believe whatever he tells them. He can tell them that he taught jujitsu in Tokyo, that he was at San Juan Hill with Teddy Roosevelt or the South Pole with Byrd or that he taught Houdini how to get out of a straightjacket. . . . [W]hatever it is, the audience is willing and eager to accept."

In keeping with Webb's vision of Belvedere, he got his haircut, after which everyone on the set referred to him as "Butch" Webb.

Shooting started on October 29, 1947. Webb was told he should meet the smallest child right away so that he wouldn't be frightened when he first saw him. Webb remembered, "My effect on him was exactly the opposite, and from the day we started to work he was my pal and buddy. He was eighteen months old."

11.1. Clifton "Butch" Webb, aka Mr. Belvedere. Twentieth Century Fox photo. The David L. Smith Collection.

Roddy McCaskill played the little boy in this film. This was McCaskill's first film, but he eventually made five films; one was *Cheaper by the Dozen*, which again starred Clifton Webb. There were two other boys in the film, age six and nine. Webb was a little apprehensive about working with children.

"My first day of shooting, having had no experience with children, I was rather nervous because they are not too easy to work with. In the afternoon of the first day, I had to do a scene with the two older boys. In this particular scene, the six-year-old had to sit on the stairs and groan from a stomachache. We went over and over and over, and Walter Lang couldn't get him to give the impression he really had a stomachache. By the time we had done the scene twelve times, and it came to one of my speeches, I forgot a word and had to stop. Much to my surprise, the young man over whom we were wasting all this time gave me my word. I think that was one of the most embarrassing moments of my life."

Webb had never met Maureen O'Hara. He said he had heard she was difficult to get along with. Webb was pleasantly surprised when he discovered this was not true. He said, "I was prepared for the worst. To the contrary, I found her most affable, willing, and helpful. The same

11.2. The oatmeal scene from *Sitting Pretty* (1948) with Clifton Webb and Roddy McCaskill. Courtesy of The Academy of Motion Picture Arts and Sciences.

goes for Robert Young, who is a first-class trouper in every sense of the word."

Webb's next scene with the youngest child became one of the most famous in cinematic history. It was the day he was supposed to dump the bowl of oatmeal on the child's head.

"Everyone was very much afraid he was going to raise hell, and kick and scream and yell. So, they tied the chair—nailed the chair to the floor, tied him in the chair, removed all the cutlery and dishes from in front of him, tied the bowl to his head, and began to pour mush all over him. Instead of crying, he began to laugh, as he was enjoying it thoroughly and kept turning to me and saying the one word that he knew, 'Man.'

"We didn't know what to do. I pretended to scold him, and he continued laughing. The director scolded him, the assistant director scolded him, but to no avail. They were all stumped. As a final resort they turned out all the lights on the stage, and his mother called 'good-bye' to him. With this, he began to cry and they took a sound track."

Webb as Belvedere never accounts for his indifference to women and marriage. In one scene he encounters the always-prissy Richard Haydn. Haydn plays his usual self, flitting from flower to flower, lips pursed, speech affected, and hands fluttering. Haydn, as Charlie Appleton, stops Belvedere on the street and offers him a job in his household. Later, talking to Tacey (Maureen O'Hara), Belvedere explains why he refused the job.

"I shall soon be famous for writing a novel based on a fictionalized Hummingbird Hill, and it would not do for me to be discovered living with that man. Wouldn't look well at all. I might get myself branded as one of those. Do I make myself clear?"

This seems to be a declaration that Belvedere is not a homosexual or at least does not wish to be identified as such. Webb said of Belvedere, "You don't know anything about him at all. You can't put him in any pigeon-hole and that's what's intriguing." The same might be said of Webb.

The film took seven weeks to finish. Webb remembered the making of the picture fondly. "We worked in complete accord and harmony. As I look back upon that, I look back on it as the most pleasant engagement I have ever had, either in the theatre or on the screen." The film wrapped on December 16, 1947. Webb said the cast and crew were all very sad at having to leave one another.

Webb realized that he had done well with his first three films, but he was still concerned about how wide an appeal he had. "You see, I am not the formula. I don't fall in any particular category. I haven't looks. I'm not young. I am, in short, neither glamour boy nor gunman, neither dreamboat nor Boris Karloff." In his first three films, he played, as he described it, "unpleasant characters unlikely to put a Clifton Webb fan club on the boil." He therefore began to think of *Sitting Pretty* as a breakthrough film that would widen his popularity. He said, "It remained, in short, for Mr. Belvedere to make of me that one touch of nature that makes the whole world kin."

Webb described the night he attended the first preview of *Sitting Pretty:* "At my first entrance on the screen, the preview audience eked out a few uneasy laughs . . . very few. I thought, 'Oh-oh!' We arrived at the breakfast table scene and I could feel the audience feeling . . . here he comes! He's going to murder the baby! I did not, due to the limitations of the script, murder the baby; and after that, it was one perfectly mad explosion of mirth after another. Mr. Belvedere had been gathered to the bosom of his fans!"

Sitting Pretty was a huge hit. It was shot for a reputed $1,300,000. It eventually grossed over $4,000,000 in the United States alone. One poll voted it the year's most popular movie. It did what Webb hoped it would. He was nominated for an Oscar for best actor. It was the first and only time he would receive a best actor nomination. He lost to his good friend Laurence Olivier for his role as Hamlet. F. Hugh Herbert won the Writer's Guild of America award for his screenplay from the book by Gwen Davenport.

After seeing the film Noel Coward said, "[Webb] is really very good indeed and the picture is amusing if a trifle common." *Time* magazine seemed puzzled by the Belvedere character. Here was a character who coated his dialogue with a "chilly relish" but also manifested a "generally swishy aplomb." In his first three pictures, Webb was a character actor. In *Sitting Pretty* he became a star.

Sitting Pretty spawned two sequels, *Mr. Belvedere Goes to College* (1949) and *Mr. Belvedere Rings the Bell* (1951). The latter film was an adaptation of Robert E. McEnroe's play, *The Silver Whistle*.

Mr. Belvedere Goes to College marked Shirley Temple's return to Fox after a nine-year absence. She took second billing to Webb, who, as Lynn Belevedere, discovers he needs a college degree in order to qualify for an award.

There is an interesting side note to this film. A scene in the film required Mr. Belvedere to play the piano. As he is playing, he is asked, "Beethoven?" And he replies, "No, Belvedere." When Webb saw this scene in the script, he said to director Elliot Nugent, "We could play it true to type and use the concerto I wrote." Nugent asked, "Do you write music too?" Webb replied, "Certainly." Webb arranged to play his concerto for Nugent and music director Alfred Newman. Both agreed it was perfect for the film. Webb told them he had written it many years ago as a tribute to Jeanne Eagels, to whom he was greatly devoted. He named it "Rain," after her greatest stage play. He said he hadn't written it down yet, but could if he wanted to. Thus the concerto Webb plays in this film was his own composition.

Critic John Bainbridge wrote in *Life* magazine, "Mr. Belvedere is a piece of pure Americana. He is an elegant addition to U.S. folkfore." Another reviewer commented, "The film gets its comedic value almost entirely from Webb's presence."

The Belvedere character was an endearing one, and there were several attempts to cash in on its notoriety. Webb was offered a television series based on the character. In a 1961 interview, Webb said, "I've done almost everything there is to do in show business. The only thing I haven't tackled is television. I was offered part ownership in a *Mr. Belvedere* TV series, but turned it down. They made two pilots with other actors but they never sold them. Frankly, I didn't want to work that hard, and I realize no one can come up with a good script every week."

Webb had very few appearances on television. He did appear on *Ed Sullivan's Toast of the Town* three times: 1953, 1955, and 1957.

After three films, Webb became weary of the Belvedere character. He said, "I must say the character of Belvedere swept the world. I played him three times in films. I don't ever expect to play him again."

In 1956, Reginald Gardiner did a *Belvedere* pilot for Fox. Nothing came of it. In 1965, Victor Borge shot a pilot for a *Belvedere* television series. The pilot was aired but no series evolved. In 1985, a television series entitled *Mr. Belvedere* starred British actor Christopher Hewitt. It ran for about five years.

By now, Webb was on solid footing at Twentieth Century Fox. In 1950, he and Betty Grable were the only Twentieth Century Fox performers on the *Motion Picture Herald*'s roster of "Top Ten Money-Making Stars." He was now a proven moneymaker and, as such, was considered a certifiable "star." A star is someone who *opens*. When a movie opens and no one comes, then "it didn't open." Because he had become a favorite of moviegoers, Clifton Webb's movies always seemed to open. Additionally, his pictures didn't cost much to make. Zanuck liked him for the aforesaid reasons, but he also liked him as a person.

Zanuck carved out a contract for Webb that was one of the best in Hollywood. In 1951, Zanuck tore up Webb's old contract and gave him a new fourteen-year deal. At age sixty, Webb was committed to do two pictures a year for the length of his contract. Reflecting about how the contract came into being, Webb said it was "one of those heaven-sent deals. It was Zanuck's idea, as a Christmas present. Took fourteen months to draw up too."

There is no question he was happy with his movie career. He now had no desire to return to the stage, where he toiled for more than forty years.

"When I go to plays in New York, I look up at the actors and say, 'You poor devils. You have to do the same tomorrow . . . perhaps twice if it's a Wednesday or a Saturday.' The trouble with doing a play nowadays is this: if you're in a hit, you have to play it over and over for two years or more. If you're in a flop, your ego is damaged. You can't win either way."

After just six years in Hollywood, Webb appeared on the list of the top ten box-office favorites. When a film executive patted him on the back and said, "Well I don't suppose you'll be speaking to us now that you've

11.3. Party time with Gilbert Roland and Constance Bennett. The John and Betsy Neylon Collection.

had this big success," Webb replied haughtily, "My dear man, I have always been a success. One more will not unsettle me in the slightest."

After reluctantly leaving their house in Greenwich, Webb and Mabelle rented a house in Hollywood. They soon regretted their haste. Webb said, "I rented it sight unseen. Had I seen it, I'm sure I would never have made such a mistake. I gave several dinners in the house.

"The dining room always caused a great deal of laughter, for it was furnished very much like a French bordello. The walls were mirrors, great candelabra, and very bad imitation French furniture. Everybody who saw it went into screams of laughter. When the candles were lighted, the reflections in the mirrors gave it the appearance of some early Shubert revue."

Webb and Mabelle continued to go to lunches, dinners, and cocktail parties. He enjoyed some, but others he considered a "waste of time." Among those he considered worthwhile were the "charming dinners at the home of Mr. and Mrs. Samuel Goldwyn. I always felt that Frances

Goldwyn was one of the most charming hostesses. Her house is beauti-fully run, and she manages to get the right assortment of people. Also Otto Preminger, who has the happy gift of knowing how to blend his people. Every Sunday I spent with the Zanucks at their charming house in Santa Monica. Darryl had a croquet lawn built with imitation grass, that rather reminded me of one of the early Belasco productions. We would play in the afternoon, dine, and run possibly two or sometimes three pictures. It was all very pleasurable."

When the rented house became too much for him, Webb decided to look for something he could buy.

"Suddenly I got the bright idea, or perhaps it wasn't too bright, time alone will tell, that I should buy a house and settle in California. Mabelle and I looked and looked, and I had about eight real estate agents work-ing on it. I had almost given up in despair when Millicent Rogers, who had rented Tyrone Power's place, put me onto a new real estate agent.

"On July 23, 1947, I bought the first adobe house built in Beverly Hills some twenty-five years ago, at 1005 North Rexford Drive. It was owned by Gene Lockhart. Mabelle and I arrived with the agent and after a half hour we said we'd take it, a very quick sale.

"By this time Tyrone Power and Annabella had separated, much to all their friends sorrow. Tyrone found that Lana Turner was tugging at his heartstrings. I had never met her before and had only seen her in one picture, but I found her charming. On August 30, 1947, Tyrone and Lana gave a joint party at the Mocambo. It was a farewell party before he took off for South America. That, I believe, was the end of that romance."

Webb had always been a music devotee, thus, when he heard that President Truman's daughter was to give her first concert, he decided to see what kind of singer she was.

"On Saturday, August 23, 1947, I went to the Hollywood Bowl to hear Margaret Truman give her first concert. The place was filled with Helen Hokinson–type of women, who had come with granite faces and a determined desire that Margaret was going to get her just dues. [Hokin-son was a cartoonist for twenty-five years for the *New Yorker* magazine, specializing in plump and befuddled society matrons.] She opened her program with a selection by Mozart, which was a courageous thing to do. Her voice showed possibilities, but one could tell that she had been unwisely taught. Her manner was most gracious and unaffected, but one felt that she was hardly ready to appear in the Hollywood Bowl. By the end of the program, her determined, hatchet-faced supporters had dropped their eyes and found it wiser to leave quietly."

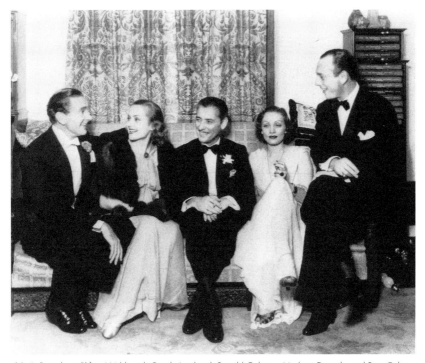

11.4. Party host Clifton Webb with Carole Lombard, Ronald Colman, Marlene Dietrich, and Russ Colum-
bo. The John and Betsy Neylon Collection.

Webb began to make some changes in his new home. He wanted to
ensure that it would be something fit for proper entertaining. He and
Mabelle were anxious to put the image of the laughable rental home
behind them. He liked the location and design of his new house but de-
tested the Spanish motif.

"On September 3, 1947, Tom Douglass, the ex-actor, who through the
years had become one of Hollywood's top decorators, and I went to my
new house to meet a gentleman whom I had been told was an architect
and whom I had engaged to make some changes for me. Walls were
taken out, windows put in, all the arches were squared, steel beams were
put in, fireplaces removed, fireplaces squared. The builder that the supposed architect brought on the job made himself very impressive, called
me by my first name, and told me how it was going to be a little bit of
heaven. Before the job was over I found, through inefficiency, it was a
little bit of hell." Before the house was finished to his satisfaction, Webb
had spent as much as the house originally cost in changing it to a more
pleasing and subdued modern design.

Webb and Mabelle moved to the Beverly Hills Hotel while their house was being renovated. "I would come over at night with a candle to try and find out what was happening to my house. Trying to rebuild a house by night and do a picture in the daytime was no easy job." Despite his difficulties, Webb managed to finish a home that became one of the most well known "party houses" in Hollywood. Everyone came to the house on Rexford Drive. Living in the eleven-room house were a secretary, his manservant/valet Romano (real name, Hoyt Grant), and a cook. He also had a pool and a tennis court.

Romano had been with Webb for quite some time. In April of 1931 the *Indianapolis Star* reported, "For the present Webb's mother, and his three dogs, Lulu, Kiki and Squealer, must suffice, not forgetting of course, his Negro valet, Ramona [*sic*]. It is Ramona's nightly duty to give Webb a rubdown and a glass of meat juice between acts of the show [*Three's a Crowd*].

Webb and Mabelle had guest books for each party and asked all guests to sign them. Some of these guest books were dated in the late 1930s, thus they reflect guests who came to Webb's parties in Greenwich and New York City. These books were part of the John and Betsy Neylon collection and the names in them were a veritable "Who's Who" in the entertainment industry. Just a partial listing of the personal signatures of those who attended these parties is staggering.

Noel Coward	Gloria Swanson
Moss Hart	Judy Garland
Jean Harlow	Mary Pickford
Clark Gable	Ray Bolger
Marlene Dietrich	Bea Lillie
Greta Garbo	Gary Cooper
Cole Porter	Joan Crawford
Dorothy Parker	Alfred Lunt
Fanny Brice	Lynn Fontanne
Humphrey Bogart	Fritz Lang
Lauren Bacall	Richard Rodgers
Irving Berlin	Helen Hayes
Laurence Olivier	Vivien Leigh

When someone praised Webb about the interesting and famous guests that were always present at his parties, he replied, "Naturally, old boy.

Fascinating people always attract fascinating people." He had a remarkable talent for friendship. No one, not even Elsa Maxwell, had a wider circle of friends, both in theatre and the *haut monde*. Someone once asked a friend to list Webb's intimates. The reply was, "The simplest way to put it is that he knows *everyone*."

In 1949, Warner Brothers was preparing to film Ayn Rand's *The Fountainhead*. King Vidor was to direct and Henry Blanke was to produce. Gary Cooper was set for the lead and Patricia Neal was to play opposite him. One important part, that of Toohey, had not been cast. Both Henry Blanke and Ayn Rand wanted Clifton Webb. However Warner Brothers refused to consider him. Warners felt he had been hugely successful in several comedies, but they believed his public would not want to see him as a villain. Finally, Robert Douglas was selected for the role. Rand said, "He was too forceful for Toohey, and too strong for the rest of the cast. He should have been slippery and snide, not so openly villainous." Rand was describing exactly how Clifton Webb would have played the part.

With the success of the *Belvedere* series, Darryl Zanuck started looking for another moneymaking vehicle for Webb. He believed that Webb's special personality and his superior acting ability might be expanded into more clear-cut heterosexual roles. He found what he thought might be just the thing in a book by Frank B. Gilbreth Jr. and his sister, Ernestine. Zanuck felt that the character of Father Gilbreth was so different from that of Lynn Belvedere that he might be able to keep Webb working in a series of similar movies. This was a time when sequels and series were popular. *Tarzan* was doing well as was the *Andy Hardy* series. Additionally, Webb made it known that he had his fill of Belvedere. He made three movies as the prissy babysitter, and it appeared the public was getting a little bored with this character. The first two *Belvedere* movies did well at the box office but the third one did not.

Adding to Webb's reticence was that, as Belvedere, he had secured a reputation for being one of the foremost child psychologists in the nation. He said, "I want to resign from that job right now." His mailbox was jammed with mail from parents wanting to know how to handle their children. "Mothers decided I knew how to handle children. Since then I have been called on for assistance in rearing the bubble gum youth of the nation. I regret to say I am a mere mortal man who knows less about children than anyone in the country."

Because of this reaction from the public, Webb looked upon his next role as the father in *Cheaper by the Dozen* with some trepidation. He said,

11.5. Webb as the fertile father in *Cheaper by the Dozen* (1950). Twentieth Century Fox photo. The David L. Smith Collection.

"With twelve children I will be expected to know even more. The fact that I am a bachelor, always have been a bachelor, and always will be is beside the point."

Before starting *Cheaper by the Dozen*, Webb was interviewed by fan magazine writer Gladys Hall. He mentioned a film he was going to make in England. "I shall play, while in England, in the film tentatively titled *21 Bow Street*." He seemed to be looking forward toward playing "the part of the obsessed murderer, an extraordinary Jekyll and Hyde character." Much to Webb's disappointment, the film was never made. Apparently Twentieth Century Fox had misgivings about Webb playing this type of part. He was now too valuable a property to allow him to do anything that might reduce his now established appeal.

Despite his protestations, Webb might have known more about child psychology than he was willing to admit. A co-worker reported, "He maintains good discipline. The kids and their stand-ins are quiet and well behaved. They call him 'Uncle Clifton' and come to him with the funny papers to read, skates to fix, and buttons to be buttoned. He talks to them as though they were adults." Webb commented, "No one has tried to burn down the stage, and no one has attempted to assassinate me with a BB gun. I like children and they like me. We get on famously. But I'll always be a bachelor."

Myrna Loy was Webb's wife in *Cheaper by the Dozen*. Loy, like Webb, had no children. Here then are two people with no personal experience raising children playing the ideal, devoted Mother and Father. It's a testament to their acting prowess that they were wonderfully believable. Loy enjoyed working with Webb, but she did have some problems. In her autobiography she said: "As a stage-trained actor of the old school, he considered scene-stealing his duty. Apparently it was kosher to do this on stage in his day. It isn't in films. You are absolutely nose-to-nose and cannot move or you've turned your partner around with the back of his head or some awkward angle to the camera.

"During one of my scenes with Clifton our cameraman Leon Shamroy suddenly hurled his hat to the floor. 'Goddamn it, Myrna! When are you going to learn? Look at your marks.' He was absolutely right. I had moved way back to keep up with Clifton. 'I've marked you both three times, but he keeps moving back on you and you don't know it!' Leon stormed off the set in utter disgust. It was a bad moment, but I went out and convinced him to come back.

"When I returned to Clifton, he was standing stock-still where I'd left him. We finished our scene without a hitch. There was no apology, no reference to Leon's outburst, but I sensed a touch of sheepishness cracking Clifton's otherwise imperturbable veneer. We had no more stage tricks, and our friendship stayed intact. I went to his house for bashes where his mother, Mabelle, who looked like Clifton in drag, held court. They used to say Clifton and Mabelle were Hollywood's happiest couple. Everybody went to their house. He was very social and very dear in his way . . . it just had to be his way."

Loy said that after she shot the touching ending where she became a widow, Webb came to watch the filming. She said, "The scene took a lot out of me, and I was resting in my dressing room when Clifton started hammering on the door. 'My dear Myrna,' he intoned, 'what are you trying to do? Take the picture away from me?'"

Cheaper by the Dozen was released in April 1950. It was one of the biggest moneymakers of the year. That same year, Clifton Webb was listed in the annual *Motion Picture* list of top box-office stars. He was number seven. Ahead of him were such people as John Wayne, Bob Hope, Bing Crosby, Betty Grable, and James Stewart. He had defied the odds. He told reporters he couldn't play murderers anymore because he would be committing professional suicide if he did. He announced, "I'm now America's sweetheart."

Since Webb's character died at the end of *Cheaper by the Dozen*, he could not make the sequel, *Belles on Their Toes* (1952). This didn't stop Darryl Zanuck from capitalizing on the success of *Cheaper by the Dozen*. He managed to talk Myrna Loy into carrying on as the determined widow. The film was able to retain enough charm to be reasonably successful at the box office.

Although Clifton Webb did not venture far from his own personality, he nevertheless managed to play a wide variety of roles. Webb has said he thoroughly enjoyed playing Clifton Webb, but he also expressed the opinion that he tired of doing the same type of character and wanted more diversity in his parts. In late 1950, writer-director George Seaton (a fellow Hoosier from South Bend, Indiana) came to Webb with a script he had written based on a play by Dorothy and Harry Segall. It was unlike anything Webb had done (unless you count his stage appearance in *Blithe Spirit* that had him talking to the ghost of his late wife). Seaton wanted Webb to play a cowboy who also happened to be an angel. The title of the movie was *For Heaven's Sake*. Seaton seemed to be attracted to supernatural stories. As a writer-director, he had already won an Oscar for *Miracle on 34th Street* (1947). He also wrote the screenplay for *A Cock-eyed Miracle* (1946), in which Frank Morgan returns from Heaven to right some of his wrongs.

Seaton thought Webb would be perfect as "Slim" Charles, an angel disguised as a crusty old cowboy. Slim is sent to earth to help find suitable parents for an unborn child. When Webb was approached by Seaton to play the role of Slim he said: "I had not anticipated such a role, not in this life at least. I always had hopes, naturally, that in the next life I might get such an assignment. My problem is in the preparation of the role. It seems that nobody knows just how an angel talks and acts."

Webb even agreed to appear on screen for the first time (other than his silent films) without his mustache. He was given a haircut that was supposed to resemble Gary Cooper's. Seaton said he watched at least two-dozen cowboy films to pick out the cowboy talk that pleased him the most. One of Webb's favorites was this: "I ain't a-lookin' for trouble stranger, but if trouble comes a-lookin' for me, I won't be hard to find." Speaking to villain Jack LaRue, Webb says, "I got a feelin' this place ain't big enough for both of us. You better take your saddlebag and git." When another bad guy makes advances toward Joan Blondell, Webb gets to

11.6. Clifton Webb as "Slim" Charles in *For Heaven's Sake* (1951). Twentieth Century Fox photo. The David L. Smith Collection.

say, "Wouldn't molest the little lady mister, if I were you." To Joan Bennett he spits out this old cliche, "Strikes me you're well worth waitin' for ma-am."

Needless to say, Webb had a lot of fun with this role. The film was certainly not a blockbuster, but it turned out to be a charming comedy with a bravura performance by Webb.

In November of 1951, Twentieth Century Fox announced that Clifton Webb would be starred in *The Ransom of Red Chief*, one of five O. Henry stories to be packaged together as a movie. The title was set as *O. Henry's Full House*. Unfortunately, Webb did not make the film. Instead, Oscar Levant played the character originally assigned to Webb. When the film was previewed for critics, it was felt that *Ransom of Red Chief* was weak. It was cut from the official premiere prints. When it was released for television in the 1960s, the sequence was restored. This incident begs the question, What if Webb had played the part instead of Levant?

Elopement, released in November of 1951, was a bit of nonsense that did not match the caliber of film upon which Webb had based his career. Webb played a successful, functional designer whose daughter (Anne Francis) elopes with William Lundigan. Along with the groom's parents, father Webb chases the fleeing couple and tries to annul the marriage. Francis would play Webb's daughter again in *Dreamboat* (1952). The latter proved to be a unique and successful satire on television. As usual, Webb received good notices for his performance in *Elopement.* One critic said the film was amusing only because of the "haughty playing of Webb."

In 1951, Gloria Swanson appeared in *Twentieth Century* on Broadway with Jose Ferrer. Swanson had been a friend of Webb's since the 1930s. Webb heard she might be coming back to Hollywood for the Oscars. In her autobiography, Swanson talked about her old friend, "We had seen a lot of each other again when I was making *Sunset Boulevard,* and since then we had stayed in close touch. He hadn't been well for the past month, but near pneumonia hadn't dulled his tongue."

Webb wrote the following note to Swanson:

> As yet I have not taken a quiet ride to Forest Lawn, but I have had one hell of a siege. . . .
>
> Now that you are the new "Baby Wampas" star on the silver sheet, "La Reine du Theatre," "Empress of the Air Waves," and the "Little Princess of Publicity," will you please saturate your beautiful body with some of that Jergens lotion and get the hell out here. I want to see you get your satiny little hand on that nude little Oscar. After it is all over we can elope to that famous Pasadena clinic and you can teach me the joys of high colonics and fruit juices.

Swanson had been doing a radio show sponsored by Jergens lotion in addition to appearing on Broadway. She wrote to Webb, assuring him they would get together when she returned.

Webb was very grateful when he was presented with another departure from the stereotypical image frequently associated with him. *Dreamboat* (1952) was a delightfully clever satire on television. It was based on a *Collier's* magazine serial entitled *The Love Man,* by John D. Weaver.

At this time, Hollywood was beginning to experience a loss of audience to television. This film provided a chance to level some derision at this burgeoning competitor. Who was more able to do this than, as critic Bosley Crowther put it, "that able exponent of loftiness and disdain . . . that master of withering sarcasm, the serene and eloquent Clifton Webb."

Webb played a long-retired silent movie idol, now a respected college professor, who wants to keep his past a secret. The role required him to

11.7. Clifton Webb as a "legionnaire," kissing Ginger Rogers in a black wig, in *Dreamboat* (1952). Twentieth Century Fox photo. The David L. Smith Collection.

be involved in several barroom brawls, wield a sword with the precision of an Errol Flynn, jockey a galloping horse through walls of fire, and leap through second-story windows—among other things. He also was given the opportunity to dance briefly with, of all people, Ginger Rogers.

In preparation for the role, Webb said it was deemed advisable for him to "undergo special athletic training." His preparation involved "doing roadwork, twirling Indian clubs, and getting battered by a medicine ball." Webb complained, "I never realized the human body was comprised of so many muscles, all sore." Fred Cavens, Hollywood's fencing master, who taught such people as Fairbanks, Flynn, and Cornel Wilde, said, "Mr. Webb was a remarkable pupil. He possesses great body coordination."

Since he was supposed to have been a silent screen actor when those sequences were shot, there was no sound equipment used. Director Claude Binyon even ordered mood music to be played while the actors went through their paces. Although he made several silent films, Webb said, "I realize now what a cinch silent actors had. Why, this is nothing compared to doing a sound picture. There are no lines to learn, no scripts to study. All you have to do is show up on the set every day. It's a dream!"

Since he was to dance briefly with Rogers, Webb decided to get himself in shape in that respect as well. "I did a rather foolish thing when I put away my dancing shoes. I never got them down again. Oh, if I were at a party and had a few drinks and felt in the mood, I might get up and do a few steps of interpretive dancing . . . alone. But the thought of pushing another person around a crowded dance floor appalled me."

In view of the fact Webb was forever complaining about being identified as Belvedere, it was strange that he allowed the last few scenes of *Dreamboat* to show a clip from *Sitting Pretty*. The film shows Webb, Anne Francis, and Jeffrey Hunter sitting in a theatre, watching the scene where Belvedere dumps a bowl of oatmeal on the little boy's head. Francis leans over and congratulates Webb, saying, "Dad you were wonderful!"

Ginger Rogers enjoyed playing opposite Webb. She said, "Clifton was really funny in this film and played his stodgy professor role with his customary artistry." One day during shooting, Rogers said, "Marilyn Monroe dropped by the set for a visit. I was wearing a wonderful gold lame evening dress and Marilyn liked it. She got it and wore it in a brief scene in *Gentlemen Prefer Blondes*."

The reason Monroe dropped by was because she and Webb were friends. Monroe said that Webb was one of the first people who befriended her when she arrived in Hollywood. When Webb was making *Sitting Pretty*, Monroe visited the set. *Life* magazine photographer Loomis Dean was there and photographed her sitting on the floor, eating a chocolate next to Webb. This was in 1948 before Monroe was a household name. Monroe at this time was under contract to Fox and probably just dropped by for a chat with Webb. When *Life* published the story of *Sitting Pretty*, the Monroe photo was nowhere to be found. She apparently was not important enough at that time to warrant a photo in *Life*.

Almost from the beginning, there were people who ridiculed Monroe, thinking with looks like hers she couldn't be very intelligent. In *Picturegoer* magazine (June 11, 1955), Clifton Webb defended her, saying she "was very sweet, very serious. She likes to talk about the theatre and the kind of thing that makes people tick. She is intense and completely straightforward. She reads all the time. She is in complete earnest towards her career."

Monroe was invited to several of the famous parties held on Rexford Drive by Clifton and Mabelle. In an autobiography for the *Ladies Home Journal*, Judy Garland reported the following incident at a Webb party: "I knew Marilyn Monroe and loved her dearly. She asked me for help. Me! I didn't know what to tell her. One night, at a party at Clifton Webb's house, Marilyn followed me from room to room. 'I don't want to get too far away from you,' she said. 'I'm scared.' I told her, 'We're all scared. I'm scared too.' That beautiful girl was frightened of loneliness . . . the same thing I've been afraid of."

Webb was mentioned as the lead in many pictures that were never made. One he would like to have made was to feature Marilyn Monroe as his co-star. He said, "Marilyn Monroe and I were supposed to do *Hands across the Sea*. That one would have enchanted me."

When Monroe died in 1962, Webb was interviewed for his reaction to her death. He said, "I am shocked. People should have been more tolerant of her." Mel Ferrer created quite a stir when he tried to analyze Monroe's appeal. "Miss Monroe is the epitome of nothing more than a certain kind of very obvious high school physical appeal." Webb attempted to explain Ferrer's criticism. "Mature charm is a quality invented by the mature to console themselves for the loss of the powers of immaturity."

CHAPTER 12

Stars and Stripes Forever

As charming as *Dreamboat* was, it was not a blockbuster. Webb's next two films were. *Stars and Stripes Forever* and *Titanic* were big box office hits. By this time Webb was a huge moneymaker for Fox. In his memoir, Robert Wagner spoke of Webb's status: "At Fox, the elite circle was presided over by Clifton Webb. I worked with Clifton on *Stars* and *Stripes Forever*, then *Titanic*, and I was invited into his group. Clifton's friends included people like Noel Coward, and Charles Brackett, Billy Wilder's partner, who never got much credit from anyone, especially Billy. Charlie was a kind, well-educated, very bright gay man who was fairly deep in the closet."

Zanuck had a tough time getting the rights to the Sousa story. It took five years of complicated negotiations before Fox was able to get moving on the film. Zanuck paid one hundred thousand dollars for the rights and assigned Lamar Trotti to write the screenplay. It would be Trotti's last job. He died of a heart attack on August 28, 1952. The film was released in December of that year. Zanuck gave Trotti the title of the film and told him it would be shot in Technicolor and that he wanted Trotti's tradition of throat-lumping Americana prevalent throughout the script. Trotti delivered.

Shortly after its release, Howard Thompson of the *New York Times* interviewed Webb about his role as John Philip Sousa: "When I first heard about the project I thought . . . well, what on earth is there about John Philip Sousa? I had only seen photos of him, this short fellow with a bushy beard and a baton. The man not only hadn't an iota of humor but no private life. Anyway, we did some careful research, and we compromised on the beard business and we had a wonderful script by Lamar Trotti. I showed the picture recently to Artur Rubinstein and Cole Porter,

12.1. Robert Wagner and Clifton Webb, circa 1952. Courtesy of The Robert Wagner Collection.

two great friends of mine, and Artur told me Sousa was the best-known American composer in Europe."

Webb must have enjoyed being able to dance and sing in this film. Albeit the dancing and singing are meager, we at least get to hear Webb's singing voice. As Sousa, he is supposed to want to compose ballads to show people he can do more than just marches. Ruth Hussey, as Sousa's wife, plays the piano while he intones the ballad "My Love Is a Weeping Willow." Actually this tune is taken from Sousa's *Semper Fidelis*, with words by Ken Darby. Nevertheless, we hear a surprisingly deep singing voice by Webb, indicating that he, indeed, must have had a voice for opera at one time.

Stars and Stripes Forever was based on John Philip Sousa's book, *Marching Along*. However, like most movie biopics, many liberties were taken, such as the fictional character of Sousa's protégé William Little, played by Robert Wagner. The story really doesn't matter. What matters is the evocation of an era and the stirring music of Sousa. Knowing of Webb's fondness for opera and musical theatre, columnist Grady Johnson asked, "Do you like band music?" Webb deftly replied, "I never liked it until I saw it. There's something about marching musicians that stirs me." There was much of Webb's reasoning in Trotti's and director Henry Koster's handling of the film. It is filled with uniformed band members smartly marching, playing Sousa's music.

12.2. Ruth Hussey, Clifton Webb, Robert Wagner, and Debra Paget in *Stars and Stripes Forever* (1952).
Twentieth Century Fox photo. The David L. Smith Collection.

Columnist Wood Soanes had this to say about Clifton Webb's portrayal of Sousa: "At first blush the somewhat effete and suave Webb would not seem to be an ideal choice for the robust John Philip Sousa any more than he was for the rugged father in *Cheaper by the Dozen*. But after he has played his first few scenes it is difficult to imagine any player more suitable for the role."

Louella Parsons was quite taken with Webb's portrayal as well: "After seeing Clifton Webb in *Stars and Stripes* Forever, I want to say right out loud that Clifton can play any role. When I complimented Darryl Zanuck on this wonderful picture he said, 'I can't take credit for the picture. That belongs to director Henry Koster and the late Lamar Trotti. But I can take credit for choosing Clifton."

Webb received a Golden Globe nomination for Best Actor, Musical/Comedy. Golden Globe nominations for the film also included one for Best Picture and Most Promising Newcomer (Robert Wagner). With the considerable help of Darryl Zanuck, Clifton Webb seemed to be living a charmed life on the screen.

After *Stars and Stripes Forever* was released in December of 1952, Webb had a brief respite before he began his first film with director Jean Negulesco. Webb and Negulesco would make four films together, two of which would be major hits. *Titanic*, released in April of 1953, and *Three Coins in the Fountain*, released in June of 1954, solidified Webb's box-office appeal. *Titanic* was originally entitled *Nearer My God to Thee*. The

12.3. Clifton Webb as the "March King," John Philip Sousa. Twentieth Century Fox photo. The David L. Smith Collection.

title *Titanic* was owned by another producer. However, producer Charles Brackett was eventually able to negotiate the use of *Titanic* as the title of the film.

Within a framework of facts, the film centers on a fictitious family on its way home to America. Webb plays the father, who happens to be an elegant snob, if you can imagine that. Barbara Stanwyck plays his not very adoring wife. Robert Wagner, Thelma Ritter, and Richard Basehart provide solid supporting roles. Frances Bergen, wife of Edgar and mother of Candice, makes her film debut as Mrs. John Jacob Astor. Bergen was a New York model before her marriage to Edgar. Webb was very impressed with Barbara Stanwyck. He said, "That woman's an absolute dream to work with."

Titanic won an Oscar for best writing and was nominated for Best Set and Art Decoration. The film was noted for its special effects and elaborate sets. A twenty-foot model was used to depict the end of the huge liner in an icy sea. Many of the sets were used again and again in other movies through the years. Critical reviews were good. British historian

12.4. Aboard the *Titanic*, with Frances Bergen and William Johnstone as Mr. and Mrs. John Jacob Astor. Twentieth Century Fox photo. The David L. Smith Collection.

David Shipman says that the fictional family of Stanwyck and Webb "works so well due to Clifton Webb as the husband, really showing his mettle in a serious role." In the tragic last scenes Webb effectively drops his arrogance as he realizes what is about to happen. One critic said, "Webb is magnificent as the arrogant snob, graduating his performance to one of quiet nobility as he meets the common disaster."

After working in major productions like *Stars and Stripes Forever* and *Titanic*, Webb had reason to believe he didn't have to worry about being in "little pictures" anymore. He was mistaken. Zanuck found a book entitled *Be Prepared*. It was about a man who is attempting to sell breakfast food on television. He wants to better understand children, and he winds up being a scoutmaster. The title of the film was *Mr. Scoutmaster*. Much to Webb's chagrin, he found he was to play another Belvedere character. There are some differences. While attempting to lead his troop, he gets lost himself, something that would never happen to Belvedere. But, like Belvedere, he gets to dump a bowl of ice cream on a kid's head.

At this time, Webb had never made a picture in an overseas location. His next film gave him that opportunity. *Three Coins in the Fountain* (1954)

12.5. Clifton Webb learning how to make fire by rubbing two sticks together for *Mr. Scoutmaster* (1953). Twentieth Century Fox photo. The David L. Smith Collection.

teamed Webb again with director Jean Negulesco. The film was shot on location in Rome. The three girls in the film were Dorothy McGuire, Jean Peters, and Maggie McNamara. They all find their loves, including McGuire, who gradually wins the love of her writer-employer, played by Webb.

The picture was expensive, and Zanuck was anxious that it would be a commercial success. In Mel Gussow's biography of Zanuck, he gives this version of what happened after the movie was finished: "After watching the rough cut, Zanuck got up and left the projection room without saying a word. Everyone was stunned. The film seemed to be a total disaster. Jean Negulesco went out and threw up on the sidewalk. Darryl Zanuck prided himself in being a good editor. He reworked the entire script on film, redubbing new dialogue, and having other new dialogue coming from the actor's backs. He was able to convert the film into a huge commercial success. Zanuck said, 'I think if I have any talent at all, it's in editing in the cutting room.'"

Jean Negulesco, in his autobiography, has a completely different take on this event: "Next day we were summoned by D.F.Z. to his private projection room. The cutter sat to his right. Usually he nudged the cutter at places where he wanted changes. That night the nudging covered all scenes and every reel. At the end he explained to the cutter the changes and cuts he wanted. Finally he said to us, 'It's a sick baby. It needs hard work,' and he left the room.

"We saw the new version. A butchered job. A long short with nothing of the magic we thought we had achieved. A letter went to him: 'Dear Darryl, this morning we saw the new cut version of *Three Coins*. We are aware that you are one of the greatest cutters in the industry. But if you decide to release *Three Coins* as it is now, we insist that our names will not appear in the credit titles. Sol Siegel, Jean Negulesco.'"

Zanuck asked them to view the new edited version with him. After the viewing Negulesco reported, "When the lights came up, again a silence, this time shorter. Then Darryl turned to the cutter: 'Put it back as it was and ship it.'"

Like *Laura*, the film was given a huge boost by the music. The title song by Sammy Cahn and Jule Styne won an Oscar for best song. The color photography by Milton Krasner was nominated for an Oscar. Bosley Crowther summed up the appeal of the film: "*Three Coins in the Fountain* is quite clearly a film in which the locale comes first. However, the nonsense of its fable tumbles nicely within the picture frame."

Woman's World (1954), again with Negulesco, gave Webb a chance to play opposite a host of established stars of the day. The cast included Fred MacMurray, June Allyson, Van Heflin, Cornel Wilde, Lauren Bacall, and Arlene Dahl. Webb got top billing. The film was a Cinemascope production in Technicolor. The story is about an automobile manufacturer, played by Webb, who brings three of his top executives and their wives to New York to choose one as his new general manager. The Ford Motor Company built two "futuristic" cars for the film at a cost of over three million dollars. Webb was happy to be working with Lauren Bacall since he and Bogie had been good friends for many years. The Four Aces provided the theme song, "It's a Woman's World." Unfortunately, it was not the hit that *Three Coins in the Fountain* was.

During the making of this film, Webb was interviewed by columnist Bob Thomas: "Webb seated himself in a tastefully decorated dressing room. He had slipped into a robe and wore dark glasses with a piece of cardboard over his nose so the makeup would not be rubbed off. From a vacuum bottle he poured some milk . . . 'ulcer you know.' When I declined a cigarette, he sighed, 'I cannot do without them. When the doctor took me to the hospital and diagnosed the ulcer, he told me to quit smoking. I tried for two whole days, and I was miserable. The slightest noise made me jump. Finally the doctor allowed me to smoke as long as I didn't do it on an empty stomach.'"

Thomas wrote that Webb professed a dislike for the film industry's preoccupation with violence. "I liked *Three Coins in the Fountain*. It was a gentle sort of thing. Nobody was hurt in the end. But that is all too rare nowadays. The movies concentrate on murder, mayhem and other forms of violence. Television is the same. It must have a terrible effect on the children."

With the exception of his portrayal of a murderer in *Laura*, and a nefarious art dealer in *Dark Corner*, Webb's films were relatively nonviolent. He was outwardly proud of that fact, while inwardly he was yearning to play a villain at least one more time. He would come close, even being cast as such. But it was not to be.

In January of 1954, Darryl Zanuck hosted a party at Ciro's to welcome his daughter Susan and actress Terry Moore back from their tour of Korea. There was an estimated four hundred in attendance. It was an Asian-costumed affair. Midway through the event, Zanuck suddenly went up on a stage and announced that it was a lovely party and he was proud of his daughter. He said that he was full of vim and vigor and that his daughter inherited at least 40 percent of it from him. He thanked everyone for coming and then called for a trapeze that had been used earlier by some professional performers. He took off his Asian jacket and, bare-chested, began to swing on the trapeze. He said, "I hope my publicity director isn't here to stop me." He then began to do some acrobatic swings on the trapeze. It was at this point that Clifton Webb strode up to the stage and demanded that he return to the floor before he hurt himself. After a few more swings, Zanuck dismounted, re-costumed himself, and rejoined the crowd. No one but Webb would have dared to confront the boss in this manner. Webb apparently suffered no repercussions from the incident.

Webb was delighted when a film was announced that would give him a chance to return to his villainous best, a side he had not shown since his early years in Hollywood. As usual, he would retain the snobbery and superiority for which he was known. The projected film was entitled *Lord Vanity*, and he was scheduled to play Count Tromba, who was a combination of two eighteenth-century figures, Lord Chesterfield and Cagliostro. The movie was to be based on Samuel Shellabarger's novel. Webb's friend Robert Wagner was set to play the title role. Delmer Daves was the director and Charles Brackett the producer.

Robert Wagner made a test with Joan Collins as the female lead. However, Wagner said that Fox decided to postpone the film until Martine Carol, a French actress, was free to co-star as the Countess Amelia. Apparently, Carol never became available. Other reports circulating at that time were that Fox was trying to get Lana Turner for the distaff lead. The film was cancelled after several tests were made. Webb again was disappointed that he lost another chance to play a villain in what would have been his only costume epic.

On January 14, 1956, *Blithe Spirit* was televised live on CBS. The cast included Noel Coward as Charles Condomine, Lauren Bacall as Elvira, and Claudette Colbert as Ruth. Mildred Natwick recreated her role as Madame Arcati. Bacall reported that Clifton Webb gave a large party for Coward before the TV show was aired. Hedda Hopper was to be there. Bacall was on the outs with her because she'd printed some disparaging remarks about her and tried to keep William Wellman from casting her in *Blood Alley*.

Webb decided it was time for the two of them to make up. He put one arm around Hopper and the other around Bacall and said, "Come on you two, make up . . . this is ridiculous." In her autobiography Bacall said that Clifton "hated people not to like each other." Bacall fumed and told Hopper that she'd been a bitch to try to keep her from working. Hopper said, "You're right, I was. Why don't you give me a kick?" Hopper turned around and Bacall "kicked her in the ass . . . whereupon everyone laughed loudly and a truce was declared."

Another Hopper incident occurred in 1956 that allowed Webb to again turn around Hopper's opinion of someone. This incident involved a fellow Hoosier whom Webb immediately recognized as a genius. His name was James Dean.

Warners' chief public relations man asked Hopper to come and meet James Dean for lunch in the studio commissary. He told her Dean gave an outstanding performance in *East of Eden*. Hopper agreed to meet him. In her autobiography, Hopper said, "This latest genius sauntered in, dressed like a bum, and slouched down in silence at a table away from mine. Then he stood up to inspect the framed photographs of Warner stars that covered the wall by his head. He chose one of them, spat in its eye, wiped off the spittle with a handkerchief, then like a ravenous hyena, started to gulp the food that had been served him." Hopper had enough. She left the commissary without doing an interview.

When the invitation came to see the preview of *East of Eden*, Hopper refused to attend. Shortly afterward she got a call from Clifton Webb. "I heard the next day from Clifton Webb, whose judgment I respect: 'Last night I saw one of the most extraordinary performances of my life. Get the studio to run that movie over for you. You'll be crazy about this boy Jimmy Dean.'"

Hopper told Webb she'd already seen Dean and didn't want to see anymore of him. Webb replied, "Forget it . . . I read your piece. Just watch him in this picture." Hopper had great faith in Webb's judgment and called Elia Kazan and asked for a screening. He ran the film for her. Hopper said, "In the projection room I sat spellbound. I couldn't remember ever having seen a young man with such power, so many facets of expression, so much sheer invention as this actor." Hopper wrote a nice review of the film and asked Dean to come to her house for an interview. He did, and he apologized for his past behavior. Dean and Hopper became friends. He came to her for advice several times. When Dean died, Hopper begged the Academy to award him a special Oscar, to stand on a plain granite shaft as a headstone to his grave in Fairmount, Indiana. The Academy declined.

In 1956, Webb was offered the lead in a film that was based on a true story and would provide him with the chance to go overseas again for location shooting.

Ewen Montagu was working in the British Naval Intelligence during World War II when he came up with a piece of contrived deception that proved to be more ingenious than anything Alfred Hitchcock could have cooked up. Montagu wrote a book about his plot to fool the Nazis into believing that the invasion of southern Europe was to take place through Greece. The book was entitled *The Man Who Never Was*. The movie retained that title.

Clifton Webb was delighted to be cast as Montagu. It was a much "heavier" role than he had been playing for the past three years. After his admirable dramatic performance in *Titanic* he was disappointed to be placed in a series of rather "light" films.

The film was a scrupulous re-enactment of Montagu's true-life story. Stephen Boyd was cast as a Nazi spy who almost discovers the plot. Gloria Grahame is supposed to be the sweetheart of the fictitious courier with "top secret" information. Ronald Neame, a former cinematographer, directed.

12.6. Clifton Webb with Stephen Boyd on location for *The Man Who Never Was* (1956). Twentieth Century Fox photo. The David L. Smith Collection.

Some felt that Webb might have been miscast in this role. Bosley Crowther said, "Clifton Webb in the role of the sorcerer who plots this trickery is too lofty and prim. There is not enough about him to excite you with the devilish cleverness of this man." Other critics differed from Crowther's evaluation. "Clifton Webb as Montagu is at his best. He plays the part wonderfully and is absolutely convincing." Another said, "Clifton Webb gives an entirely new characterization for him . . . that of Lt. Commander Montagu . . . masterfully played by Webb."

During most of his Hollywood career, Webb gave private screenings of his films for his friends. This time Webb invited not only his friends but members of the press as well. Bob Thomas was one of those. He reported, "Oh, it was very chic. Clifton was there at the door of the projection room to plant a kiss on the cheek of pals like Barbara Stanwyck, Marlene Dietrich, and Dorothy McGuire. Others paying homage were Van Johnson, Jeanne Crain, Patricia Morrison, and old-time star Richard Barthelmess." Thomas mentions others in attendance, such as Jeffrey Hunter, Lauren Bacall, Humphrey Bogart, and Frank Sinatra. Thomas asked Webb, "What happens if guests don't like the picture?" Webb replied, "Nothing can be done. It's in the can. Besides they always use superlatives in referring to my performance."

Webb not only managed to play a "nasty" in his next film, but also finagled a way to use his mother's maiden name, which was also his middle name. In *Boy on a Dolphin* Webb plays Victor Parmalee (this time spelled with an "a" instead of "Parmelee," as Webb uses in his autobiography). His co-stars were Alan Ladd and Sophia Loren. Ladd got top billing. Cary Grant was originally scheduled for the lead, then Robert Mitchum. Gina Lollobrigida was to play Loren's part, but the twenty-three-year-old Loren, who had made only one other American movie, *The Pride and the Passion* (1957), was cast as the female lead. The film was shot on location in Greece and its Aegean Islands. Webb played an unscrupulously wealthy collector of art treasures. Ladd is an archeologist and Loren is a Greek Island girl who dives for sponges and stumbles upon the famous lost statue of a boy astride a dolphin. Webb offers her a fortune for it, but Ladd has other ideas.

Jean Negulesco again directed. The film was a moderate hit. Webb attempted to keep the film moving with his usual haughty manner and sardonic barbs. Most of the difficult location work took place on the Aegean Sea, off Hydra, a little island located four miles by boat from Athens. Unfortunately, the little island did not have appropriate housing facilities for a Hollywood company. The studio decided to rent some luxury cabin cruisers to serve the cast and crew. Webb and Mabelle were assigned to the S.S. *Neraida*, owned in prewar years by Mussolini's son-in-law. The only problem was that in bad weather the yachts would roll and bounce around, sending furniture, china, and food flying in all directions.

The film was described by one critic as "a stunning picture and one of the visual delights of the year for the armchair traveler." Robert Wagner reported that Webb brought a lot of "souvenirs" back from Greece and created a "Greek Room" in his house, where he displayed his treasures.

When Webb returned to Hollywood, the first thing he did was to call to inquire about the health of Humphrey Bogart. He had been told that Bogie was very ill again. Webb was an old friend of Bogie's and had been very close to both Bogie and Bacall ever since their marriage. Bacall gave this account of his phone call in her autobiography: "He became very emotional, kept saying, 'Oh, poor Bogie . . . I can't bear it,' got weepy on the phone. I told him he could not come unless he could hold himself together, that seeing Bogie after so many months would be a terrible shock to him, but Bogie was very alert and would notice the slightest suggestion of emotion."

It was decided that Webb should not come alone. George Cukor was asked to accompany Webb. Cukor had seen Bogie recently and thus would not be as shocked as Webb might be. Bacall related the scene: "Clifton got through it somehow, but as Bogie was being wheeled out of the room, Clifton totally collapsed . . . started to cry, moan. I was trying to keep him quiet so Bogie wouldn't hear him. One had not only one's own emotions to contend with, but also those of friends who couldn't deal with the facts. Clifton was a special friend . . . cried easily . . . so there was no point to being angry with him. That afternoon, however, he was definitely more of a problem than Bogie ever was."

Humphrey Bogart died January 14, 1957. He·always told Lauren Bacall not to mourn, that it did no good for the dead and was just self-indulgent. That is all well and good for some, but Clifton Webb was not one of those who could contain his grief.

Following Bogart's death Bacall sent Webb a note thanking him for the long friendship he and Bogie enjoyed. She said Bogey adored him and she envied Webb for all those extra years he had with Bogey.

In 1959, Buddy Adler, who was picked by Zanuck to succeed him, bought the rights to a 1953 Broadway play by Liam O'Brien entitled *The Remarkable Mr. Pennypacker*. Webb and Dorothy McGuire were cast in the roles played by Burgess Meredith and Martha Scott in the Broadway production. At first blush, it appeared this would be another film in the stereotypical mode of *Sitting Pretty* and *Cheaper by the Dozen*. However, there were a few differences. Webb said, "I play a bigamist who is the head of an enormous sausage factory. I still maintain an attitude of elegance. And that is a very difficult thing to do." Also, instead of a dozen children, he is the father of a pack of seventeen youngsters. Once again the question was asked of Webb, "How can a life-long bachelor get along with all those kids?" Webb replied: "There's a great legend about my hating children. While I have no kids of my own, I must say that I bear no grudge toward the small fry. On the contrary, for some reason children love me. It must be because I have a very sweet nature. Even dogs come to me for attention."

As the irrepressible Pa Pennypacker, Webb roller-skates to work and maintains two families so he won't have to travel back and forth to kiss his children good night. Reviews were good for this light-hearted bit of nonsense. "Laughs come so fast and furious that the story enters the kind of insane no man's land that only the incomparable Clifton Webb can travel through."

12.7. Clifton Webb in *The Remarkable Mr. Pennypacker* (1959) with Dorothy McGuire. Twentieth Century Fox photo. The David L. Smith Collection.

Ray Stricklyn, who played one of Webb's children in *The Remarkable Mr. Pennypacker*, was invited to a party at Rexford Drive. He describes the scene: "The grand piano was covered with photographs of his famous friends . . . Vivien Leigh and Laurence Olivier, Fred Astaire, Noel Coward, Gertrude Lawrence, and Cary Grant. He [Webb] was really very sweet, not at all like the acerbic characters he played in most of his films. He was very affectionate towards me, but other than a goodnight kiss on the cheek, more like a father and son, he was never aggressive in any way."

Stricklyn also tells of a smaller dinner party given by the actor Richard Deacon. Both Stricklyn and Deacon were gay. Deacon had particularly planned the evening for Webb, thinking he might take a shine to one of the actors invited. That actor is described by Stricklyn as a TV soap opera star named "Val." Stricklyn said, "Val showed up wearing very short, very revealing, ripped-off jeans, frayed at the bottom. Clifton was appalled, thinking him quite crude, and refused to have anything to do with him the rest of the evening. So much for blind dates." Apparently, Deacon had misinterpreted Webb's socializing within the gay circles in the film colony.

Another story that surfaces frequently concerning Webb's sexuality centers around one of Bob Newhart's appearances on the *Tonight Show*. He told Johnny Carson of his first meeting with Clifton Webb. Newhart was a young up-and-coming comedian at the time. His *The Button-Downed Mind of Bob Newhart* had just hit the record charts. While playing at the Hungry Eye in San Francisco, Vivien Leigh visited him backstage and invited him to a party at the Fairmount Hotel. In his autobiography Newhart describes the scene: "She introduced me around the room, and I began chatting with some of the guests. Clifton Webb sidled up next to me and introduced himself. Then he asked me if I would like to dance. As hard as I tried to reverse roles and quickly come up with a line like, 'my dance card is full,' I couldn't. Not-withstanding the fact that he had been a professional ballroom dancer since the age of nineteen, I politely declined. From then on, whenever I saw a Mr. Belvedere picture, my mind would wander back to that time."

The author wrote to Newhart and asked if Webb said or did anything else. Did he feel Webb was simply using his "wicked sense of humor" to shake up a rookie comedian or did he think there was something else to it? Mr. Newhart's response follows:

Dear Professor Smith:

    I really can add little further information on Mr. Webb other than contained in my book.

    I am not sure of Mr. Webb's sexual orientation other than I had never been asked to dance by a man before.

    I don't know if this is of any help to you.

Sincerely,

Bob Newhart

It appears that Webb was doing nothing more than shaking up a young novice comedian.

The Remarkable Mr. Pennypacker was released in January of 1959, and Webb was scheduled to start almost immediately on another film. He was to play Sir Oliver S. Lindenbrook in Jules Verne's *Journey to the Center of the Earth*. Unfortunately, he became ill and was hospitalized for a brief time. Doctors told him he should take an extended rest. James Mason replaced Webb in the film. Webb rested for about six months and then began work on *Holiday for Lovers*, which was released in September of 1959.

It was in 1959 that Webb found he was the inspiration for a popular cartoon character. Jay Ward created a cartoon series entitled *Rocky and*

12.8. Clifton Webb in *Holiday for Lovers* (1959) with Jill St. John and Carole Lynley. Twentieth Century Fox photo. The David L. Smith Collection.

His Friends for the ABC network. One of the main characters was an intelligent, talking beagle who owned a small orphan boy named Sherman, whom he found on the streets. Together they traveled through time to set straight the outcome of history. According to Bill Hurtz, the program's director, the character of Mr. Peabody was inspired by Clifton Webb, whose screen characters were often "smug, snide, and condescending." While announcer Durward Kirby tried to sue Ward for using the name "Kirward Derby" as a cartoon character, there is no evidence that Clifton Webb did anything to dissuade Ward from imitating him in the form of Mr. Peabody.

In 1959, Clifton Webb was seventy years old. Mabelle was now in her ninetieth year. He must have been aware of his mortality. It would only be natural then to hope for a wonderful film to close out an amazingly diversified career. Unfortunately, his next film was not one that would fill that bill. *Holiday for Lovers* had Webb playing in his familiar straight-laced, tilt-nosed, and waspingly stinging style. Webb's co-star in *Laura*, Gene Tierney, was set to play his wife. However, illness forced her to drop out of the production and Jane Wyman took over the role. Carol Lynley and Jill St. John played his two daughters. In an interview with Jill St. John, she said the film was shot entirely in the studios. Scenes of Sao Paulo, Rio de Janeiro, and Lima, Peru, were all simply inserted. The film was photographed nicely in color and Cinemascope.

CHAPTER 13

Clifton and Mabelle, Together Forever

On October 17, 1960, Mabelle died of a heart attack at Cedars of Lebanon Hospital. She was ninety-one. Needless to say, Webb was devastated. In his diary Noel Coward said: "Mabelle Webb died a couple of days ago. I had a cable from Clifton. Poor dear, I'm afraid he will feel dreadfully lonely without her. The late sixties is rather late to be orphaned [actually, Webb was seventy-one at this time]. I hope he will rise above it and not collapse into aimless melancholia."

Coward's hope that Webb would not spend a lot of time grieving was not realized. He was inconsolable. The next month, a group of his friends talked him into hosting his annual birthday party for himself. They were able to convince him that Mabelle would have wanted it that way. Reports were that it was a "swinging party," but the next day Webb had to take to his bed.

Noel Coward invited Clifton to spend Christmas with him at his Jamaican villa, Blue Harbor. With some apprehension Coward contemplated the visit: "He was seventy-one, but he looked ninety. Poor Clifton is still, after two months, wailing and sobbing over Mabelle's death. As she was well over ninety, gaga, and had driven him mad for years, this seems excessive and over-indulgent. He arrives here [Jamaica] on Monday and I'm dreaming of a wet Christmas. Poor, poor Clifton. I am, of course, deeply sorry for him but he must snap out of it."

He didn't "snap out of it." Jean Howard reported that at a New Year's Eve party celebrating the arrival of 1961, she invited Webb along with Coward, Cole Lesley (Noel's secretary), producer Charles Russell, British heiress Blanche Blackwell, and her son Chris, who became a big movie producer. She said that when the New Year arrived, the guests all hugged, kissed, and lifted their glasses. "Poor Clifton disappeared into his own room, hugging only his grief."

Several of Webb's friends called regularly to try to cheer him up. Noel Coward phoned Webb and tried to talk to him, but he wept so uninterruptedly that Coward finally lost his temper and said, "Unless you stop crying I shall reverse the charges!" Webb tried to be cheerful during the day and succeeded most of the time. But after about the second martini before dinner, he began to tell sad stories about the death of his many friends: Valentino, Eagels, di Frasso, Lilyan Tashman, and more. As the dinner progressed, he talked of how Mabelle was buried in her favorite evening dress (by Norman Hartnell) with all the correct accessories. Helen Matthews, Webb's secretary, at the very last moment realized they had forgotten the earrings to match. Webb never forgot how Helen drove all the way back to Rexford Drive and then back to the funeral home so that Mabelle could have her earrings. At this point he'd break down and sob and, as Coward said, "There was nothing to do except gaze at him in wild surmise and give him another drink."

In Cole Lesley's biography of Coward, Lesley (Coward's secretary) was given the job of getting Webb home and into bed. He said getting Webb undressed and into his pajamas was only half the job. Webb would then sit on the bed and repeat word for word each night the same monologue.

"Ah, Coley, you don't know. Nobody knows. Nobody understands. Nobody understands what it's like. Only Gloria [Swanson] understands. Marlene never called, did I tell you? Not one word from Marlene. You know what Gloria said when she called? She said, 'Clifton, you've lost more than a mother. You've lost a sister, a friend and a lover as well.' Only Gloria understands. Can you imagine, not one word from Marlene."

At one point, Coward became so frustrated with Webb's incessant mourning that he said sharply, "It must be tough to be orphaned at seventy-one!"

By July of 1961, Webb had moved to London in anticipation of shooting *Satan Never Sleeps*. It was to be filmed in England, using sets built for *The Inn of the Sixth Happiness*. Webb hadn't worked in eighteen months, but under the terms of his contract, he collected his salary regularly even during a bitter actors' strike. Vernon Scott interviewed him in his Dorchester Hotel suite. Scott pointed out that many people thought he bore a resemblance to the Duke of Windsor, one of Webb's good friends. Webb replied, "Perhaps that's why everyone believes, wrongly, that I'm an Englishman. No matter how many times I tell people I'm a Hoosier

13.1. Clifton Webb, France Nuyen, and William Holden in *Satan Never Sleeps* (1962). Twentieth Century Fox photo. The David L. Smith Collection.

from Indiana, no one remembers it for long. Even here in England they're convinced I'm one of them."

Scott asked about Webb's next role, that of a priest in Leo McCarey's *Satan Never Sleeps*. Webb said, "For the first time I will be seen in a picture without my customary elegance. It is indeed a far cry, but a challenge. The part was written especially for me. He is a caustic man of the cloth, but with a warm heart."

Satan Never Sleeps was not only Clifton Webb's last film, it was also director Leo McCarey's last film. In an analogous vein, the film was a departure from the norm by both Webb and McCarey. McCarey was known for absurd, screwball romances like *The Awful Truth* or generational conflicts between Catholic priests like *The Bells of St. Mary's* or *Going My Way.* Webb was always elegantly dressed and had never played anything close to a clergyman. Here he was to appear without his mustache (he appeared sans mustache only one other time in *For Heaven's Sake* in 1951) and in priest's clothing that was considerably rumpled after spending time in a Chinese Communist prison. He even decided that his costume was not "rumpled" enough and said, "I put it under my mattress so it was all wrinkled up and not like it came from a tailor."

The theme of *Satan Never Sleeps*, based on a Pearl Buck story, is a touchy one. William Holden and Webb play missionaries caught in the Red Chinese sweep. One of the refugees in their charge is France Nuyen, who falls in love with Holden. Holden insisted on Nuyen as the female lead. Her career had languished after she was replaced by Nancy Kwan in *The World of Suzie Wong*.

In Bob Thomas's book, *Golden Boy: The Untold Story of William Holden*, McCarey is quoted with this version of the controversial love story between Nuyen and Holden, "He thinks he can handle the situation but Webb warns him he is getting into quicksand, and he does." McCarey ran afoul of the Johnston office with this film. Eric Johnston had taken over the job of film censorship czar after Will Hays resigned. McCarey said, "I showed it to Catholic authorities, both in the United States and here. Both approved it. But those jerks in the Johnston office wouldn't allow it."

McCarey described the scene that caused the problem: "I have a scene in the picture in which a young Red Chinese army officer rapes France Nuyen in front of the priest, played by William Holden. The young Chinese does it to taunt the priest, whose spirit he can't break. The scene isn't played for sensation; the rape is never seen."

McCarey said, "I'm going to be the Catholic Otto Preminger." He meant that he was going to shoot the scene as written and release the film without code approval. That is what Preminger did with *The Moon Is Blue*. But in addition to his problems with Johnston, McCarey also complained of constant interference from the Fox front office. With five shooting days left, McCarey quit the film. An assistant finished it.

McCarey was caught up in the "Red Scare" of that day. He had already made an anti-communist film, *My Son John* (1952). Many thought it was a McCarthyist film. *Satan Never Sleeps* was also criticized for being nothing more than an anti-communist diatribe. *Variety* said, "The modern film audience is not apt to accept a two-dimensional portrait of the Communist as merely a bumbling, irrational, arch-villain."

Contributing to the problems experienced in the making of this film was the fact that both Holden and McCarey were heavy drinkers. Holden thought he was drinking heavily until he saw McCarey drinking more than two quarts of brandy a day. Unfortunately, the film reflected the debasement of these two major participants. Just before making this film, Holden told his good friend Joel McCrea, "I just can't get excited about making pictures anymore."

It was unfortunate that Clifton Webb had to end his career working in a troubled film. However, looking much older than his seventy-three years, Webb again received good reviews. Some critics thought he showed more depth in this role than any he had ever played and that perhaps the full range of his acting talent had never been realized.

After this film, Webb was not well enough to make another picture. He suffered from abdominal problems. In 1963, he underwent surgery to correct an abdominal aneurysm on a weakened blood vessel. Famed heart specialist Dr. Michael DeBakey performed the Houston operation, during which he and other doctors grafted a length of Dacron into the damaged artery. He had a second operation in May of 1966 to remove an intestinal block. He had been suffering from a heart condition for several years.

During his last years, Clifton Webb was virtually a recluse. He was unable to enjoy the social scene he loved so much. The wonderful parties he and Mabelle hosted were now just a memory. The operations and the heart disease had sapped his strength and withered his frame. His friends were well aware that his absence from the screen signaled a serious illness. Robert Wagner was one of many who came to visit. Wagner said he used to sit by Webb's bed, chatting and enjoying a glass of wine.

Death finally came to Clifton Webb in his sleep at his home on Rexford Drive, in Beverly Hills, October 13, 1966. Webb's secretary, Helen Matthews, his physician and his nurse were with him when he died at 9:00 p.m. Matthews said she didn't think he could endure another anniversary of his mother's death (Mabelle died on October 17). He was interred next to his beloved mother at the Sanctuary of Peace in the Abbey of the Psalms Mausoleum at Hollywood Forever Cemetery.

On October 16, 1966, Noel Coward made the following entry in his diary: "Poor Clifton died two days ago. Another old friend gone. For his sake I'm glad. He's been miserably ill for a long time now. He was dreadfully preoccupied with his own health, poor dear. If Mabelle had died ten years earlier he might have survived better, but she left it too late and he wrapped himself in grief and dread every morning when he woke. He used to be such good company in the past. Age defeated him. I wonder if it will defeat me? I feel it won't, but you never know. Invalidism is a subtle pleasure."

Columnist William E. Sarmento reflected on Webb's career: "To be sure no one could deliver a verbal thrust with more venom than Mr. Webb and he could handle comedy well. But Clifton Webb was more than just a stereotype. He was a fine actor.

"Webb never gave a bad performance although he was saddled with some bad scripts. He was always more than adequate whether a leading performer or a supporting star. Clifton Webb was first rate. He had class. There are not many actors left in Hollywood who can match his professional skill."

Clifton Webb was a most unlikely movie star. In a day when all leading men were supposed to be strong, virile, and brave, he was a misogynist hero. Most male movie stars of his day were supposed to have women melting in their arms. Webb had a considerably different approach. He said proudly, "I have destroyed the formula completely. I'm not young, I don't get the girl in the end and I don't swallow her tonsils, but I have become a national figure."

He was one of the most consistent moneymakers in Fox history. The moviegoing public loved him, overlooking his well-known status as a bachelor and the fact that he lived with his mother all his life. For more than fifteen years, he was a top-billed leading man who rivaled most other leading men of that day. Not bad for an actor who made his first major movie at age fifty-five.

On October 18, 1966, services for Clifton Webb were held at All Saints Episcopal Church in Beverly Hills. Over two hundred people attended, including such names as Katharine Hepburn, Rosalind Russell, Tony Curtis, Raymond Massey, Janet Gaynor, Richard Zanuck, Robert Wagner, Natalie Wood, Otto Preminger, Alfred Lunt, and Lauren Bacall.

Samuel G. Engel, who was the producer for three Webb films, *Sitting Pretty, Mr. Belvedere Goes to College,* and *Boy on a Dolphin,* delivered the following eulogy:

> Six years ago, almost to the day on October 20th, I was your spokesman when we said good-by to Clifton's gallant mother, Mabelle. Today we have come together to say good-by to our friend, Clifton.
>
> The extraordinary theatrical team of Mabelle and Clifton . . . for they were just that . . . was severed by her death. Now . . . with Clifton gone . . . a very significant chapter in the annals of SHOW BUSINESS is ready for entry into the history books.
>
> Mabelle will perhaps receive but a footnote in all these books (though she deserves infinitely more), but no responsible historian of the theatre and the motion picture dealing with the last three decades can do even a remotely creditable and authentic job without the name Clifton Webb appearing on many a page of his work.

For, from boyhood on until the very twilight of his years, Clifton has been an actor of stage and screen . . . honoring his profession, as it honored him. But let us leave the recounting of Clifton's illustrious career, and the dynamic role Mabelle played in making it so . . . to the historians.

Let us pause, briefly, and reflect on those traits and attributes of our friend, who so endeared himself to those of us who were privileged to know him and work with him, and to the countless numbers around the globe who watched him across the footlights and on the screen, as he pursued the profession to which he was sacredly dedicated.

Clifton was no child prodigy who burst like a rocket into the firmament. His climb up the slippery ladder of success was not without its accompanying struggles. He was no stranger to reverses and even failures; his inherent gifts and talents were hammered out on the anvil of trial, error and experience.

Thus he gained a healthy respect for hard work, perseverance, integrity, and above all self-discipline, which earned him the right to wear the time-honored masque and mantle of a professional actor . . . which he wore with pride, distinction and nobility.

Thus, he was a great debunker, who loathed arrogance, pomposity and hypocrisy. He could detect a phony a mile away. He had no time for the sordid, the sloppy, the cheap, the second rate . . . for he was a gentleman . . . in the finest sense of the meaning of the word.

He could, and would consort with the so-called high and mighty, yet had the rare faculty of moving among the so-called masses . . . accepting and dispensing friendship and kindness in a manner all his very own.

He was ever alert to encourage and praise, as he was quick to admonish and reprove. No one however great and famous, or lowly and unrenowned, could escape his sharp, discerning eye, his critical tongue if he thought their conduct needed sensible guidance or advice. And . . . unhesitatingly it would come forth with candor, but always delivered with genuine concern . . . and always enveloped in a protective coating of true charity and affection.

I can attest that there are more than a handful among us, and I can head the list, who have been on the receiving end of his gunfire, and who have profited immeasurably from such an experience.

For Clifton, when he cared about a person, could not abide standing by silently and watching him carelessly or thoughtlessly cast his talent, his career, or even his personal life to the four winds.

And many a talent, a career, a reputation was not ruined or wrecked because Clifton cared enough to speak up. And since he instinctively knew the difference between superb quality and tawdry mediocrity, what he had to say merited being heard and heeded.

Like his mother, Mabelle, he too was blessed with a zest for life; the many rich rewards it can provide; and the remarkable capacity to enjoy them to the fullest.

Anyone who has ever been warmed by his hospitality, or has traveled with him on plane or ship, or has worked with him in this country or abroad, knows that while he would never permit happy times and jolly moments to interfere for one split second with his work, he would never overlook a single opportunity to surround himself with congenial company.

In his world there was no room for gloom and doom. Like the bon vivant extraordinaire that he was, he graciously, gracefully, gratefully danced his way along the stage of life.

And all these pursuits he performed with an exquisite style and elegance: CLASS . . . from head to toe, and in every bone of his lithesome body. He could step out from a battered, dilapidated car, but when he closed its door and walked away, it took on the appearance of a custom-built Rolls Royce.

Come upon him in his garden, wearing a dirty sweat shirt, worn denims and work shoes, and find him ministering to a plant with tender care . . . yet when he turned to greet you . . . somehow the entire setting looked like a color ad in "House and Garden." He was to the manor born.

So . . . the indivisible team of Mabelle and Clifton are now re-united. And, if I knew our Mabelle, she was waiting to greet him with a giant-sized Scotch extended in one hand, the other clinging to a huge black purse filled with offers, bookings and engagements, and cackling out a cheery, resounding "Welcome Webb!"

All of us . . . especially you, dear, devoted Helen . . . have ample cause for sorrowing that Clifton is no longer with us. But can't the burden of our hearts somehow be alleviated . . . though he is gone, though he has left no kith or kin . . . by the happier thought that he has left us a rich heritage . . . one his colleagues to honor; one, his friends to remember and treasure.

There is one star less blinking in the entertainment galaxy, but while it was up there, there was no mistaking its sparkle and radiance.

God bless, old boy! YOU'RE HOME!

Stage Appearances

Present Laughter
Plymouth Theater, New York, Oct. 29, 1946–March 15, 1947, 158 performances; *Garry Essendine*

Blithe Spirits
Variety show put together by the cast of *Blithe Spirit* to entertain service personnel, circa 1942–1943

Blithe Spirit
Morosco Theater, New York, Sept. 6, 1943–Oct. 2, 1943, 32 performances; *Charles Condomine*

Blithe Spirit
Morosco and Booth Theaters, New York, Nov. 5, 1941–June 5, 1943, 657 performances; *Charles Condomine*

The Man Who Came to Dinner
On tour, various theaters, circa 1939–1940; *Sheridan Whiteside*

Burlesque
Stock revival, summer of 1939; *Skid*

The Importance of Being Earnest
Vanderbilt Theater, New York, Jan. 12, 1939–circa March 19, 1939, 61 performances; *John Worthing*

You Never Know
Winter Garden Theater, New York, Sept. 21, 1938–Nov. 26, 1938, 78 performances; *Gaston*

Room Service
National touring company with Joey Faye, 1937. No other information, and only source for this is Joey Faye's obit in the *New York Times*.

And Stars Remain
Guild Theater, New York, Oct. 12, 1936–circa Nov. 1936, 78 performances; *Overton Morrell*

As Thousands Cheer
Music Box, New York, Sept. 30, 1933–Sept. 8, 1934, 400 performances; *Mahatma Ghandi, Douglas Fairbanks Jr., Mons. Peppiton, Henry Perlmutter, John D. Rockefeller Sr.;* dance partners, Marilyn Miller, Tamara Geva

Flying Colors
Imperial Theater, New York, Sept. 15, 1932–June 25, 1933 . . . 88 performances; *Dr. Eric Trevelyan*

Three's a Crowd
Selwyn Theater, New York, Oct. 15, 1930–circa June, 1931, 272 performances; dance partners, Amy Revere, Margaret Lee, Tamara Geva

The Little Show
Music Box Theater, New York, April 30, 1929–circa Feb. 1930, 321 performances; dance partner, Libby Holman

Treasure Girl
The Alvin Theater, New York, Nov. 8, 1928–Jan. 5, 1929, 68 performances; *Nat McNally;* dance partner, Mary Hay

She's My Baby
The Globe Theater, New York, Jan. 3, 1928–March 3, 1928, 91 performances; *Clyde Parker*

In the Old Days and Today (nightclub revue)
Des Ambassadeurs Club, Paris, May 10, 1928–? dance partner, Dorothy Dickson

Sunny
The New Amsterdam Theater, New York, Sept. 22, 1925–Dec. 11, 1926, 517 performances; *Harold Harcourt Wendell-Wendell;* dance partner, Mary Hay

Les Acasias (Paris nightclub), circa 1925;dance partner, Mary Hay

Les Acasias (Paris nightclub), circa 1924;dance partners, the Dolly Sisters

Parasites
39th Street Theater, New York, Nov. 19, 1924–Jan. 19, 1925, 54 performances; *Eliot Phelps*

Meet the Wife
Klaw Theater, New York, Nov. 26, 1923–circa Jan. 1924, 232 performances; *Victor Staunton*

Jack and Jill
The Globe Theater, New York, March 22, 1923–June 9, 1923, 92 performances; *Jimmy Eustace;* dance partner, Ann Pennington

The Fun of the Fayre
The Pavillion Theater, London, October 21, 1922–closing date unknown, 239 performances; dance partners, the Dolly Sisters

Phi-Phi
The Pavillion Theater, London, Aug. 16, 1922–closing date unknown, 132 performances

As You Were
Central Theater, New York, Jan. 27, 1920–May 29, 1920, 143 performances; *Ki Ki, Mark Antony*

Piccadilly to Broadway
The Globe Theater, Atlantic City, NJ, Sept. 27, 1920 (closed during try-out)

Listen Lester
The Knickerbocker Theater, New York, Dec. 23, 1918–Aug. 16, 1919, 272 performances; *Jack Griffin;* dance partners, Ada May Weeks, Gertrude Vanderbilt White

It Pays to Flirt
1918, this production closed out of town. No other information.

Love O' Mike
Shubert Theater, Maxine Elliott's, The Casino, New York, Jan. 15, 1917–Sept. 29 1917, 233 performances; *Alonzo Bird;* dance partner, Gloria Goodwin

See America First
Maxine Elliott's Theater, New York, March 28, 1916–April 8, 1916, 15 performances; *Percy*

Very Good Eddie
Note: This was listed in Webb's credits in the Playbill for *Blithe Spirit* Jan. 5, 1942. This production ran on Broadway Dec. 23, 1915–Oct. 14, 1916. No other information on this appearance can be found.

Ned Wayburn's Town Topics
Century Theater, New York, Sept. 23, 1915–Nov. 20, 1915, 68 performances

Nobody's Home
Note: This was listed in Webb's credits in the Playbill for *Blithe Spirit* Jan. 5, 1942. Performance date was listed as April 1915. No other information on this appearance can be found.

Various clubs and theaters, 1915; dance partner, Mae Murray

Dancing Around
Winter Garden Theater, New York, Oct. 10, 1914–Feb. 13, 1915, no. of performances unknown; *Clarence;* dance partner, Eileen Molyneux

Keith Vaudeville Circuit, various theaters, circa 1914; dance partner, Bonnie Glass

The Purple Road (operetta)
Liberty Theater, New York, April 7, 1913–June 16, 1913; Casino Theater, New York, June 16, 1913–Aug. 2, 1913, 136 performances; *Bisco-Vestris.* Also traveled to Boston with this production in September 1913. Mabelle Parmelee was in the cast as *Ophelia*

Mignon
The Aborn Opera Company; appeared in this opera as *Laertes* and also in *The Bohemian Girl, Madame Butterfly,* and *Hansel and Gretel,* circa 1911–1913.

Huckleberry Finn
Klaw and Erlanger production, five weeks in Philadelphia, 1901; *Sid Sawyer.*

Brownies
The Children's Theater at Carnegie Hall Theatre (Lyceum), circa 1896–1900. Other dramas included *Oliver Twist, The Master of Carlton Hall,* and more.

Filmography

Satan Never Sleeps (1962) as Father Bovard
William Holden, France Nuyen; director: Leo McCarey; Twentieth Century Fox Film Corporation

Holiday for Lovers (1959) as Robert Dean
Jane Wyman, Jill St. John, Carole Lynley; director: Henry Levin; Twentieth Century Fox Film Corporation

The Remarkable Mr. Pennypacker (1959) as Horace Pennypacker
Dorothy McGuire, Charles Coburn, Jill St. John; director: Henry Levin; Twentieth Century Fox Film Corporation

Boy on a Dolphin (1957) as Victor Parmalee
Alan Ladd, Sophia Loren; director: Jean Negulesco; Twentieth Century Fox Film Corporation

The Man Who Never Was (1956) as Lt. Cmdr. Ewen Montague
Stephen Boyd, Gloria Graham; director: Ronald Neame; Twentieth Century Fox Film Corporation

Woman's World (1954) as Ernest Gifford
Lauren Bacall, June Allyson, Arlene Dahl; director: Jean Negulesco; Twentieth Century Fox Film Corporation

Three Coins in the Fountain (1954) as John Frederick Shadwell
Dorothy McGuire, Jean Peters, Maggie McNamara; director: Jean Negulesco, Twentieth Century Fox Film Corporation

Mister Scoutmaster (1953) as Robert Jordan
George Winslow, Edmund Gwenn; director: Henry Levin; Twentieth Century Fox Film Corporation

Titanic (1953) as Richard Ward Sturges
Barbara Stanwyck, Robert Wagner, Thelma Ritter; director: Jean Negulesco; Twentieth Century Fox Film Corporation

*Stars and Stripes Forever (1952) as John Philip Sousa
Robert Wagner, Debra Paget, Ruth Hussey; director: Henry Koster; Twentieth Century Fox Film Corporation

Dreamboat (1952) as Thomas Sayre/Bruce Blair
Ginger Rogers, Anne Francis, Jeffrey Hunter; director: Claude Binyon; Twentieth Century Fox Film Corporation

Belles on Their Toes (1952) as Frank Bunker Gilbreth (uncredited)
Myrna Loy, Jeanne Crain, Debra Paget; director: Henry Levin; Twentieth Century Fox Film Corporation. Note: Webb's only appearance is in a few photographs and a flashback scene near the end of the movie.

Elopement (1951) as Howard Osborne
Anne Francis, William Lundigan, Charles Bickford; director: Henry Koster; Twentieth Century Fox Film Corporation

Mr. Belvedere Rings the Bell (1951) as Lynn Belvedere
Joanne Dru, Hugh Marlowe, Zero Mostel; director: Henry Koster; Twentieth Century Fox Film Corporation

For Heaven's Sake (1950) as "Slim" Charles
Joan Bennett, Robert Cummings, Joan Blondell; director: George Seaton; Twentieth Century Fox Film Corporation

Cheaper by the Dozen (1950) as Frank Bunker Gilbreth
Myrna Loy, Jeanne Crain; director: Walter Lang; Twentieth Century Fox Film Corporation

Mr. Belvedere Goes to College (1949) as Lynn Belvedere
Shirley Temple, Tom Drake, Alan Young; director: Elliott Nugent; Twentieth Century Fox Film Corporation

*Sitting Pretty (1948) as Lynn Belvedere
Maureen O'Hara, Robert Young; director: Walter Lang; Twentieth Century Fox Film Corporation

The Razor's Edge (1946) as Elliott Templeton
Tyrone Power, Ann Baxter, Herbert Marshall; director: Edmund Goulding;
Twentieth Century Fox Film Corporation.

The Dark Corner (1946) as Hardy Cathcart
Mark Stevens, Lucille Ball; director: Henry Hathaway; Twentieth Century
Fox Film Corporation

Laura (1944) as Waldo Lydecker
Gene Tierney, Dana Andrews, Vincent Price, Judith Anderson; director:
Otto Preminger; Twentieth Century Fox Film Corporation.

The Still Alarm (1930) as a fireman
(Short film based on a scene from "Three's a Crowd") Fred Allen; director:
Roy Mack; The Vitaphone Corporation

The Heart of a Siren (1925) as Maxim
Barbara LaMarr, Conway Tearle; director: Phil Rosen; Associated Pictures
Productions/First National Pictures

New Toys (1925) as Tom Lawrence
Richard Barthelmess, Mary Hay; director: John S. Robertson; Inspiration
Pictures/First National Pictures

Let Not Man Put Asunder (1924) as Major Bertie
Pauline Frederick, Lou Tellegen; director: J. Stuart Blackton; Vitagraph
Company of America

Polly with a Past (1920) as Harry Richardson (uncredited)
Ina Claire; director: Leander De Cordova; Metro Pictures Corporation.

National Red Cross Pageant (1917) as a dancer in "The Pavane"
French episode; director: William Christy Cabanne

---

*   **Oscar nominations**
Best Actor in a Leading Role, *Sitting Pretty* (1948)
Best Actor in a Supporting Role, *The Razor's Edge* (1946)
Best Actor in a Supporting Role, *Laura* (1944)
   Golden Globes
Nominated Best Motion Picture Actor, musical/comedy, *Stars and Stripes Forever* (1953)
Won Best Supporting Actor, *The Razor's Edge* (1946)

Bibliography

BOOKS

Allen, Fred. *Much Ado about Me.* Little Brown and Company, 1956.
———. *Treadmill to Oblivion.* Little, Brown and Company, 1954.
Ball, Lucille, with Betty Hannah Hoffman. *Love Lucy.* G.P. Putnam's Sons, 1996.
Bankhead, Tallulah. *Tallulah: My Autobiography.* Harper & Brothers, 1952.
Baral, Robert. *Revue: The Great Broadway Period.* Rev. ed. Fleet Press Corporation, 1962.
Barrios, Richard. *Screened Out.* Routledge, 2003.
Basinger, Jeanine. *The Star Machine.* Alfred A. Knopf, 2007.
Behlmer, Rudy. *Memo from Darryl F. Zanuck, the Golden Years at Twentieth Century Fox.* Grove Press, 1993.
Bergreen, Laurence. *As Thousands Cheer: The Life of Irving Berlin.* Viking Penguin, 1990.
Bloom, Ken. *American Song: The Complete Musical Theatre Companion.* Vols. 1 and 2. Facts on File Publications, 1985.
Bloom, Ken, and Frank Vlastnik. *Broadway Musicals: The 101 Greatest Shows of All Time.* Black Dog and Leventhal Publishers, 2004.
Boardman, Gerald. *American Musical Theater.* Oxford University Press, 2001.
Bosworth, Patricia. *Montgomery Clift: A Biography.* Harcourt Brace Jovanovich, 1978.
Bradshaw, Jon. *Dreams that Money Can Buy: The Tragic Life of Libby Holman.* William Morrow and Company, 1985.
Branden, Barbara. *The Passion of Ayn Rand: A Biography.* Doubleday, 1986.
Brassai [Gyula Halasz]. *The Secret Paris of the 30's.* Translated from the French by Richard Miller. Pantheon Books, 1976.
Brian, Denis. *Tallulah, Darling.* Pyramid Books, 1972.
Brown, Gene. *Show Time: A Chronology of Broadway and the Theatre from Its Beginnings to the Present.* MacMillan, 1997.
Capsuto, Steven. *Alternate Channels: The Uncensored Story of Gay and Lesbian Images on Radio and Television.* Ballantine Publishing Group, 2000.

Cassini, Oleg. *In My Own Fashion: An Autobiography.* Simon & Schuster, 1987.

Coward, Noel. *Noel Coward Autobiography: Consisting of Present Indicative, Future Indefinite, and Uncompleted Past Conditional.* Methuen, 1986.

Custen, George F. *Twentieth Century's Fox, Darryl F. Zanuck and the Culture of Hollywood.* Basic Books, 1997.

Day, Barry. *The Letters of Noel Coward.* Alfred A. Knopf, 2007.

Dietz, Howard. *Dancing in the Dark: Words by Howard Dietz.* Quadrangle, The New York Times Book Co., 1974.

Dyer, Richard. *Heavenly Bodies: Film Stars and Society.* St. Martin's Press, 1980.

———. *Now You See It: Studies on Lesbian and Gay Film.* Routledge, 1990.

———, ed. *Gays and Film.* New York Zoetrope, 1984.

Eels, George. *The Life That Late He Led: A Biography of Cole Porter.* G. P. Putnam's Sons, 1967.

Ewn, David. *Complete Book of the American Musical Theater.* Holt, Rinehart and Winston, 1960.

Fehl, Fred (photographs), William Stott with Jane Stott (text). *On Broadway.* University of Texas Press, 1978.

Freedland, Michael. *Jerome Kern: A Biography.* Stein and Day, 1978.

Furia, Philip. *Irving Berlin: A Life in Song.* Schirmer Books, 1998.

Green, Stanley. *Ring Bells! Sing Songs!* Arlington House, 1971.

Guiles, Fred Lawrence. *Tyrone Power, The Last Idol.* Doubleday & Company, 1979.

Gussow, Mel. *Don't Say Yes until I Finish Talking: A Biography of Darryl F. Zanuck.* Doubleday, 1971.

Hadleigh, Boze. *Hollywood Gays.* Barricade Books, 1996.

———. *Hollywood Lesbians.* Barricade Books, 1994.

Harriman, Margaret Case. *Blessed Are the Debonair.* Rinehart & Company, 1956.

Harris, Marlys J. *The Zanucks of Hollywood: The Dark Legacy of An American Dynasty.* Crown Publishers, 1989.

Harris, Warren G. *The Other Marilyn.* Arbor House, 1985.

Hart, Dorothy. *Thou Swell, Thou Pretty: The Life and Lyrics of Lorenz Hart.* Harper & Row, 1976.

Harte-Harrington, Fynes. *After Dark: The Nocturnal Adventures of Fynes Harte-Harrington.* http://fynesharteharrington.wordpress.com/.

Hirsch, Foster. *Otto Preminger: The Man Who Would Be King.* Alfred A. Knopf, 2007.

Hoard, Philip. *Noel Coward: A Biography.* Simon & Schuster, 1995.

Hofler, Robert. *The Man Who Invented Rock Hudson: The Pretty Boys and Dirty Deals of Henry Willson.* Avalon Publishing, 2005.

Hopper, Hedda, and James Brough. *The Whole Truth and Nothing But.* Doubleday & Company, 1963.

Howard, Jean. *Jean Howard's Hollywood: A Photo Memoir.* Harry N. Abrams, 1989.

Israel, Lee. *Kilgallen.* Dell Publishing Co., 1979.

Kantor, Michael, and Laurence Maslon. *Broadway: The American Musical.* Bulfinch Press, 2004.

Lackmann, Ron. *The Encyclopedia of Radio.* Checkmark Books, 1996.

Lahr, John. *Notes on a Cowardly Lion.* Alfred A. Knopf, 1969.

Lesley, Cole. *Remembered Laughter.* Alfred A. Knopf, 1976.

Loos, Anita. *A Girl Like I.* Viking Press, 1966.

Loy, Myrna, and James Kotsilibas. *Myrna Loy: Being and Becoming.* Alfred A. Knopf, 1987.

Malnig, Julie. *Dancing Till Dawn: A Century of Exhibition Ballroom Dance.* Greenwood Press, 1992.

Mann, William J. *Behind the Screen: How Gays and Lesbians Shaped Hollywood, 1910–1969.* Viking, 2001.

Marchant, William. *The Privilege of His Company.* Bobbs-Merrill Company, 1975.

Mast, Gerald, and Bruce F. Kawin. *A Short History of the Movies.* Pearson Longman, 2006.

Maxwell, Elsa. *R.S.V.P. Elsa Maxwell's Own Story.* Little, Brown and Company, 1954.

McBrien, William. *Cole Porter.* Vintage Books, 1998.

McCann, Graham. *Marilyn Monroe.* Rutgers University Press, 1988.

McGilligan, Patrick. *A Double Life: George Cukor.* Harper Perrenial, 1992.

Minelli, Vincent, with Hector Arce. *I Remember It Well.* Angus & Robertson (U.K.) Ltd., 1975.

Moore, Grace. *You're Only Human Once.* Garden City Publishing Company, 1946.

Mordden, Ethan. *Make Believe: The Broadway Musical in the 1920s.* Oxford University Press, 1997.

———. *Sing for Your Supper: The Broadway Musical in the 1930s.* Palgrave MacMillan, 2005.

Negulesco, Jean. *The Things I Did and Things I Think I Did.* Linden Press/Simon & Schuster, 1984.

Newhart, Bob. *I Shouldn't Even Be Doing This!* Hyperion Books, 2006.

Payn, Graham, with Barry Day. *My Life with Noel Coward.* Applause Books, 1994.

Payn, Graham, and Sheridan Morley, eds. *The Noel Coward Diaries.* Phoenix Press, 1982.

Pratley, Gerald. *The Cinema of Otto Preminger.* A. S. Barnes & Company, 1971.

Price, Victoria. *Vincent Price: A Daughter's Biography.* St. Martin's Press, 1999.

Riva, Maria. *Marlene Dietrich.* Alfred A. Knopf, 1993.

Russo, Vito. *The Celluloid Closet.* Rev. ed. Harper & Row, Publishers, 1987.

Shipman, David. *The Story of Cinema.* Vol. 2. Hodder and Stoughton, 1984.

Silverman, Stephen M. *The Fox That Got Away, The Last Days of the Zanuck Dynasty at Twentieth Century Fox.* Lyle Stuart, 1988.

Stricklyn, Ray. *Angels and Demons: One Actor's Hollywood Journey.* Belle Publishing, 1999.

Suskin, Steven. *Show Tunes: The Songs, Shows, and Careers of Broadway's Major Composers.* 3rd ed. Oxford University Press, 2000.

Thomas, Bob. *Golden Boy: The Untold Story of William Holden.* St. Martin's Press, 1983.

————. *Joan Crawford.* Doubleday & Company, 1978.

Thomas, Tony. *Music for the Movies.* A. S. Barnes and Company, 1975.

Thompson, David. *A Biographical Dictionary of Film.* 3rd ed. Alfred A. Knopf, 1994.

Tierney, Gene, with Mickey Herskowitz. *Self Portrait.* Simon & Schuster, 1979.

Tyler, Parker. *Screening the Sexes: Homosexuality in the Movies.* DeCapo Press, 1993.

Wagner, Robert, with Scott Eyman. *Pieces of My Heart: A Life.* HarperCollins Publishers, 2008.

Waters, Ethel, with Charles Samuels. *His Eye Is on the Sparrow.* Doubleday & Company, 1951.

Wood, Peggy. *How Young You Look: Memoirs of a Middle-Sized Actress.* Farrar & Rinehart, 1941.

NEWSPAPER ARTICLES (IN CHRONOLOGICAL ORDER)

"Miss Mitchell's Entertainment." *Indianapolis Evening News,* April 18, 1882.

"Miss Mitchell's Entertainment." *Indianapolis Evening News,* May 26, 1882.

"Opera House: Rebellion of the Daisies." *Indianapolis Sentinel,* August 9, 1885.

"Child Actors in Grown-Up Plays." *Brooklyn Eagle,* March 16, 1902.

"New Musical Play Smartly Staged: 'Love O' Mike.'" *New York Times,* January 18, 1917.

"Dances and Puns Galore: 'Listen Lester.'" *New York Times,* December 24, 1918.

"How the Young Stage Dancer Won the Leading Lady." *Syracuse Herald,* July 17, 1921.

Woodward, Jean Davis. "Names of Joe Cook, Clifton Webb, Hoosiers, Shine Brightly in New York's Theater Lights." *Indianapolis Star,* April 19, 1931.

"3,000 Attend Ball in Circus Setting." *New York Times,* April 26, 1933.

Maxwell, Elsa. "Come As Your Opposite Reveals Celebrities Natures." *Jefferson City Post-Tribune,* July 30, 1937.

"Clifton Webb Was Born in Indianapolis." *Indianapolis Star,* October 27, 1940.

"Hoosier Likes Comedy Roles." *Indianapolis News,* November 8, 1940.

"Clifton Webb Says He Worked Hard to Avoid Being a 'Hoofer.'" *Indianapolis News,* November 14, 1940.

Fidler, Jimmy. "Jimmy Fidler in Hollywood." *Joplin Globe,* August 22, 1945.

"Williams to Star in 'A Likely Story.'" *New York Times*, November 8, 1948.

Pryor, Thomas M. "Clifton Webb Set in O. Henry Story." *New York Times*, November 13, 1951.

Thomas, Bob. "Mr. Belvedere Finally Lands in Different Role." *Long Beach Press Telegram*, January 13, 1952.

Cook, Ben. "Hollywood Film Shop." *Long Beach Independent*, February 4, 1952.

Crowther, Bosley. "The Screen in Review: Clifton Webb Sneers His Best at Television in 'Dreamboat.'" *New York Times*, July 26, 1952.

Soanes, Wood. "Hollywood Has Fun with TV." *Oakland Tribune*, August 18, 1952.

"Clifton Webb Has New Role in 'Dreamboat.'" *Oakland Tribune*, August 19, 1952.

Johnson, Grady. "And the Sousa Band Plays On." *New York Times*, September 28, 1952.

"Marilyn's Sex Appeal 'War' On." *San Mateo Times*, October 27, 1952.

Parsons, Louella. "Clifton Webb Pleased with Role in 'The Happy Scoundrel' for 20th." *Albuquerque Journal*, October 29, 1952.

Soanes, Wood. "Curtain Calls." *Oakland Tribune*, December 24, 1952.

Thompson, Howard. "Webb Spins His Own." *New York Times*, December 28, 1952.

Parsons, Louella. "Louella's Movie-Go-Round." *Albuquerque Journal*, December 29, 1952.

"Hollywood Producer Swings on Trapeze." *Joplin Globe*, January 20, 1954.

Crowther, Bosley. "Screen: 'Three Coins in the Fountain.'" *New York Times*, May 21, 1954.

Thomas, Bob. "Clifton Webb Irked by Trend toward Violence." *Oakland Tribune*, June 12, 1954.

Webb, Clifton. "He Takes Sublease on Olympus." *Chillicothe Constitution-Tribune*, August 28, 1954.

Parsons, Louella. "Clifton Webb Is Cast in Key Role in 'Lord Vanity' with Bob Wagner." *Albuquerque Journal*, October 6, 1954.

Pryor, Thomas M. "Independents Buy Two New Stories." *New York Times*, December 21, 1954.

Crowther, Bosley. "Screen: Cloak and Dagger Episode: 'Man Who Never Was.'" *New York Times*, April 4, 1956.

"Clifton Webb to Start 13th 'Show Biz' Career." *Indianapolis Star*, May 20, 1962.

Marilyn's Death Shocks World." *Gallup Daily Independent*, August 6, 1962.

"Clifton Webb, Stage and Film Star, Dies." *Indianapolis News*, October 14, 1966.

Vogel, Carol. "Home Design: In the Dunes." *New York Times Magazine*, August 25, 2008.

OTHER SOURCES

1880 Census, Twelfth Ward. Indianapolis, Marion County, Indiana, 379A.

Bainbridge, John. "Mr. Belvedere and Mr. Webb." *Life Magazine*, May 30, 1949.

Birth Records, 1882–1920, Marion County, Indiana, Book H-3, 369.

Dancer History Archives by StreetSwing.com. http://streetswing.com/hist mai2/d2movetl.htm.

The Family Parmelee. http://www.thefamilyparmelee.com/a-maybelle.html.

Garland, Judy. Autobiography in *Ladies Home Journal*, August, 1967.

Hall, Gladys. Interview with Clifton Webb. 1949. Academy of Motion Picture Arts and Sciences.

Holland, Larry Lee. "Clifton Webb." *Films in Review*, April 1981.

Hooey, Charles. "An American Original—Orville Harrold." Music Web International. http://www.musicweb-international.com/hooey/harrold.htm. This is a reworking of an article that appeared in *For the Record* 24 (Winter 2007): 8.

The John and Betsy Neylon Clifton Webb estate collection, Chagrin Falls, Ohio.

Last Will and Testament of Clifton Webb, filed October 25, 1966.

Leff, Leonard. "Becoming Clifton Webb: A Queer Star in Mid-Century Hollywood." *Cinema Journal* 47, no. 3 (Spring 2008): 3–28.

Marquis Who's Who in America, News Communications, Inc.

Marriage Records, January, 18,1888, Marion County, Indiana, Book 21, 8.

The Metropolitan Opera Database. http://archives.metoperafamily.org.

Newhart, Bob. Letter to author. May 22, 2010.

Pierce, Max. "Sitting Pretty . . . The Talented Mr. Webb." *Films of the Golden Age*, Summer 2000.

Playbill for the Plymouth Theatre "Present Laughter." March 3, 1947.

Price, Victoria. Interview by author via e-mail. May 24, 2010.

St. John, Jill. Phone interview by author, Los Angeles. July 15, 2008.

Wagner, Robert. The Clifton Webb collection. Formerly housed at Boston University.

Wagner. Robert. Phone interview by author, Los Angeles. July 10, 15, 2008, and June 28, 2010.

www.VintageRadioPlace.com/broadcast. Jerry Haendiges Productions.

Zanuck, Richard. Phone interview by author, Beverly Hills. June 30, 2010.

Index